Understanding Islam

Through History
Through Theology
and
Through Daily Life

Second Edition
2013

Roland Müller

Understanding Islam

by Roland Müller

Copyright © CanBooks 2013
Printed in Canada

Sources

Scripture quotations marked (NLT) are taken from the Holy Bible, New Living Translation, copyright © 1996. Used by permission of Tyndale House Publishers, Inc., Wheaton Illinois 60189. All rights reserved.

Scripture quotations marked (ESV) are from the Holy Bible, English Standard Version, copyright @ 2001 by Crossway Bibles, a division of Good News Publishers. Used by permission. All rights reserved.

Scripture quotations marked (NIV) are from the Holy Bible, New International Version, copyright © 1973, 1978, 1984 by International Bible Society. Used by permission. All rights reserved worldwide.

Other books by the same author:

- The Messenger, the Message and the Community
- The Man from Gadara
- Missionary Leadership by Motivation & Communication
- Missions: The Next Generation
- Honor and Shame, Unlocking the Door
- Tools for Muslim Evangelism

ISBN: 978-1-927581-12-4

Table of Contents

Acknowledgements

This book has come about through thirty years of exposure to Islam and Muslim people. A comment made here, or a tidbit dropped there, opened up subjects for further research. It would be impossible to name every person who said or did something that helped in compiling the research. Besides those who provided input on sources and subjects, there are those who have quietly encouraged me along the way, often without their knowing it. They are as important as the others. Then there are those who had a direct impact on the production of the manuscript. Here I must thank Jennifer May, Eldon Bottger, Tilda Dafoe, Dave Ginter, Melissa Tomblin, and others. Without their eyes and comments this manuscript would have remained a dismal collection of notes full of spelling and grammar errors. A special thank you must go to Colin Bearup who provided the bulk of chapter fourteen, taken directly from his book: *Keys, The Gospel for Muslims*. And then there is you, of course, the reader. Books without readers are just space fillers, waiting for the recycling bin. And I do hope that one day this book will end in a recycling bin. I look forward to the day when the need for this book has ceased, and every knee has bowed, and every tongue has confessed that Jesus Christ is Lord.

Abbreviations

Abu Daood	Sunan of Abu Dawood, with reference to volume and hadith number
Ali	Maulana Muhammad Ali's translation of the Qur'an (1917)
Asad	Muhammad Asad's translation of the Qur'an, 1980
Bukhari	Sahih al-Bukhari, with reference to volume and hadith number
Ishaq	The *Life of Muhammad*, Translated by A. Guillaume, by Ibn Ishaq, with reference number to the section in the Arabic text. Oxford University Press, 1955,1967
KJV	King James Version of the Bible
NIV	New International Version of the Bible
Pickthall	Muhammad Marmaduke Pickthall's translation of the Qur'an (1930)
AlTabari	*The History of Al-Tabari*, State University of New York Press series with reference number to the section in the Arabic text
Yusif Ali	Abdullah Yusuf Ali's translation of the Qur'an (1934)

Understanding Islam
(Through History)

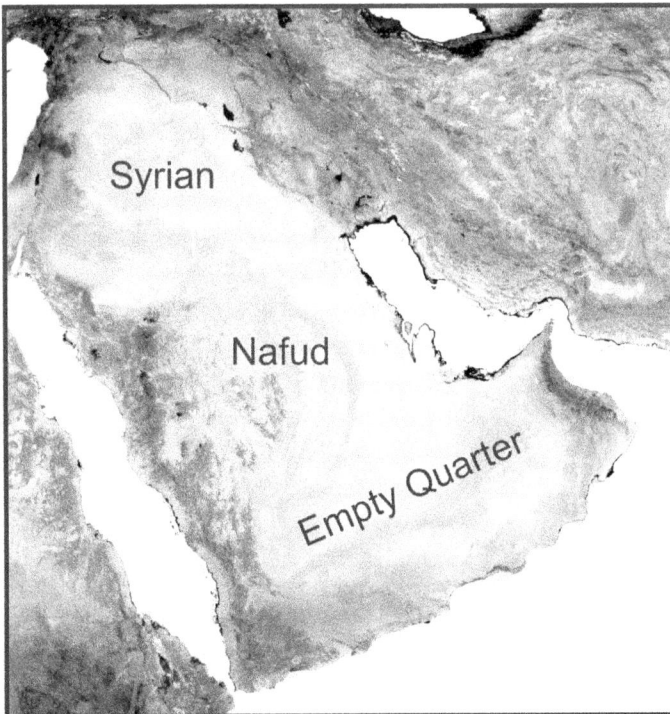

Chapter One
The Importance of Arabia in History and God's Plan

Introduction

Every day, five times a day, almost a billion Muslims bow down and recite a prayer to Allah, given to them by Muhammad, their prophet. Every day, five times a day, they face a black rock in far off Mecca and submit themselves afresh to the religion of Islam. Every day, five times a day, they bow as a corporate group, all around the world, to express their solidarity as followers of Islam, for whom Muhammad is their prophet, and the Qur'an is their scripture. And every day, their numbers grow.

Islam is now considered by some to be the greatest challenge that the Christian church is facing all around the world. Next to evangelicals, no other religious group is growing at such a rapid rate. Not only is the population of Muslim countries expanding, fervent Muslims are sharing their message all around the world. Most cities in the world now have mosques or Muslim places of prayer. While many Christians feel inhibited about sharing their faith, Muslims are often bold and excited. As a community, they reach out to those around them, offering support and encouragement to those that need it. In a time when the West is struggling with broken families and sexual immorality, Muslims uphold their strict code of conduct as an example of what true religion should be.

Even China has its Muslim groups. The first Muslims arrived in China around the time of the death of the prophet Muhammad. Since then Muslim merchants have spread their religion and founded communities along China's coasts and along the Silk Road trade route through Central Asia.

Sometimes it is hard for us to grasp just how large and important the Muslims are. Unlike many other people who have a Christian church among them, there are millions of Muslims who have no Christians near them. Many Muslims have never met a Christian. Most have never seen a Bible. Many will pass into eternity having never heard the gospel, simply because no one cared enough to go and tell them.

On the other hand, most Christians have never reached out to Muslims and have no idea what Muslims believe and how they are different from Christians.

That is where this course will help. It is designed for Christians everywhere who want to become more aware of Islam and the specific needs and opportunities that exist when ministering to Muslims.

This book is the one of several aimed at helping Christians reach out to Muslims. Each book has a very specific aim and purpose. This book, *Understanding Islam,* introduces the student to the religion of Islam. *The Messenger, the Message and the Community* highlights some of the struggles that exist when doing evangelism and church planting among Muslims. The online *Toolbox* provides students with Bible-based tools and other resources that have proven effective when ministering to Muslims.

We trust that God will use these books to inform and prepare Christians as they reach out to Muslim people everywhere.

Arabia

The land of Arabia is a vast place with rocky plains, rugged mountains, burning deserts, and huge sand dunes; all of it without rivers and virtually unknown to the outside world until recent years.

Three great deserts exist in Arabia. All of them are barren wastelands, the Syrian Desert is in the north, the Nafud Desert is in the interior, and the Empty Quarter is in the south east.

Each of these deserts consists of extremely hot, dry spans of barren rock and sand. Each of these deserts is formidable, except to the few nomads who live in central Arabia.

The Syrian Desert in the north is a flat plain covered with sand and pebbles. Travelers as early as Abraham would journey around it rather than try and pass through it. (Genesis 11:31)

The Nafud Desert in the center of Arabia alternates between fields of rock and fields of sand. It is known to some of the Arabs as "God's Anvil." Its particularly harsh environment makes it a place that even nomads avoid if possible. From an airplane, it appears as rivers of rock flowing in fields of sand.

The Empty Quarter in the south of Arabia is filled with great sand dunes. It is known as the Empty Quarter because it is just that, empty, and avoided by nomads because it is almost impossible to pass through let alone live there.

Along the west side of Arabia lie mountains, great piles of silent rock surrounded by a sea of desert. Blistering hot during the day, and bitterly cold during the night, their valleys are home to some greenery and wild life.

And yet, for all this barrenness there is some life. Rain visits these deserts several times a year. Most of the rain is quickly absorbed into the sand, but sometimes there is enough water to encourage plants to rise, flower, produce seed and then die. Sometimes there is enough water to provide patches of green for a few weeks. After it rains, some of the rain water collects in rocky areas and valleys. The places where the water collects and life can exist are called *oases*. Sometimes the water source is surrounded by small bushes; sometimes there is a grove of trees. Small groups of Bedouin often huddle around these oases. These nomads carefully watch the sky for indications of a burst of rain. The clouds are carefully noted so several weeks later they can visit these locations with their small herds of sheep and goats, hopeful to find green grass and bushes.

The camel is the Bedouin's key to life in the desert. Its soft padded feet are perfect for walking in the sand and its capacity for storing fat in its hump have made the camel capable of needing water only every three days. The Bedouin love the camel, and much of their diet is based around products produced from the milk of camels. So, using the camel as their chief mode of transport and a source of food, Bedouin have moved across the deserts of Arabia for many centuries.

Arabia connects Asia, Africa, and Europe. This land mass should have acted as a bridge between continents. But history has proven otherwise. For many centuries, Arabia was a barrier between the great continents and their civilizations. Its vast deserts proved to be the graveyard of many armies. And so the deserts separated humanity. On both sides civilizations rose and fell, many of them unaware of the others presence.

For thousands of years these deserts were only traversed by Arab merchants and their camel caravans. It was these merchants who conquered the deserts. For them the desert was a place of refuge and safety where they could travel in relative freedom from one civilization to another. Everywhere the merchants traveled, they were welcomed for they brought goods from other places, and, more importantly, they brought news, ideas and knowledge.

In their own quiet way these desert merchants wielded immense power. Being the only contact between civilizations, they brought news that influenced world leaders, be it truth or lies.

And so it is even today. Arabia continues to play an important role in world events. Be it trade, oil, or the Islamic religion, Arabia is a key to many major events in the world.

And yet, for most westerners Arabia continues to be an unknown. Its history is obscure, its regions untraveled, its culture misunderstood, and its importance in world history ignored by the historians of the great nations that surround it.

Christians, Jews and others focus their attention on the nation of Israel. Israeli history is studied and expounded on in most universities around the world. Jewish history and religion are studied and expounded on by countless millions of pastors, theologians and interested Christians. Egyptian and Babylonian history are carefully studied but few western people know anything about the history of Arabia and how Arabia has influenced and shaped events in the Bible and even in world history.

How much do you know about Arabian history? If you answer, "Not much," you are in good company. Most people know very little. We trust that when you finish reading this book, Arabia, its history, people, and religions will be much more familiar to you.

The Founding of the Nations (Genesis 10 & 25)

The history of Arabia goes back to the very earliest moments of recorded time. All peoples of the world are descendants of Noah and his three sons, Shem, Ham and Japheth. The descendants of these three sons spread out over the whole world. In time, different languages, cultures, worldviews, and even skin color would vary, but all human beings are linked together through the three sons of Noah.

The book of Genesis provides us with a picture of how the nations developed from these three sons. This information appears in Genesis chapter 10, and you can reconstruct this chart by simply following through what Genesis 10 teaches.

The sons of Japheth moved east into Asia, inhabiting India and the nations beyond. The sons of Ham originally moved into northern Arabia and then migrated into Egypt, Ethiopia and eventually Africa.

The sons of Shem lived in the Middle East. Most of this chart deals with the sons of Shem.

Genesis 10 contains many names of people in a genealogical list. While some people may find this information very boring, it is vitally important to historians and to the Arabs in particular.

A reconstruction of Genesis 10 (on the next page) provides us with some fascinating information. It shows us that Shem's line continued through Salah and Eber until Joktan. The sons of Joktan listed in Genesis 10 became the tribes that settled in southern Arabia or present day Yemen.

If you visit the Middle East you will find that the old tribal historians and poets can recite their tribal lineage all the way back to Noah and from there to Adam. The tribes in Yemen all trace their histories back to Joktan (Jahtan) the descendant of Shem, the son of Noah. This explains why the people of Yemen had a distinct culture and a very distinct language until the coming of Islam which forced the Arabic language on everyone.

If we continue constructing a chart from the information in Genesis it will eventually look like the chart on the next page. The descendants of Shem continue on through Peleg until we come to Terah. Terah was the father of Abraham.

Genesis 11:27-30 tells us about Terah:

This is the account of Terah. Terah became the father of Abram, Nahor and Haran. And Haran became the father of Lot. While his father Terah was still alive, Haran died in Ur of the Chaldeans, in the land of his birth. Abram and Nahor both married. The name of Abram's wife was

Sarai, and the name of Nahor's wife was Milcah; she was the daughter of Haran, the father of both Milcah and Iscah. Now Sarai was barren; she had no children. (NIV)

The Bible continues on to tell how Terah took his family and moved away from the great city of Ur to the land of Haran:

Terah took his son Abram, his grandson Lot son of Haran, and his daughter-in-law Sarai, the wife of his son Abram, and together they set out from Ur of the Chaldeans to go to Canaan. But when they came to Haran, they settled there. Terah lived 205 years and he died in Haran. (11:31-32, NIV)

The whole purpose of Genesis 10 is to show the reader how the tribes and peoples of the Middle East are related. Terah's sons and grandsons all became the fathers of great nations.

- From Haran's son Lot – the nations of Moab and Ammon.
- From Nahor's sons - the Buzzites, the Syrians, and others.
- From Abraham came many nations.
- Abraham's first son, Ishmael was the father of many Arabian tribes.
- Abraham's second son Isaac was the father of the Israelites, the Edomites, the Temanites and the Amalekites.
- Another of Abraham's sons, Midian, was the father of the Midianites.

So from this chart we can see that the following tribes were all closely related, finding their roots in Terah.

- Israelites
- Ishmaelites
- Moabites
- Edomites
- Ammonites
- Buzzites
- Syrians
- Tenanites
- Amalekites
- Midianites

Originally all these tribes spoke the same language and related together as cousin tribes. Early on in their existence there must have been alliances and support for one another. This affected history, as we shall see a bit later.

NOAH

JAPHETH
- GOMER
  - ASHKENAZ
  - RIPHATH
  - TOGARMAH
- MAGOG
- MADAI
- JAVAN
  - ELISHAH
  - TARSHISH
  - KITTIM
  - DODANIM
- TUBAL
- MESHECH
- TIRAS

TRIBES IN INDIA

SHEM
- ELAM
- ASSHUR
- ARPHAXAD — SALAH — EBER
  - PELEG — REU — SERUG — HAHOR — TERAH ——————
  - JOKTAN
    - ALMODAD
    - SHELEPH
    - HAZARMAVETH
    - JERH
    - HADORAM
    - UZAL
    - DIKLAH
    - OBAL
    - ABIMAEL
    - SHEBA (Yemen)
    - OPHIR
    - HAVIEAH
    - JOBAB
- LUD
- ARAM
  - UZ
  - HUL
  - GETHER
  - MASH

ARABIAN TRIBES

HAM
- CUSH
  - SEBA
  - HAVILAH
  - SABTAH
  - RAAMAH
  - SABTECHA
  - NIMROD —— BABYLONIANS
- MIZRAIM —————————— CASLUHIM & CAPHTORIM (PHILISTIM) (Philistines)
- PHUT (Lybia)
- CANAAN
  - SIDON (Phoenicians)
  - HETH
  - JEBUSITES
  - AMORITES
  - GIRGASITES
  - HIVITES
  - ARKITES
  - SINITES
  - ARVADITES
  - ZEMARITES
  - HAMATHITES

LAND OF CANAAN

ABRAM (ABRAHAM)
- ISHMAEL
  - NABAJOTH (Nabataeans)
  - KEDAR
  - ABDEEL
  - MIBSAM
  - MISHMA
  - DUMAH
  - MASSA
  - HADAR (HADAD)
  - TEMA
  - JETUR
  - NEPHISH
  - KEDEMAH

  ISHMALITES or HAGARITES

- ISAAC
  - ESAU
    - ELIPHAZ
      - OMAR
      - TEMEN (Temanites)
      - ZEPHO
      - GATAM
      - KENAZ
      - AMALEK (AMALEKITES)

      EDOMITES
    - REUEL
    - JEUSH
      - NAHATH
      - ZERAH
      - SHAMMAH
      - MIZZAH
    - JAALAM
    - KORAH
  - JACOB
    - REUBEN
    - SIMEON
    - LEVI
    - JUDAH
    - DAN
    - NAPHTALI
    - GAD
    - ASHER
    - ISSACHAR
    - ZEBULUN
    - JOSEPH
      - MANASSEH
      - EPHRAIM
    - BENJAMIN

    ISRAELITES

- ZIMRAN
- JOKSHAN
  - SHEBA
  - DEDAN
    - ASSHURIM
    - LETUSHIM
    - LEUMMIM
- MEDAN
- MIDIAN
  - EPHAH
  - EPHER
  - HANOCH
  - ABIDAH
  - ELDAAH

  MIDIANITES
- ISHBAH
- SHUAH

NAHOR
- HUZ
- BUZ — BUZITES
- KEMUEL — ARAM SYRIANS
- CHESED
- HAZO
- PILDASH
- JIDLAPH
- BETHUEL
- TEBAH
- GAHAM
- THAHASH
- MAACHAH MAACHATHITES

HARAN — LOT
- MOAB MOABITES
- BEN-AMMI AMMONITES

Names

Names are important to God. In some cases God changed people's names to new names. This is important because it alerts us to the fact that these are very important people in the Bible.

While God changed the names of several people in the Bible, God gave names to four people before they were born. Others had their names changed later, but four very important people were named before they were born. Two of them are in the New Testament. The most well known was Jesus, the promised Messiah. He was the son of promise, and so God named him before he was born. The second was John the Baptist. The angel announced before he was born what his name would be. Why did God choose John the Baptist? Why this man who was wearing hairy clothing and living in the wild? The Bible tells us that this wild looking man was the fore-runner of Jesus.

Now, who were the two people in the Old Testament who were named before they were born? In Genesis 17 God told Abraham to name his promised child Isaac. This made Isaac the son of promise.

But who is the other person in the Old Testament that God named before he was born? In Genesis 16:11 the angel of the Lord tells Hagar "that his name will be Ishmael" even before he is born. And, the angel adds, "he will be a wild man living in the desert."

Imagine that! The fore-runner of the son of promise is a wild-looking man: both in the Old Testament and in the New Testament.

Why did God name these four before they were born? It would seem that from God's perspective they are the four most important people in the Bible. The second most important people like Abraham, Jacob, Paul, and others, had their names changed, but they were not named before they were born.

Out of the four who were named before they were born, Christians know the most about three of them. John the Baptist was the fore-runner for Jesus. His ministry prepared the way for Jesus' ministry. Jesus is the promised Messiah and he is the central figure in the Bible, so we understand his name being announced before he was born. Isaac was the son of promise to Abraham. It was from Isaac that the Children of Israel would come. These three names we understand, but why Ishmael?

How much do you know about Ishmael? How many sons did he have? Who were they? Where did they live?

Most Christians have never considered that Ishmael had 12 sons, all of them the fathers of tribes and nations. You will find their names listed in Genesis 25:12-18. The names of these tribes re-appear in many other places in Scripture.

These tribes settled in Arabia. The descendants of Johtan lived in southern Arabia while the descendants of Ishmael lived in northern Arabia.

Ishmael

The 12 sons of Ishmael are listed in Genesis 25:

> "*Now these are the generations of Ishmael, ... The firstborn of Ishmael, Nebayoth, Kedar, Adbeel, Mibsam, Mishma, Dumah, Massa, Hadad, Tema, Jetur, Naphish and Kedmah. These are the sons of Ishmael, and these are their names, by their towns and by their encampments; twelve princes according to their nations.*" (Genesis 25:12-16, KJV)

It was these 12 tribes that settled in northern Arabia. There are still towns and areas that bear their names today. These 12 tribes of Ishmael are the origins of many of the Arabs of Saudi Arabia, Jordan, Syria, Iraq and the Gulf countries on the east side of Arabia.

Most of these tribes are only mentioned a few times in history, but the tribes that descended from the two eldest sons of Ishmael are mentioned over and over again. Nebayoth and Kedar became the major tribes in Northern Arabia. The black tents of Kedar were known from Iraq to Israel, and they are mentioned in many places in the Old Testament.

The Nabayoth became the desert merchants who moved goods from one end of Arabia to the other. It was from this tribe that Muhammad the founder of Islam would eventually emerge.

In the beginning, the sons of Ishmael all began worshiping the Lord Jehovah. We can understand this from the angel's message to Hagar in Genesis 16:10-15. The angel said to Hagar:

> "*I will so increase your descendants that they will be too numerous to count.*" The angel of the LORD also said to her: "*You are now with child and you will have a son. You shall name him Ishmael, for the LORD has*

heard of your misery. He will be a wild donkey of a man; his hand will be against everyone and everyone's hand against him, and he will live in hostility toward all his brothers." She gave this name to the LORD who spoke to her: "You are the God who sees me," for she said, "I have now seen the One who sees me." That is why the well was called Beer Lahai Roi; it is still there, between Kadesh and Bered. So Hagar bore Abram a son, and Abram gave the name Ishmael to the son she had borne. (NIV)

Hagar received a promise that was very similar to Abraham's. The angel promised Hagar that her children would also greatly multiply. The big difference was that there was a covenant with Abraham and the promise of God's blessing (messiah) through his line. When Hagar received God's promise she acknowledged God as her Lord, and the one who saw her and watched over her, so Ishmael would have grown up following God. However, in time, worship of the one true God, Jehovah, grew distant in the minds of his descendants and they began to adopt the gods of the people around them.

This happened in several places in the Bible. Look at I Chronicles 1:28 -41. This list begins with the children of Ishmael. It then goes on to tell us about the sons of Esau and those that ruled over Edom. Verse 49 tells us that the seventh ruler of Edom was named Baalhanan. His name included the name of Baal, a pagan deity. This demonstrates how even the sons of Esau gradually moved away from worshiping Jehovah God, and began to follow other gods. The descendants of Ishmael also did the same.

Ishmael's Place in Bible Prophecy (Isaiah 60)

The tribes of Ishmael are mentioned in many places in the Bible, including Bible prophecy. One of the most interesting of these is found in Isaiah 60.

Isaiah looks far into the future and foretells what will happen in the Middle East during the last days. He tells of the days when Israel will be restored. In verses 6 - 7 he foretells an amazing thing. He says in verse 6 that someday Midian, Ephah and Sheba will come, bearing gold and incense and proclaiming the praise of the LORD (Jehovah). Verse 7 goes on:

"Kedar's flocks will be gathered to you, the rams of Nebaioth will serve you; they will be accepted as offerings on my altar." (NIV)

This is an amazing prophecy. Midian, Ephah, Sheba, Kedar, and Nebaioth will all be praising the LORD Jehovah in the last days!

Who are these people? All of them are Muslim nations today but Isaiah tells us that before the Lord returns, these Muslim nations and people groups will come to Christ. I wonder who will bring the gospel to the tribes of Ishmael?

Nebaioth

In the list of the 12 tribes of Ishmael you will notice that Nebaioth was the eldest son of Ishmael and Kedar was the second son. What do you know about Nebaioth and the tribe that grew from his line? If you study history you will find that by the time of Christ, they had become a powerful nation known as the Nabataeans. They only bowed their heads to the Roman Empire 100 years after the time of Christ. The Bible mentions the Nabataeans in 2 Corinthians 11:32 when Paul escaped from the governor who represented the Nabataean king, Aretas. The Nabataeans, not the Romans, controlled Damascus at this time.

The Kedarites are also found throughout the Bible and are mentioned in the records of many of the old civilizations of the Middle East. Whenever ancient civilizations attempted to enter the deserts of Arabia they clashed with the Kedarite tribesmen. These people lived in black goat-haired tents, and their way of life has changed little from the time of Abraham to today.

According to the prophecy in Isaiah 60:6-7 the Islamic nations of the Arabian Peninsula will all come, proclaiming praise to the Lord God Jehovah. This means that there will someday be a major turning, where Muslims will change from following Allah and his prophet Muhammad to becoming followers of the one true God and Father of our Lord Jesus Christ.

In this we can take hope. Christ will do his work and bring millions of fanatical Muslims to himself. We have his promise. Now we need to serve him faithfully until he brings it about.

Questions for Reflection and Group Discussion

1. Discuss Ishmael and his offspring. Was Ishmael loved? (by Abraham? by God?) How do you know? Did God curse Ishmael or did he bless him?

2. Read I Peter 1:16-19. Does God love one person more than another? Compare Isaac and Ishmael. Was one son of Abraham loved more than another? Does God love some people more than others? Does God love Muslims?

3. Read Galatians 4:21-31. Paul draws a spiritual lesson from the two women. Hagar was called a slave woman, and she is a picture of everyone who is born on earth. We are all slaves to sin and to our earthly passions. Read Romans 7:14-15. Sarah on the other hand was a free woman, and she represents those that have been set free. Read Galatians 5:1. In this spiritual picture, whose children are we born of? How do we move from one spiritual lineage to another? Is the Bible here speaking against the children of Hagar, or is it identifying us as children of Hagar until Christ changes us?

4. Read Isaiah 54:1-8. Who are the deserted and disgraced ones? Which woman had no husband to look after her? Does this verse speak of the children of Hagar or Sarah? Is the Lord calling the children of Sarah or the children of Hagar back to himself? Can this apply to both? What is the promise given in Isaiah 60?

5. Read Genesis 12:2-3. Consider the founding of the nations chart and the many great nations that came from Abraham. Think especially of the promise to Abraham that any one who cursed him would have the curse turned back on him. Now read Genesis 16:1-5. Sarah despised Hagar and called her a slave, and she despised the son of Abraham and had them cast out. Did Sarah heed God's warning not to curse Abraham and his seed? Did Sarah's children receive a curse because of her actions? Whose sons ended up as slaves first?

6. Did Jesus come to redeem just the sons of Sarah or also the sons of Hagar?

Chapter Two
The Nabataeans, Merchants of Arabia

Most accounts of the founding of Islam give the impression that before the coming of Islam, Arabia was devoid of civilization. They suggest that a few warring tribes occupied the scattered oases. Nothing can be further from the truth. Arabia was home to a great civilization that impacted Muhammad and the founding of Islam. Here then, is a quick account of the founding of that empire.

The ancient civilizations of Egypt and Babylon both record dealings with Arab merchants who would come out of the desert with camels laden with goods from distant lands. These Arabs were called Nabayat, Nabatu, or Nabataeans. They were the descendants of Nebaioth, the eldest son of Ishmael.

These Arab merchants did not start a kingdom or establish a great civilization. Instead, a few families of Nabataean Arabs would live near the outskirts of each of the great cities of the Middle East. These merchants would then buy and sell in the local markets and would become part of the local community, while living separate from them. In this way, the Nabataeans established small communities all over the Middle East, and even into Europe and Asia.

The map on the next page shows us cities where archaeologists have discovered Nabataean communities from very early in their history. This allowed the Nabataeans greater trade advantages. When the Nabataean camel caravans arrived in a city they traded or sold their goods to the local Nabataean merchants, who would have bought up local goods at cheap prices. The camel caravans would then take these goods to other cities. In this way the camel caravans could quickly unload and load, and then head off again for the next city. The local

Nabataeans would then take the new goods to market and sell them.

Because the local Nabataeans would remain living in the same city, they often became well-known and very wealthy. Sometimes they became powerful businessmen within the city, even though their allegiance was primarily to the Nabataeans and not to the local people.

This form of trade is still practiced in the Middle East today by gypsies and Turkomen merchants. Although they live in tent communities near the major urban centers and buy and sell in the local markets, they are supplied by other gypsy and Turkomen people who transport goods from town to town.

Initially the Nabataeans received little respect from the populations around them. They were nomads, and whenever possible they took advantage of local situations to raise their prices to whatever the market would bear. Sometimes they provided luxury goods to the wealthy, but sometimes they dealt in prostitution and gambling. For this reason, the Nabataeans never mixed well with the local people. They usually lived in small communities outside of the city limits, often several miles away in an isolated area.

Above: Bozrah was the Edomite capital city on a flat mountain top.

A good example of this is found at the Edomite capital Bozrah. This ancient city was located on the top of a flat-topped mountain. Steep hillsides surrounded the city. The only access was via a narrow place where the mountain connected to the hills behind it. This made the Edomite capital city a natural fortress where the people could live in safety and security.

The Nabataeans settled nearby on a smaller mountain known as Sela. This was the place where King Amaziah of Judah took 10,000 Edomites prisoners and threw them from the summit of Selah. (II Kings 14:7) Since so many Edomites had been killed at this location, the Edomites seldom visited this rocky place. So the Nabataeans located here, building high-places, stairs and caves to store their goods. From Sela they visited the local towns and markets.

Over the years that followed, the Nabataean merchants slowly grew in wealth. Although they appeared poor to outsiders, their storerooms were filled with expensive goods, and they demanded high prices wherever they went.

The Nabataeans were always quick to earn money. Ancient records from Egypt demonstrate that the Nabataean merchants traded in exotic foreign goods, incense, medicine, and also in exotic foreign women. (Gibson, Dan, *The Nabataeans, Builders of Petra*, CanBooks, 2003 pp 24-25 concerning the archives of Zenon papyri) Within their own communities, however, the Nabataean always treated women with special honor, women and men were equals in business and in leadership in the home. The Nabataeans also practiced a form of democracy where decisions were made at a gathering of tribal elders and leaders. Everyone was free to voice his or her opinion, and the decisions of the leaders were discussed and challenged in their leadership forum. However, once a decision was made, everyone participated.

The Nabataean Problem

The Nabataean merchants were faced with several major problems. In order to trade sucessfully in the Arabian Peninsula they had to have regular supplies of water for their camel caravans.

All of the waterholes in the Middle East were claimed by tribal people, many of them zealously protecting their source of water. These tribes would attempt to charge the Nabataean merchants very high prices if they attempted to water their camels at their wells. The tribal rulers would also try and tax the caravans, requiring payment before they could pass through their lands.

In response the Nabataeans developed a brilliant strategy that provided them with water in the desert. They designed and built hidden water collection systems throughout the desert. These systems were designed to catch the occasional rainfall and store the water in underground cisterns.

Imagine traveling through the desert, winding your way between great mounds of rock searching for a source of water. How sad it would be to die unaware of water so close at hand. Unknown to those who traveled nearby, channels were dug into the rocks, high on the tops of the mounds and hills. Smaller rocks were strategically placed to direct rainwater.

At one end of the hill the water drained into a bell shaped cistern with a small opening in the ground just large enough for a man to get through. This led to a very large underground cistern. Small channels were cut into the mountains to direct the water towards the cistern. The Nabataeans would place a rock over the opening, allowing water to get into the cistern but blocking the hot sunlight and preventing most of the evaporation. The Nabataeans could then leave these collection systems to slowly collect and store water until they passed by. In this way, they conquered the desert, making it a place of refuge and protection for their camel caravans.

Navigation

From very early times Arabs used the stars for navigation. While other nations turned to the stars for fortune telling as astrology, the Arabs used the stars for navigating in the trackless deserts. Before the invention of the compass and the sextant, Arab merchants obtained latitude by measuring the altitude from the horizon to the Pole Star, (since the Pole Star did not move in the night sky). This was the simplest method, and was known as the science of *qiyas*. The easiest method was to use the width of a finger. When held at arm's length, the width of four fingers was considered to measure 4 *isba'*. In a 360 degree circle there were 224 *isba'*. The *isba'* was further divided into 8 *zam*. Thus land distances were often measured in *zams*. Later, when the Nabataeans took to sailing, they considered that a day's sailing due north would raise the Pole Star 1 *isba'* from the horizon.

Eventually the Nabataean merchants developed an instrument called a *kamal*. The end of a string was held in the teeth. The lower edge of a square was placed on the horizon while the square was moved along the string until the upper edge touched the required star. The knot at which the square stopped signified a certain number of *isba'* of altitude of the star. The altitude of the Pole Star could then be deduced from this.

In this way, the Nabataean merchants could navigate in the desert, using the altitude of the Pole Star and the steps counted from the last stop. This would always provide them with their exact position.

The Trade Routes

Eventually trade routes were developed throughout the Arabian Peninsula. Because of the mountains and deserts, all of the trade routes passed through the land of Edom, near to the Edomite capital city, Bozrah. Outside of Bozrah, the Nabataeans continued to use their mountain fortress 'Sela.'

The Bible tells us that King Solomon gained tremendous income from taxation:

> Now the weight of gold that came to Solomon in one year was six hundred and sixty six talents of gold. Beside this he received from the merchantmen, and of the trade of the spice merchants, and of all the kings of Arabia, and of the governors of the country. (1 Kings 10:14 KJV)

Six hundred and sixty six talents of gold is around 23 metric tons! The Bible tells us that to this total was also added the tribute paid by the Arab merchants and the leaders of the Arabs. Since many of the caravans traveled up the King's Highway and through the land of Edom, Edom played an important role in

23

the merchant world. As a result, Edom was conquered by the Israelites, the Assyrians, then the Babylonians, the Persians and even the Greeks.

Nabataean Trade Items

The Nabataeans traded in many items. Whatever was in demand in one area was obtained from somewhere else and transported to where it could be sold. Eventually the Nabataeans discovered that they could purchase most items very cheaply at their source, and sell them for exorbitant prices in foreign markets. Some examples of the goods they might have carried include vanilla, ginger, nutmeg, cloves, pepper, and leather.

Even silk from China was transported and sold to the Greeks, Egyptians and Romans. The Nabataeans would purchase silk garments from China and then take them apart and re-sew them into the types of clothes that the Romans would wear. Two centers were set up in the Middle East, one in Damascus and one in Gaza, which produced damask silk and gauze silk. These became famous in the western world.

However, there was one item that was more important to the Nabataeans than all of their other trade items. This was incense.

Incense

Incense was produced from sap taken from the Frankincense tree. This sap was dried in the sun and broken up into lumps. It was relatively light to transport, and when burned it gave off a fragrant smell. All of the civilizations of the world had a demand for incense because frankincense was used in many different ways.

First, people used it in temple worship. Ancient temples were erected to worship gods. Most cities had many temples, each focused on a different god. There were thousands of temples across Egypt, Greece, Rome, India, and beyond. Each of these temples required incense for their worship. Added to this, there were also many small altars in homes where people burned incense to their gods.

Incense was also a popular deodorant. Small incense burners would be lit, and people would stand over the burner allowing the incense smoke to flow through their clothing.

Additionally, Roman rulers customarily cremated the bodies of important people. During the funeral incense was burned to mask the smell of the burning flesh. Incense was so expensive that when the Roman Emperor Nero burned his wife's body at her funeral, he used so much incense that the Romans objected to the cost. The Greeks also discovered several medical uses for incense.

Incense became a highly valued commodity and the Nabataean merchants kept their sources secret. Since they were the only suppliers, they could charge whatever they liked. Like all good businessmen, the Nabataeans never told their buyers where they had obtained the incense. They closely guarded this secret for many generations.

The Incense Road

The incense road began in southern Arabia. Here, along the edge of the desert, frankincense trees grew in an area called the Hadramaut. Initially there was only one frankincense harvest, but as demand grew during the time of the Roman Empire, that harvest was increased to twice a year. Because of the successful trade the Yemenis grew wealthy and built cities with great mud buildings up to nine stories high, such as the city of Shibam.

From Shibam incense moved to the kingdom of Sa'aba, whose capital city was Yathul. The walled city of Yathul still lies in the desert, much the way it was during the time of the incense trade. It has long been abandoned, and few people know of its existence.

From Yathul the incense route extended north along a narrow route between the mountains and the Empty Quarter. This route passed through modern day Saudi Arabia and into Jordan.

Yathul, a walled city in Yemen

At the north end of the route, the caravans converged on Sela very near to the Edomite city of Bozrah. From this point caravans went to Gaza, Alexandria and Damascus. This trade route was the backbone of the Nabataean Empire's commerce.

Founding a Kingdom in the Land of Edom

In 586 BC everything in the Middle East changed. The Babylonian army marched through the Holy Land besieging cities, burning crops and destroying everything in its path. After conquering all the cities, including Jerusalem, they took Israelites captive. Hundreds of thousands were killed, and thousands upon thousands were forcibly taken back to Babylon. After the Babylonians returned, the land lay empty, with only a few of the very poorest people left. The Edomites then decided to move into the land of Israel. After all, the land of Israel was much more fertile than the Edomite land.

As the Edomites moved north, the Nabataeans from the Negev and from Arabia began migrating into the land of Edom. Before long the Nabataeans had completely occupied Edom, and for the first time in history the merchants of Arabia had a homeland.

Now, flush with money from centuries of trade, the Nabataeans began to build homes and erect cities. Eventually the Nabataeans also expanded their control northwards, and in 85 BC they took control of the ancient city of Damascus. At this point they controlled all trade between the east and the west.

The overland Silk Road between China and Rome was established at about the time that the Nabataeans took control of Damascus and the Middle Eastern section of the trade route. Now, with the Silk Road and the Incense Road firmly in their grips, the Nabataeans' wealth continued to grow. Around this time they also monopolized trade on the Red Sea and parts of the Indian Ocean, and also made contact with the Chinese. Shih Chi & Chien Hans Shu both mention Nabataean and Chinese contact as early as 100 BC.

The best records we have of Chinese and Nabataean contact comes from *Xiyu chuan* ("Chapter on the Western Regions") taken from *Hou Han shu 88.* The *Hou Han shu,* the official history of the Later (or 'Eastern') Han Dynasty (25-221 AD), was compiled by Fan Ye, who died in 445 AD. Fan Ye used a number of earlier histories, including the *Shi ji* by Sima Qian and the *Han sh*u by Ban Gu plus many others, most of which have not survived intact. During the Han dynasty Chinese maritime activity increased with Chinese junks meeting Arab dhows and trading in Sri Lanka's northern port of Balk Bay.

Nabataeans on the High Seas (India and China)

Very early in their history, a group of Nabataeans settled on the sea shore near Paran on the Sinai Peninsula. This group of Nabataeans herded sheep in the mountains and fished in the Red Sea. They kept a wary eye on the sea, for the storms that frequent the Red Sea would sometimes cause passing boats to capsize or be dashed on the rocks. The Nabataeans were always quick to take whatever they could from these shipwrecks. Eventually the Nabataeans obtained small ships of their own and used them to attack passing boats, taking their goods. The piracy grew so bad that the Egyptians dragged several military boats overland from the Nile River to the Red Sea so that they could protect their waters from these Nabatatean pirates. However, in time the Nabataeans defeated the Egyptian boats, and by the time of Christ they had taken complete control of all of the trade on the Red Sea.

Around 30 BC, Cleopatra and Anthony tried to escape from Egypt to India by dragging 60 ships from the Nile River to the Red Sea. The Nabataeans, however, alarmed at such a large force, armed their own boats and attacked and destroyed the Egyptian fleet. Upon hearing this news, Cleopatra and Anthony opted for suicide.

With no one to oppose them, the Nabataeans began to use maritime shipping in earnest, making frequent trips to India and beyond. Nabataean boats, (dhows) first made contact with Chinese ships at Palk Bay in Ceylon. Here a trading Emporium was set up, and Nabataean merchants traded goods with Chinese merchants.

In time, even the overland frankincense route declined, as boats rather than camels were the principle means of transporting incense from Arabia.

Nabataean Language

The Nabataeans spoke Aramaic, the same language that Jesus spoke. Over the centuries, however, they developed their own dialect, which eventually became its own language. During the time of Christ, however, most Middle Eastern people could still understand one another, despite the strong dialectic differences.

The Nabataeans, however, developed several clever writing systems. As merchants, they were always interested in keeping their trading and transactions as secret as possible. Since their spoken language was easily detectable they disguised their written language by using other language scripts. The most popular was the script used by the people in southern Arabia. Other scripts were also added, so that the Nabataeans could write in ways that the people around them could not read. They then used these scripts to leave messages in the desert. Today, over 30,000 desert messages have been found by archaeologists, using three different scripts, Nabataean, Thamudic, and Safaitic. The use of three different scripts helped form the image that the Nabataeans were secretive people.

Nabataean Religion

The Nabataeans traveled to many lands. As good merchants, they would pay homage to whatever god ruled over the various places that they visited. When passing through the Edomite area, they would pay homage to Dushares the god of the rocks and mountains. When passing through Egypt they would pay homage to the Egyptian gods, and when passing through Rome to the Roman gods. To the Nabataeans, a god was simply a deity that ruled over a particular place. In their own lands, they believed in many gods. Six of these gods became the pantheon of gods which was the Nabataeans primary religious focus. These gods were:

Al-Uzza	(The God of Power)
Al-Dushares	(The God of Rocks & Mountains)
Al-Kutbe	(The God of Writing)
Al-Qaum	(The God of War, Protection)
Al-Manaat	(The Goddess of Fate)
Al-Lat	(The Goddess of Fertility)

Unlike other nations, the Nabataeans were reluctant to give their gods human or animal form, so they used squares, triangles, circles, crescents and other shapes to represent their gods. The most common form was a square block. Outside of the Nabataean capital city of Petra there are over 20 huge square blocks known as jinn rocks. It is believed that these rocks represented Al-Qaum, the God of Protection, who watched over the city.

Within the city one can find niches in walls and rocks that have several blocks in them, each block representing a different deity. Eventually temples and holy places were constructed throughout Arabia to honor these gods. These gods are very important, as we will see later, as their characteristics influenced the later Muslim concept of Allah.

Nabataean Capital City

Around 100 years before Christ the Nabataeans decided to build a capital city. They chose a place in the Edomite mountains where they could construct a brand new city. This place was located at the edge of a very mountainous and rough area. They chose a valley between two huge rock mountains. The ends of the valley were closed off by city walls, but the people could enter and exit through a crack that ran through one of the mountains. This crack was known as the *siq*. At its narrowest point five soldiers could stand side by side across the entrance.

Inside the Nabataeans built spectacular buildings, many carved into the sides of the mountains. The first building, known today as the Treasury, stands at the end of the *siq*. Carved into solid rock, it towers above the visitors, awing them with its size and beauty. As visitors move farther along, they pass many tombs carved into the rocks, as well as a large theater. All of these buildings were designed to impress the visitor. Eventually the visitor would come to a column lined street that went through the center of the city. Temples, houses, and government buildings rose on every side. The road ended at the foot of the far mountain, where paths went up into the mountains to other great and impressive monuments.

The city had fresh running water and sewers. Water came in clay pipes from distant springs and cisterns providing the city with a constant supply of water. Eventually the Nabataeans built swimming pools and lush gardens.

Everything was designed to impress visitors with the Nabataeans' wealth and prosperity. Through this the Nabataeans wanted to impress upon others

Below: A monument in Petra. The door is over 2 stories tall!

that they were an important and honorable people, not just camel drivers from the desert.

Nabataean Burial Practices and Pilgrimage

Since the Nabataeans traveled to many different places, they wanted something that would keep them together as a nation, even though they were spread across the face of the earth. Their language was very important to them, but more important to them was that they were a tribal family that should be together in death. So when one of their members died, they would send the bones back to their country to be buried in a family grave.

There were several Nabataean burial cities where families maintained large and impressive tombs. When a Nabataean died, his body would be placed on a high place where the birds could strip the body of its flesh, leaving behind the bones. These bones would then be collected and placed in the family tomb. When someone died in a far country their bones were brought back to the family tomb so that the Nabataeans could all rest together in death.

Each family maintained its tomb, carefully looking after the bones of its dead ancestors. Beside each of the tombs, the families prepared a place where they could meet and remember the dead. Eventually the Nabataeans developed the practice of returning home to their family tomb for a remembrance meal. These were known as pilgrimages or 'hajs'. There was one important pilgrimage each year that everyone would try to attend if possible. There was also a lesser pilgrimage a half year later. If possible, Nabataeans from distant lands would try to visit their family burial place and remember the dead at least once during their lifetime.

During the pilgrimage the Nabataeans would gather at their family tomb. Here they would recite their family's lineage from Adam to themselves. They would remember the exploits of their dead relatives, and then they would eat a meal in celebration of their family. At the end of the meal, all of the dishes would be broken and discarded. Eventually great mounds of broken pottery were deposited around and outside of Petra.

Years later, when Muhammad brought the religion of Islam to the Nabataeans, he maintained the concept of a greater and lesser pilgrimage, although he changed what the Muslims did during their time at the holy city.

Nabataean Culture

The Nabataeans were obsessed with honor. For centuries they had been treated with contempt by the civilizations around them. Eventually they were able to build their own cities and have their own kings. When they did this they openly displayed their wealth and success. They began riding Arabian horses, dressing in silk, wearing gold, decorating their faces and hair, and living in large houses. Most Nabataean houses ranged from 600 to 2000 square meters in size, many of them with two stories, making some of them nearly 4000 square meters. These houses would usually be occupied by an extended family, but were built to a high quality and decorated with brightly colored painted patterns, all designed to impress.

Things went well for the Nabataeans until 70 AD, when the Romans sent a large army to put down a rebellion in Jerusalem. Following this the Roman army

Below: Ancient trade routes in Arabia

slowly moved around the countryside until all of Israel was brought under their control. Then the Romans turned their attention to the wealthy Nabataeans.

Roman Domination

There are no records of any war between the Nabataeans and the Romans. With a huge army on their borders, the Nabataeans simply negotiated with the Romans.

Four things happened to the Nabataeans when the Roman armies marched into their kingdom:

1. Many of the wealthy merchant families moved to Alexandria and even Rome where they became Roman citizens and began acting as the merchants of the Roman Empire.

2. Other Nabataean merchants moved much farther south to the port of Mocha (Mozza), which was outside of Roman control. From Mocha they continued their trade with ships to India and China, becoming the maritime merchants for the Roman Empire. The Romans never traded directly with India or China because the Nabataeans did it for them.

3. Some of the poorer Nabataeans stayed, raising horses, and continuing with local trade. Petra continued as an important local city for many years as capital of the Roman province of Arabia.

4. Some Nabataeans moved to Iraq and continued the overland trade with Asia.

Whenever the Romans conquered a new area, they usually produced a set of coins that would read "*Conquered ...*" such as "Conquered Egypt" or "Conquered Carthage." After the Roman armies marched into Arabia, however, Roman Emperor Trajan minted a set of new coins that had written on them, *Arabia adquista* or *Acquired Arabia* (pictured below). As good merchants the Nabataeans bought and sold everything, including their empire. In the end, the Nabataeans remained merchants, continuing their business, but without having their own empire or special identity.

Christianization and Byzantine Empire in the North

We are told in Acts 9 that the apostle Paul went to the city of Damascus seeking to persecute Christians. After his conversion he attempted to leave the city. Paul relates the story to us in II Corinthians 11:32: *"In Damascus the governor under King Aretas had the city of the Damascus guarded in order to arrest me, but I was lowered in a basket from a window in the wall and slipped through his hands"* (NIV). King Aretas was a well-known Nabataean king living in Petra. His governor was in charge of the city of Damascus. So at this point the Apostle Paul was in the Nabataean kingdom.

Later, Paul went into Arabia. Galatians 1:15-18 tell us the story:

> But when God, who set me apart from birth and called me by his grace, was pleased to reveal his Son in me so that I might preach him among the Gentiles, I did not consult any man, nor did I go up to Jerusalem to see those who were apostles before I was, but I went immediately into Arabia and later returned to Damascus. Then after three years, I went up to Jerusalem to get acquainted with Peter and stayed with him fifteen days. (NIV)

Scholars are unsure how many years he spent in Arabia, but estimates put it at somewhere between three years and twelve years. Then he returned to Damascus and stayed there for three years. Later friends took him to Jerusalem.

From a Judean perspective, there was only one Arabia at that time: the Nabataean Empire. Surely Paul must have had some impact on the Nabataean lives that he touched during the years of his sojourn in their empire.

First Persecution

During the next two hundred years, the church in the Roman Empire slowly grew. The first major persecution of Christians took place under the Roman Emperor Diocletian around 284 AD and continued for thirty years. In Arabia, some Christians were martyred although churches continued to be built in the various Nabataean cities in the Negev. Not long after this persecution, the Christian chronicler Eusebius thundered against the Nabataeans in Petra for being filled with superstitious Christians who had sunk into theological error.

Byzantine Empire Starts

In 330 AD, Emperor Constantine the Great transferred the capital of the Roman Empire to the Greek city of Byzantium and rebuilt it as a Christian city. It was then renamed Constantinople. As soon as Constantine began to encourage Christianity, construction of churches began everywhere in the Middle East.

Jerome of Stridonium

One of the oldest references to Christianity and the Nabataeans comes from a description written by Jerome in 390 AD in Bethlehem. Jerome was born in 342. He was a gifted and diligent scholar, a master of languages, and a lover of books. Jerome was educated in Rome and in his mid-twenties was baptized as a believer. Several years later he was secretary to Pope Damasus until his death. Under Damasus' encouragement, he started work on a Latin translation of the Scriptures, which would one day become the Vulgate translation of the Bible.

After the death of Damasus, Jerome left Rome and settled near Bethlehem, building a school for study and translation. From this point he not only worked on his translation, but also directed young men in Christian outreach. One of the men studying under him was Hilarion. In one of his writings, Jerome describes the role of Hilarion as he ministered to the Nabataeans at Elusa, a Nabataean city in the Negev:

> *"... the journey which he (Hilarion) once undertook in the Kadesh desert in order to visit his pupils. He reached Elusa with a great following of his disciples, and this happened on the day on which all the people had gathered in the temple for the annual festival ... When it became known that Hilarion was journeying by (he had recently healed many Saracens possessed by demons), they went to welcome him. They bowed their heads and called in the Syrian (Nabataean) language 'Barech,' i.e. 'Bless us.' He received them politely and modestly and prayed that they should serve God and not the stone. Crying copiously, he looked up to heaven and promised that if they believed in Christ, he would visit them often. Through the wonderful mercy of God, he stayed there and did not leave them until they had drawn up the plan of a church and their priest had been instructed and given a wreath with the symbol of Christ."* (Nicene and Post-Nicene Fathers*, Ph. Schaff and H. Wace)

Pagan worship, however, continued in the city of Petra. A man called Mar Sauma felt called upon to change this situation. He and his forty brother evangelists were traveling around the area converting pagan temples into churches. They arrived in Petra in 423 AD to find the gates shut against them. Their demands to be let in, accompanied by threats if they were not, coincided with a rainstorm of such intensity that part of the city wall collapsed and they managed to get in anyway. The whole episode was deemed to be of truly miraculous significance, as there had been an unbroken drought for four years. The impressed pagan priests converted to Christianity. A few years later, Christians in Petra converted what is now known as the Urn Tomb into a cathedral and Asterius was appointed as a bishop.

On July 9, 551, a great earthquake leveled Petra. The temples collapsed, and thousands of people were killed. While people continued to live there, the city started to decline rapidly. The Prophet Muhammad was born around 570 AD, 19 years after this great earthquake.

The Divided Kingdom

The church in the north of Arabia had lost the power of its message and the missionary zeal to proclaim it. Churches had become traditional and ritualistic. While a few people might become Christian through conversion, most people officially became Christians at birth and were baptized as infants into the church. Most Christians belonged to the Nestorian, Monophysite or other sects. The Bible was not well known nor available to the common people. Most religion was learned from priests.

There was also a considerable Jewish presence in north Arabia. Most Jews in the Middle East were involved in trade, commerce, goldsmithing and jewelry manufacturing. As merchants they competed directly with the Nabataean merchants. Many of the Jews in Arabia had fled there after the Roman invasion in Israel in 70 AD.

The Roman Empire and the subsequent Christian Byzantine Empire only penetrated isolated areas of Arabia. Most people were pagans, and temples to Al-Uzza, Al-Dushares, Al-Kutbe, Al-Qaum, Al-Manaat, and Al-Lat were common. The Qur'an speaks a great deal about the gods Al-Uzza, Al-Manaat and Al-Lat. In the Qur'an they are called Uzza, and Lat.)

Nabataean and Greek Names

When the Nabataeans started building their impressive cities, they began adopting the dress and culture of the western civilized world. They began wearing western dress, riding horses instead of camels and using Greek and Roman names instead of Arab ones. This has created problems for historians, as they have problems distinguishing between Greeks and the Nabataeans, especially in the northern part of the empire. Many Muslim Arabs today do not recognize that there ever were Christian Arabs because most of the names found in church records in Northern Arabia are Greek names rather than Arab names. In central and southern Arabia where the Nabataeans remained pagan, they continued to use their traditional names plus names related to their gods.

Eventually there were two churches, the Romanized western church, which acknowledged the leadership of the pope in Rome, and the Eastern Byzantine church, which had patriarchs for leaders.

In time the Byzantine churches grew very ornate, but their understanding of the Bible dwindled. People were impressed with the churches and decorative services rather than with the simple, life-changing message of the Bible. Eventually church traditions would have equal value with Scripture, and in some groups greater value. As the Byzantine Empire spread across the northern part of the Middle East, worship was always in the Greek language which was regarded as the proper Christian language for worship. Slowly churches became more formalized, and the use of icons was adopted. Icons were pictures of biblical events that were painted on the walls of churches. Eventually these paintings took on special meaning, and were incorporated into the worship of the church. Later people started praying before icons. The church leaders encouraged this, as they taught that icons helped people concentrate on spiritual things. Eventually icons became objects of prayer itself, and people began praying to the saints in the Bible. Priests also began charging people money when they came to ask for help or special blessings. Prayers for the dead were also incorporated into church life, usually for a price. In time, the church lost its power and evangelistic zeal.

Some of the Nabataeans moved east to Iraq. Their pagan religion developed into something that others called devil worship. These are now known as the

Yezidi people of Iraq and Turkey. In central Arabia many Nabataeans remained pagans worshiping Al-Uzza, Al-Manaat and Al-Lat.

Questions for Reflection and Group Discussion

1.   Review the Nabataean pantheon of Gods:

      a.   Al-Uzza   (The God of Power)

      b.   Al-Dushares   (The God of Rock & Mountains)

      c.   Al-Kutbe   (The God of Writing)

      d.   Al-Qaum   (The God of War, Protection)

      e.   Al-Manaat   (The Goddess of Fate)

      f.   Al-Lat   (The Goddess of Fertility)

      Do any of these attributes reflect the true nature of God as revealed to us in the Bible?

2.   Think about how the Nabataeans portrayed their gods. What shapes did they use? Why do you think they did not use human or animal shapes?

3.   How did the pursuit of honor and wealth corrupt the Nabataeans?

4.   Read I Timothy 6:10 and Hebrews 13:5. Why do you think the Bible warns us of pursuing wealth?

Chapter Three
Abdul Mutalib, Rebuilding a Lost Empire

Abdul Mutalib belonged to the distinguished Beni Hashim tribe, a subgroup of the Quraysh tribe of Mecca, which traced its genealogy back to Ishmael and Abraham. In 497 AD, just before he was born, Abdul Mutalib's father died while doing business in Palestine. He was given the name "*Shayba*", meaning "old man" in Arabic, because he was born with a few white hairs. After his father's death he was raised in the north Arabian city of Yathrib with his mother and her family until about the age of eight, when his uncle Mutalib came to take him to Mecca. When he first arrived in Mecca, people assumed the unknown child was Mutalib's slave, and they gave him the name Abdul Mutalib which means "slave of Mutalib." When Mutalib died, his son succeeded him as the chief of the Beni Hashim clan.

Many of the great rulers of the Middle East today trace their heritage back to the Beni Hashim tribe. (Examples include the ruling family of the Hashemite Kingdom of Jordan and the late Saddam Hussein of Iraq.)

Zamzam

Hundreds of years before, the ancient well or cistern of Zamzam was filled up and its location was forgotten. One day, Abdul Mutalib had a series of four dreams directing him to the location of the Zamzam well. Abdul Mutalib began to dig, with his only son Harith standing guard over him because people objected to the idea of disturbing the ground next to their temple, known as the Ka'aba. It was a tense moment, until Abdul Mutalib's tools struck the covering of the long-lost well. Not only had he found the well, but all through history people had occasionally dropped valuables down the well, so Abdul Mutalib recovered considerable wealth.

At this success, the Quraish tribe argued that since the well was the property of Ishmael, it and the valuables belonged to the whole tribe. Abdul Mutalib rejected their claim, saying that it was given to him by the gods.

They agreed to present their case to a wise woman of the tribe of Sa'd in far off Syria. During the trip, Abdul Mutalib's water reserves were depleted, and his group began suffering from thirst. The leaders of the other group refused to give them water and Abdul Mutalib advised his group to dig graves so that when someone died others could bury him.

The next day as they dug their graves, Abdul Mutalib exhorted his companions that it was cowardice to succumb to death. According to Muslim tradition, he mounted his camel, and its foot hit the earth, producing a stream of water. The two groups drank from the fountain, and the group that opposed him said, "The gods have decided between you and us. We will never dispute with you about Zamzam." (Isn Isaq, *The Life of Muhammad*, #93, translated by A. Guillaume, Oxford University Press, 1955 p 63)

Abdul Mutalib's experience at the well made him long for more sons who could stand beside him when the need arose. He prayed to the gods to give him more sons, and vowed that if he were blessed with ten sons, he would sacrifice one of them to gods at the Ka'aba. His prayers were answered, and over the years he had nine more sons, the most favorite of whom was his youngest, Abdullah, whose name means "slave of Allah." He did not forget his vow, and when all his sons had grown up, he took them to the Ka'aba and had lots cast to determine who would be sacrificed. Abdullah was chosen.

The entire community was in an uproar over the situation. The wives and daughters of Abdul Mutalib were upset and they called upon their families for support. The other brothers asked Abdul Mutalib to sacrifice something else instead of their youngest brother. Abdul Mutalib was upset because he had made a vow and must keep it, but he did not relish the idea of sacrificing his favorite son.

Finally he agreed to consult the wise woman about whether a replacement could be provided, and what form it should take. After a long trip they reached

Sa'd. The wise woman provided the solution to the problem. She told Abdul Mutalib to cast lots between Abdullah and ten camels. If Abdullah were chosen, then he should add ten more camels, and continue until his Lord accepted the camels and the lot fell to them. So they returned to the Ka'aba and cast lots, but Abdullah was chosen. They added ten more camels.

But again Abdullah was chosen. This continued until there were one hundred camels. Only then did the lot fall to the camels. Abdul Mutalib had the test repeated a second and a third time, and each time the lot fell to the camels. Finally Abdul Mutalib was convinced that the hundred camels were acceptable to Allah as a replacement for his son. The camels were sacrificed and Abdullah was spared.

Persecution of Christians in Yemen

Dhu Nawâs was the last king of the Arab Himyarite kingdom of Yemen. According to the Christian historian, John of Ephesus, Dhū Nuwas converted from paganism to Judaism. Soon after this he announced that he would persecute the Christians living in his kingdom because Christian countries had persecuted his fellow Jews in their realms. Simon, the bishop in Arabia in 524 AD, wrote a letter where he told the story of the persecution in Najran.

After seizing the throne of the Himyarites around 518 AD, Dhū Nuwas attacked the Christians at the town of Zafar, capturing them and burning their churches. He then moved against the area known as Najran, a Christian stronghold. After accepting the city's surrender he massacred those inhabitants who would not renounce Christianity. Estimates of the death toll from this event range up to 20,000 people.

Dhū Nuwas then proceeded to write a letter to the king of Hira and the king of Persia, informing them of his deed and encouraging them to do likewise to the Christians under their dominion. The King of Hira received this letter in January 519 AD as he was receiving an embassy from the Christian Byzantine Empire seeking to forge peace with Hira. He revealed the contents of the letter to the Christian ambassadors, who were horrified at its contents. Word of the slaughter quickly spread throughout the Byzantine and Persian realms, and refugees from Najran even reached the court of the Byzantine emperor, Justin I, begging him to avenge the martyred Christians.

Several Christian kingdoms, including Ethiopia, cooperated together to form an army, and their fleet arrived off the shores of Yemen around 520 AD. A Christian from south Arabia named Sumuafa' Ashawa' was appointed to rule Yemen and a battle ensued.

Arab tradition states that when Dhū Nuwas realized that he was losing the battle he committed suicide by riding his horse into the sea. Archeologists understand from an inscription that he was killed in the battle.

Many of the Christians in the attacking army realized that Yemen was a very fertile land. According to the historian Procopius, one of the generals, Abraha, seized control of Yemen from Sumuafa' Ashawa' with the support of dissident elements within the occupation force that were eager to settle in the Yemen. An army sent by the Byzantines and Ethiopians to subdue Abraha joined his ranks so everyone had to accept Abraha as the ruler of Yemen.

Abraha became a prominent figure in Yemen's history, promoting the cause of Christianity in the face of the prevalent Judaism and the paganism of Central Arabia. A zealous Christian himself, he is said to have built a great church at Sana'a' and to have repaired the principal irrigation dam at the city of Ma'rib.

Many of the pagan Arabs continued to take pilgrimages to the Ka'aba in Mecca even after Abraha built his cathedral in Sana'a, the capital city of Yemen. It is said that this church was so large that its roof could not be seen from the ground and that it was decorated with gold, silver and pearls. Abraha then forbade the Arabs to travel to the Ka'aba.

Some of the Quraysh tribe of Mecca traveled secretly to Yemen and desecrated the cathedral with dung, and tried to burn it. Abraha swore that he would take apart every brick of their holy Ka'aba and destroy it. He began gathering a large army. According to Islamic tradition an elephant led the army and several Arab groups were defeated on the way to Mecca. When news of the advance of Abraha's army came, the Arab tribes united in defense of the Ka'aba.

Near the city of Mecca the Yemeni army captured a large herd of camels. Two hundred of the camels belonged to Abdul Mutalib, the leader of the Quraysh clan.

A man from the Himyar tribe was sent by Abraha to advise the Meccans that Abraha only wished to demolish the Ka'aba, and if they resisted, they would be crushed. Abdul Mutalib told the Meccans to seek refuge in the mountains, while he with some leading members of Quraysh remained near the Ka'aba.

When the messenger returned, Abdul Mutalib went with him to meet Abraha and demanded that his camels be returned. Abraha was very surprised at this and replied, "I thought you were a very respectable and honorable man, but the first thing you have said has made me change my mind. I have come to destroy your Ka'aba and all you are worried about is your camels!"

Abdul Mutalib replied, "The owners of the Ka'aba are its defenders, and I am sure they will save it from the attack of the adversaries and will not dishonor the servants of this temple."

Abraha replied, "Your gods cannot defend it from me." Abdul Mutalib said, "Then do as you wish." So Abraha gave back the camels and Abdul Mutalib returned to Mecca. The people then fled the city and waited in the mountains to see what would happen.

When the army arrived, the elephant refused to break down the Ka'aba. It sat down and refused to move. When beaten it bolted, killing several people. Their army was then defeated and Abdul Mutalib was declared a hero.

That year came to be known as *Amul Fil* or *The Year of the Elephant,* and the years afterwards were numbered as being so many years after the year of the Elephant. This practice ended when it was later replaced with the Islamic calendar.

The Qur'an refers to this event in Sura105 (The Elephant) where it is recorded that when the Abraha's forces neared the Ka'aba the soldiers of Allah appeared in the form of a dark cloud of small birds that destroyed Abraha's army by dropping pebbles from their beaks. Abraha was seriously wounded and retreated towards Yemen but died on the way. The Qur'an then says:

> *"Have you not seen how your Lord dealt with the owners of the Elephant? Did He not make their treacherous plan go astray? And He sent against them birds in flocks, striking them with stones of baked clay, so He rendered them like straw eaten up."* (Sura 105)

This conflict occurred in 570 AD the same year that Muhammad was born.

Restoration Attempt

Abdul Mutalib desired to see the old Nabataean kingdom restored to its former glory. He and his sons visited all of the areas where the Nabataeans had settled and endeavored to unite the Nabataean tribes, but they could not.

An old Jewish rabbi told Abdul Mutalib that he could never unite the Arabs, because the Arabs had no prophet. The Jews had David, and the Christians had Jesus, but the Arabs had never had a prophet. The attempt at reuniting the empire had failed because religion split the Nabataeans. Those in the north were Christians, and those in the south were pagans.

Abdullah, the son of Abdul Mutalib who had been spared from being sacrificed, was married to a young woman named Aminah. Shortly after their marriage, Abdullah left with a caravan to trade in Palestine and Syria. On the way home he stopped in Yathrib to visit his family members who lived there. He took sick and died during his visit. Aminah was deeply grieved over the death of her husband. Her only consolation was the knowledge that she was carrying his unborn child. Sometime later her son, Muhammad, was born.

Aminah died when Muhammad was five years old, so Muhammad went to live with his grandfather, Abdul Mutalib, until he was eight. Then he was given to his uncle Abu Talib, a prominent Quraish chief and custodian of the Ka'aba.

Weakening of Christianity in the North

Ever since the time of the New Testament, there have been Christians in Northern Arabia. The early church was vibrant and alive, but after many centuries, tradition replaced faith, and children were assumed to be Christians because their parents were. Eventually Christianity became the religion of the state, and Christianized Byzantine Empire ruled most of Northern Arabia. While these people professed the name of Christ, true faith was slowly replaced by religious activities.

Icons

Byzantine Christians liked to decorate the walls of their churches with pictures that depicted scenes in the Bible. Eventually it became customary to have pictures of Bible characters as well as church leaders painted on walls. Five hundred years after Christ, the Byzantine Empire began to discourage all paintings of humans that were not religious people.

In European churches, statues were slowly adopted as aids for worship, supposedly helping the Catholic Christians to focus their prayers, either to

God or to the saints portrayed in the images. The Eastern Church abhorred the use of statues - but continued with the use of paintings. Very often Christians faced these paintings, or icons as they called them, and addressed their prayers to the saints portrayed in them. Over time reports were made of miraculous icons that gave off fragrant smells, healing oils, or performed miracles. The leaders of the Byzantine churches gave the credit to the saints portrayed by the icons, rather than to God alone.

Eventually icons became a major focus of worship in Middle Eastern Greek Orthodox and Russian Orthodox churches.

When Islam was founded, the prophet Muhammad was shocked by the church's adoration of images. To him this was equal to worshiping idols. Muhammad urged his followers to worship only the God of heaven, who created the world and who would judge mankind. He commanded his followers never to make an image, not of a human being, nor of an animal. Thus when Islam emerged as a great religion, the walls of its buildings were decorated with geometric shapes rather than images or statues. Later, when Muslims occupied Byzantine lands, they forced churches to remove their icons and cover their mosaic floors with plain tiles.

Prayers for the Dead

Around 600 AD Pope Gregory the Great accepted and developed the doctrine of purgatory. This new teaching was then introduced into the Byzantine Empire. While the church taught that sins were pardoned by a loving God, the law required that sin be punished. Therefore, they believed that Christians would suffer punishment at the hands of God, and after some time of suffering, they would pass into heaven. To support this, the church used the verse in the Bible where Jesus Christ declares in Matthew 12:32, "And whosoever shall speak a word against the Son of man, it shall be forgiven him: but he that shall speak against the Holy Ghost, it shall not be forgiven him, neither in this world, nor in the world to come." According to the Church these words prove that in the next life "some sins will be forgiven and purged away by a certain purifying fire." They argue "that some sinners are not forgiven either in this world or in the next" would not be truly said unless there were other sinners who, though not forgiven in this world, are forgiven in the world to come. (*City of God* XXI.24) Thus they taught that man would pay for his sins in a place called purgatory. It fell to reason that if Christians go to purgatory first, then those still on earth should pray for them, that God would have mercy on them and speed or lighten their punishment.

As Islam was founded, the prophet Muhammad was shocked by the teaching of purgatory and praying for the dead. He taught that when men die they immediately face judgment. God would weigh their good and bad works. He taught that all through life their deeds were noted and one day they would be judged. Those who had truly submitted to God's religion as brought by Muhammad would be granted access to paradise. Those who failed would be cast into hell.

Ritual Fasting

Fasting has always been seen as a religious activity. The pagan people of Nineveh declared a fast after Jonah preached to them. The Jews of Persia fasted for three days before Queen Esther went in to the King. The Pharisees in Jesus' time fasted regularly. So the Byzantine church followed suit, and encouraged the faithful to fast on a regular basis. Eventually the church proclaimed four main fasts, which generally meant that the person fasting abstained from meat, dairy, fish, olive oil and wine.

1. The Nativity Fast was the 40 days preceding Christmas. It usually began on November 15 and continued through to December 24. This fast usually became more severe from December 20, until Christmas Eve.

2. The Lent Fast consisted of the 40 Days preceding Palm Sunday, and Easter.

3. The Apostles' Fast began the first Sunday after Pentecost and extended to the Feast of Saints Peter and Paul on June 29.

4. The Dormition Fast was a two-week long Fast usually from August 1 through August 14.

In addition to these fasting times, people also fasted every Wednesday and Friday, and the monks also fasted on Mondays. In essence the followers of the Byzantine Church spent almost half of the year practicing one kind of fast or another.

When Muhammad was to institute his new religion, fasting would play a large role. Instead of asking his followers to abstain from only certain items on certain days, Muhammad instituted the month long fast of Ramadan. This fast was much simpler than the Byzantine fast. Muslims fasted from the first day of the month (new moon) until the last day of the month (new moon). The fast was complete. Absolutely nothing was to be swallowed. Nothing was to pass down the Muslim's throat from sunrise to sunset. It was simple, and very effective. The fast was to be followed by several days of feasting and celebrating, which soon became a focal point in the new religion.

Honoring Mary

The ancient Byzantine church held Mary in high honor. They believed that she was conceived like any one of us, and inherited the sin of Adam, but was cleansed from it when Christ took form within her. This, coupled with the belief that she never committed any sin made her the perfect vessel. The church also believed that Mary was a perpetual virgin, in that even after giving birth to Jesus, she remained a virgin. They were perfectly aware that the New Testament has several references to the "brothers" and "sisters" of Jesus (Matthew 13:56 and Mark 6:3), who, however, are nowhere referred to as Mary's children. They believe that Aramaic, the language spoken by Jesus and his disciples, lacked a specific word for "cousin," so that the word "brother" was used instead. They also argue that the account of the loss of the twelve-year-old Jesus in Jerusalem (Luke 2:41-52) means that Jesus was an only child. Then, when dying on the cross, Jesus entrusted his mother to the beloved disciple, an action interpreted as signifying that Mary had no other children, since if there were any, one would have expected them to take her into their home.

Modern protestant theologians, however, argue that Mary did not remain a virgin and that the "brothers" of Jesus were indeed his biological half-brothers, sons of Mary and Joseph, arguing that the word for "brother" is distinct in Greek from the word for "cousin." They add that Joseph may have been a widower, making the brothers step-brothers. They also argue that since Jesus' brothers were not believers (John 7:5) until after the resurrection (Acts 1:14), Jesus entrusted Mary to the beloved disciple (traditionally John).

The Eastern churches also taught that the perpetual virgin Mary, died, after having lived a holy life. Eleven of the apostles were present and conducted her funeral. St Thomas was delayed and arrived a few days later. Wanting to venerate the body, they opened the tomb for St Thomas, but the body of Mary was gone. It was their conclusion that she had been taken, body, and soul, into heaven. While every Orthodox Christian believes this to be true, the church has never formally made it a doctrine; and so it remains a holy mystery.

The ancient Byzantine church spoke of veneration of Mary and the saints, never worship. They were always careful to separate these two terms. Worship was reserved for God, veneration for Mary and the saints. In practice however, many eastern Christians cannot distinguish between the two.

When Islam began, the church was caught up with veneration of the Virgin Mary. Islam spoke out against this, claiming that only God could be worshiped. The idea of perpetual virgins, however, did slip into Islam, when describing women who would be given as rewards to faithful Muslims in paradise. We will study more of this later.

Christian Armies

Once the Byzantine Empire was Christianized, the army of the empire became a Christian army. From that point on, they not only defended the empire, but they also fought for causes that furthered Christian agenda. Since many people were religious in a Christian way rather than true believers, they pursued wealth, power, and prestige through physical force. At this time, the world was divided into two great forces: pagan nations and Christian ones. As the church desired to take its message around the world, military forces were used to protect church workers and occupy and rule the lands that were Christianized. Once an area was converted to Christianity, the army enforced

Christian rule. In many instances lands were conquered and then pronounced Christian.

Remember what happened in Yemen? When the Yemeni ruler, Dhū Nuwas, converted from paganism to Judaism, he announced that everyone in Yemen would be Jewish. After he had massacred many Christians in Najran, the Byzantine army attacked him in order to avenge their deaths. Abraha then became the ruler of Yemen and announced that everyone was now a Christian. This practice of using force to spread religion was adopted by Islam, and was used very effectively to spread Islam across North Africa and Asia.

Questions for Reflection and Group Discussion

1. In the Middle East, the Byzantine church still exists in the form of the Orthodox Church. They claim that they are the one true church descended directly from the early church. How would you share the gospel with an Orthodox Christian who claims that his church is right because it has an unbroken line of authority right from the apostles down to the priests today?
2. How should Christians regard statues and icons? What would you say to Orthodox Christians, or to Muslims?
3. Should Christians pray for the dead? Why or why not?
4. What is a true Christian fast? What verses from the Bible talk about fasting?
5. Should Christians honor Mary? What is true honor and what is worship?
6. How should we react to persecution and trouble? Should Christians raise an army and fight for their rights? Why or why not?

Chapter Four
Muhammad, the Prophet

The Making of a Prophet (570 AD – 622 AD)

After Abdullah's death, Muhammad and his mother Aminah lived with Abdul Mutalib. When Muhammad turned six Aminah died, leaving him an orphan. His grandfather was in charge of many merchant ventures and was also acknowledged as the chief of Mecca. Muhammad lived with his grandfather until he was eight years old. This period of time had a significant impact on his life, as his grandfather was always obsessed with trying to restore the ancient Nabataean Empire.

When Muhammad was eight years old, Abdul Mutalib died, so he was sent to live with Abu Talib, because he was a brother by the same mother to Muhammad's father. During his early teens, Muhammad accompanied his uncle on several trading journeys to Busra in Syria. During one trip Muhammad made an acquaintance with Bahira, a monk who lived alone in a small cell. The two of them spoke of religion, and Bahira took a special liking to Muhammad.

Muhammad Marries Khadija

Khadija was a merchant woman of dignity and wealth, but she was a widow. She hired men from the Quraysh tribe to transport her goods to foreign markets on a profit-sharing basis. When she was prepared to send goods on another journey, several merchants approached her. One of them was Muhammad, who wanted to try his hand at foreign trade. Khadija accepted his offer and sent a young man from her household called Maysara with him. They traveled to Syria and returned after some time with trade goods, which she sold at a handsome profit. Maysara spoke highly of Muhammad, and a relationship soon formed between Khadija and Muhammad. Khadija had many suitors who wished to marry her, but she had not found any that seemed trustworthy or interested in her wellbeing rather than her riches. Muhammad was different, and eventually Khadija proposed marriage. Muhammad's uncles all agreed, and the two were married. This was very helpful for Khadija, for this secured her financial resources and stopped the interest of suitors. For Muhammad, marriage gave him instant status and financial stability. It also provided him with time to be at ease and enjoy life. After this Muhammad was known as "al Amin" or "the trustworthy one."

Rebuilding the Ka'aba

When Muhammad was 35 years old, someone entered the sacred Ka'aba and stole from the money that was gathered there. The citizens of Mecca then decided to rebuild the Ka'abah, making the wall higher and adding a roof and gates so that it could be closed.

That year a Greek ship had been cast ashore, so the Meccans hired a Christian Coptic carpenter from the ship to help them. They then divided the Ka'aba into sections, with different Quraysh tribesmen working on different sections. In rebuilding the Ka'aba a question arose as to who should have the honor of raising the black stone into its proper place. The black stone was a large meteorite that had fallen to earth many centuries before and had been revered by the Nabataeans as a representative of Al-Dushares, the god of rocks and mountains. Each tribe claimed the honor of raising the stone, so an argument broke out. A respected senior citizen advised the disputants to accept for their arbitrator the first man to enter the gate. The proposal was agreed upon, and the first man who entered the gate was Muhammad. His advice satisfied all the contending parties. He ordered the stone to be placed on a piece of cloth and each tribe to share the honor of lifting it up by taking hold of a part of the cloth.

In this manner the stone was deposited in its place, and the rebuilding of the House was completed without further interruption.

Once the Ka'aba was rebuilt, people began to flock to it to worship all the gods that it contained. During this time they would walk around the Ka'aba addressing all of the gods. Ibn Ishaq later reported that there was even a sect that did this while naked.

The renewed interest in worshiping at the Ka'aba alarmed the Christians living in Mecca, and soon a great debate arose in the city whether there was one God or many gods. The first new convert to Christianity was Suliman, a Persian young man who was drawn by the prayers he heard, as he listened outside of a church. He was followed soon afterwards by four men who broke from the Nabataean religions, claiming that they were going to follow the religion of Abraham their father. Eventually they were forced to leave Mecca.

Mount Hira experience

At 40 years of age, Muhammad decided to follow the pagan practice of *Tahannuth*, where a person would go into seclusion for one month to meditate. He left his home and went to a cave in nearby Mount Hira. One night the figure of an angel appeared to him holding a coverlet of brocade and commanded him to read. (A coverlet is a bedspread and brocade is a thick heavy fabric into which raised patterns have been woven.)

Muhammad answered, "What shall I read?"

The figure pressed it to him so tight that Muhammad thought he would die. "Read" he was commanded again.

"What shall I read?"

"Read!" he was commanded a third time.

"What shall I read?" Muhammad begged in terror. The angel answered, "Read: in the name of thy Lord who created, Who created man of blood coagulated. Read! The Lord is the most beneficent, Who taught by the pen, Taught that which they knew not, unto men."

Muhammad then awoke from his sleep, and the words would not leave him. This terrified him, and he later said, "I was afraid that I was possessed by a demon. None of God's creatures were more hateful to me than a man possessed; I could not even look at them. I thought: Woe is me. Never shall the Quraysh say this of me. I will go to the top of the mountain and throw myself down that I may kill myself and gain rest." (Ishak 153, pg 106)

So Muhammad began to climb the mountain. About midway up he heard a voice speaking, "Oh Muhammad, you are the apostle of God and I am the angel Gabriel." Where ever Muhammad looked, Gabriel stood in front of him, so he could not climb higher.

Eventually Muhammad gave up and returned back to Mecca, where he collapsed in his wife's lap and asked her to cover him for he was sick. He then confessed to her that he might be demon possessed. She tried to comfort him. Later she sent a message to Waraqa bin Naufal, who was one of the four men who had converted to Christianity, and told him of Muhammad's experience. Several days later, while Muhammad was walking around the Ka'aba praying, Waraqa bin Naufal came to him and asked him what he had seen. After he heard the account he was very impressed and told this to Muhammad.

Several days later Khadija came to Muhammad with a request. "When the angel Gabriel comes to you, can you speak and talk to people?"

"Yes"

"The next time you see him, can you call me?"

Several days later Muhammad said to Khadija, "I see Gabriel"

"Get up and sit on my left leg," she implored him. He did so. "Can you see him?" When Muhammad confirmed this she asked him to sit on her right leg. Gabriel was still there. Then she had him sit on her lap. The whole while Muhammad could still see Gabriel. Then she stripped herself of her clothing. "Can you still see him?"

"No," he replied.

"Oh Muhammad!" she exclaimed "He is an angel and not a demon for he withdrew when I exposed myself. This is an ancient test which I learned from my mother." Muhammad accepted this and from this point on never questioned Gabriel's authenticity. (Ishak 154, pg 106)

Muhammad continued to receive further revelations. Sometimes he would simply recite what he had already received, and sometimes he would go into a trance. When receiving his revelations, he sometimes closed his eyes and foamed at the mouth. Sometimes he roared like an animal. Those who saw him noted he seemed as if "his soul was being taken from him" or he was intoxicated.

(Mishqaq Vol 4) Al-Waqedi noted that Muhammad was so repulsed by the form of the cross, that he would break it whenever he came across one.

Muhammad then began to speak out against the multiple gods of the Nabataeans, proclaiming that there was only one true God. Muhammad identified this God as Allah, the god of Abraham, Isaac, and Jacob. The Quraysh were alarmed and soon they began to create trouble for those who showed interest in Muhammad's teachings. While Muhammad was protected because of his status as a wealthy merchant, many of the poorer people who were accepting his teachings were beginning to be persecuted. As this persecution grew, Muhammad advised them to move to Abyssinia (Ethiopia) in Africa, so eighty-three men and their families left Mecca.

12 Years of Persecution (Satanic Verses)

In the years that followed, persecution continued. Muhammad desired that all of his tribe should follow his new teachings. He proclaimed that there was only one God, who was a God of reckoning. He said people would either go to hell, or to a great garden of delight. The people of Mecca mocked him and threatened him.

The Satanic Verses event took place at this time. During one of his revelations in the local temple, Muhammad uttered Sura 53:19-20 "Have you then considered Lat and Uzza and the third, Manaat?" Here Muhammad seems to concede that the people could continue to worship the Nabataean god of power, and the goddesses of fate and fertility. There are some Hadiths (Traditions) that say that this verse was originally followed by "…whose intercession may be counted on." Remember, the Nabataean's believed in several gods: Al-Uzza (the God of Power), Al-Dushares (the God of Rocks and Mountains), Al-Kutbe (the God of Writing), Al-Qaum (the God of War and Protection), Al-Manaat (the Goddess of Fate) and Al-Lat (the Goddess of Fertility).

When the people of Mecca heard this they were greatly pleased at the way in which he spoke of their gods. Muhammad then prostrated himself, facing north as was his custom, and many of the people of Mecca joined him. After their time of prayer they said, "Muhammad has spoken of our gods in a splendid fashion."

Eventually news reached those in Africa that the people of Mecca had accepted Muhammad's teaching, and they decided to return. Upon their return they were shocked at the teachings of Muhammad. Muhammad then repented of what he said, claiming that Satan had put the words into his mouth. According to the Qur'an, the angel Gabriel came and chastised him for his compromise. Sura 22:52 says: "*And we never sent a messenger or a prophet before thee but when he desired, the devil made a suggestion respecting his desire, but Allah annuls that which the devil casts, then does Allah establish His messages, for Allah is knowing and wise.*"

From this situation we learn about the Muslim concept of abrogation, or the canceling of one revelation through further revelation. This was later applied to the teachings of the Old and New Testament when Muslims claimed that the Qur'an replaced them.

During the time of persecution that followed, Muhammad claimed that one evening he was carried from Mecca to the temple location on top of Jerusalem by a winged donkey. There he met with Abraham, Moses and Jesus and many of the prophets and prayed with them. When he returned in the morning, the Quraysh were angry saying that it took a long time to travel to Jerusalem and return, yet Muhammad claimed to do it in one night.

Since Muhammad had never been to Jerusalem, the people challenged Muhammad to describe different things he had seen in Jerusalem. As he did so, those who had visited Jerusalem confirmed that his descriptions were correct.

Muhammad then went on to describe a ladder that had come out of the sky, and when he climbed it he reached heaven and the Gate of the Watchers. When he entered the lowest heaven he met many angels. At one point he saw a man who met all of the spirits that came up from the earth. He was told that this was Adam, who greeted all of the spirits of his descendants. He then went around the first heaven and saw people in various forms of punishment for things they had done on earth, including those who charged interest on loans, homosexuals, and unfaithful women. He then went up to the second heaven and met Jesus and John the Baptist. In the third heaven he met Joseph son of Jacob, and in the fourth heaven he met a man called Idris. According to Muslim tradition Idris and Enoch are the same person. In the fifth heaven he met Aaron son of Imran (Moses' brother). In the sixth heaven he met Moses son of Imran. In the seventh heaven he met Abraham, who took him to see another place called Paradise, where he saw a beautiful woman who was to belong to Zayd bin Haritha, one of the people of Mecca.

Khadija Dies

Khadija and Abu Talib died the same year, and after their deaths trouble came to Muhammad. The following three years proved very difficult for him, as these two had been his main supporters and protectors in the community.

Muhammad then started visiting the surrounding markets and fairs offering himself as a prophet to the various Arab tribesmen that gathered there. Many of the low class people began to revere him, but the wealthy continued to spurn him. When Muhammad visited a fair at the port city of Aqaba, six men who were Helpers at the fair listened intently to him. The following year Muhammad returned to the fair at Aqaba, and twelve men pledged themselves to the prophet. The following year the number had grown to 73 men and two women. They all returned to their various homes, talking about Muhammad wherever they went. (Ishaq 294, pg 202)

The Hijra

Eventually trouble arose in Mecca and one Muslim man Abu Salama was so ill-treated that he and his family moved to the city of Medina in the middle of Arabia. He was well received, and soon Umar bin al-Khattab and his family followed. Ibn Ishaq in his early history of Muhammad tells us (321) that there then followed waves of emigrants leaving Mecca. Muhammad and a few close followers however stayed behind in Mecca.

The leaders of the Quraysh tribe then met and discussed imprisoning or killing Muhammad. They decided that one representative from each of the families should be chosen and when night came they would gather and all partake in the killing of Muhammad. That night Muhammad was visited by the angel Gabriel who told him to flee. He and the few followers that were left fled to a cave near Mecca and waited there several days. Eventually the searchers gave up and Muhammad and his followers moved on to Medina. Others of his followers slowly joined him. (Ishaq 339) The date of the emigration from Mecca to Medina is set by Muslims as June 20, 662, and marks the beginning of the Muslim calendar.

Mecca and Medina, Creating an Empire 622 AD – 632 AD

The followers of Muhammad prepared a house for him and then they prepared a place of worship. The city welcomed Muhammad and immediately included him among the governors of the city. The tribe of Ansar were distantly related to Muhammad and the first from Medina to embrace Islam. In Medina the Muslims began to discuss how to call the Muslims to prayer. The Jews used a trumpet and the Christians used a bell. The Muslims considered using a bell, but that night one of Muhammad's followers had a dream in which he was told a better way to call people to pray. He then shouted out the call to prayer in a sort of chant. As he shouted out the chant, another man said that he too had heard the same chant in one of his dreams. Muhammad said, "God be praised for this," and the Muslim call to prayer was official.

In order to support themselves, the Muslims often undertook raids into the desert, preying on the surrounding villages and Bedouin tents. They especially focused on the caravans on the incense road. They were particularly hostile to those going to and from Mecca. It is claimed that two years after the Hijra about 300 Muslim raiders attacked and defeated a caravan of 1000 Meccans at the Battle of Badr. When they returned triumphantly to Medina, many people were so impressed with the Muslims that they decided to join them. Many songs and poems were created, and even to this day, Muslims look back on the Battle of Badr with great pride.

The Muslims continued with their raids around the country, taking loot from many people, becoming rich and powerful in the process. Many tribesmen, seeing the power of the Muslim forces converted and joined them.

The following year, (624 AD or 3 AH) the Meccans gathered an army and attacked Muhammad and his followers at Uhud defeating him. Muhammad himself was wounded, and 70 Muslims were killed. This defeat caused many of those who were supporting Muhammad to withdraw their support. Five years after the Hijra (5 AH), the Meccans sent an army estimated at 10,000 men against Medina. That battle became known as the Battle of the Ditch or the War of the Trench because of a trench Muhammad had dug around the town. Although the siege lasted some time, it ended in failure for the Meccans, who then returned home. The Quraysh never again opposed Muhammad by force.

Muhammad and his followers called the fallen Muslim martyrs and they were given special reverence. Many songs and poems were composed for them. The Muslim forces continued to raid all through central and northern Arabia. During these raids, many people joined them because of the booty they would gain.

By 8 AH the Muslims were raiding into the old Edomite territory and eventually reached Muta the southern point of the Byzantine Empire. (Ishaq 794) From there Muhammad decided to attack Mecca, as certain Meccans had taken Muslim lives and he wanted revenge. The Muslim army then turned on Mecca, invading the city and destroying idols.

Trouble with the Jews

During their stay in Medina, the Muslims and the Jews began to clash. Jewish rabbis confronted Muhammad and accused him of misunderstanding and misquoting Scripture.

Angry with the Jews who had turned on him, Muhammad instructed his men to destroy them. In one day his men beheaded either 600 or 900 Jewish men, depending on the sources. Their wives and children were sold as slaves and their property was confiscated by the Muslim men.

Things seem to have gone down-hill, morally, from this point. The Muslim army's attention began to focus on capturing material goods and taking women captive. This obsession with sex was encouraged by Muhammad's behavior. Two months after Khadija died, Muhammad remarried. He then took other wives, not just four as his revelations permitted, but many during in his lifetime.

Muhammad's Marriages

All together Muhammad married 11 or 13 women depending upon the differing accounts of who were his wives. After the death of Khadija, Muhammad began to marry many different women, but he did not marry them all at one time. Below is a list of Muhammad's wives.

Khadija: At the age of 25, Muhammad married a woman named Khadija who was 40 years old at the time and this marriage lasted for 25 years. She was the first woman he married and his only wife until she died. Their sons were Qasim and Abd-Allah (who were nicknamed al-Tahir and al-Tayyib). Their daughters were Zainab, Ruqaiya, Umm Kulthum and Fatima. There is some dispute between Muslim scholars regarding the four daughters of Khadija. Were they born to Khadijah from an earlier marriage, or were they in fact the daughters of a widowed and dead sister of Khadija? Most Sunni Muslims believe Muhammad had four daughters with Khadija, while the Shi'a Muslims do not.

Sawda: The death of Khadija left Muhammad lonely and it was suggested to him that he marry Sawda, who had suffered many hardships after she became a Muslim. Muhammad married her one month after Khadija died when she was about 55 years old, in the tenth year after the Hijra.

Aisha: Aisha was the daughter of Abu Bakr, a close friend and confidant of Muhammad, and a controversial figure in the differing records of the Shi'a and Sunni narratives. Muhammad married Aisha before the Hijra, but Muslim scholars differ on whether Muhammad married Sawda or Aisha first. Muhammad married Aisha when she was six years old but did not consummate this marriage until she reached the age of nine. Aisha lived with Sawda during this time.

Hafsah: Muhammad married Hafsah daughter of 'Umar bin Al-Khattab three years after the Hijra. Her husband had been killed in the battle of Uhud. She was 18 at the time.

Zaynab: Muhammad married Zaynab four years after the Hijra, but she died two or three months after marriage. She was nicknamed *Umm Al-Masakeen* (roughly translated as "the mother of the poor"), because of her kindness and care towards them. She was the widow of a man who was martyred at the battle of Uhud.

Umm Salama Hind: Umm Salama Hind was the widow of Abu Salamah. She married Muhammad in the fourth year of Al-Hijra.

Zaynab: Muhammad took another wife named Zaynab. She was his cousin, being the daughter of one of his father's sisters. At the time of the Hijra she was likely a widow, and had probably emigrated with her brothers who were also Muslims. Upon arriving in Medina, she was forced by Muhammad, against her will, to marry his adopted son Zayd. In the year 626 Muhammad went to visit Zayd at his house to talk to him. Zayd was not there, but, according to traditional Muslim sources, Muhammad saw Zaynab scantily clad, and he greatly desired her. Muhammad did not force Zaynab but left, saying to himself, "Praise be to God, praise to the manager of hearts!" Zaynab told her husband about this, and Zayd at once offered to divorce Zaynab, but Muhammad told him to keep her. After these events, life with Zaynab became unbearable for Zayd, and he divorced her. When her waiting period was complete, Muhammad married her. Muhammad's contemporaries criticized him for this marriage because of its incestuous character. It was considered incest for a man to marry a woman who had once been married to his son, and an adopted son was counted the same as a biological son. However, this marriage was justified when the angel Gabriel revealed another verse in the Qur'an:

> "So when Zeyd had performed the necessary formality (of divorce) from her, We gave her unto thee in marriage, so that (henceforth) there may be no sin for believers in respect of wives of their adopted sons, when the latter have performed the necessary formality (of release) from them. The commandment of Allah must be fulfilled." (Sura 33:37)

This verse implied that treating adopted sons as real sons is objectionable, and that there should now be a complete break with the accepted morals of the past.

Juwayriya: Juwayriya was among the booty that fell to the Muslims from a raid. She was a portion of one of the Muslim raiders who made her a covenant to set her free at a certain time. When she was set free, Muhammad married her, in the sixth year of Al-Hijra.

Ramlah: Ramlah was married and emigrated with her husband to Ethiopia. When her husband converted to Christianity, she stood fast to her Muslim religion and refused to convert. When her husband died, Muhammad dispatched someone to the king of Ethiopia with a letter asking for Ramlah. He married her in the seventh year of Al-Hijra.

Safiyya: Safiyya was a Jewess captured in the battle of Khaybar. Her father had been beheaded before the battle. Muhammad also married her in the seventh year of Al-Hijra.

Maymuna: Muhammad married Maimunah after the Lesser Pilgrimage, also in the seventh year of Al-Hijra.

Maria: Maria was a Coptic Christian slave, sent as a gift from a Byzantine official. Muhammad later freed her, and upon marriage she assumed the title, "Mother of the believers" like all his other wives.

Raihanah: Raihanah was captured as a slave after the defeat of the Bani Qurayza tribe. She later became a Muslim but remained a slave in Muhammad's household.

Children and Grandchildren

None of Muhammad's sons lived to marry but he did have two grandsons, Hassan and Husayn, born to his daughter Fatima and his son-in-law Ali.

Muhammad's widows

The prophet's wives were all revered as *Mother of the Believers*. It was considered tantamount to incest for a Muslim to marry one of Muhammad's widows, so none of his widows remarried after his death.

Abu Bakr and the succeeding rulers known as *caliphs* made provision for Muhammad's widows and relatives out of the proceeds of the Muslim conquests. One-fifth of the spoils were to be given to the ruler, as public funds. Part of this was devoted to pensions. Neither the wives nor the relatives were satisfied with this decision, and there are many traditions recounting their complaints to Abu Bakr and the succeeding caliphs.

Was Mohammed Illiterate?

Muslim people are divided on this issue. Most Muslims, however, believe that Mohammad was illiterate and thus could not have written the Qur'an, proving that it was a revelation from God. In order to prove this they use Sura 7:157. Some read this verse as saying, "The unbooked prophet" and claim that this means "the prophet was unbooked" or was illiterate; however, others argue that it could mean he was a "prophet to those who did not have a book or a scripture of their own." The Jews and Christians already had a book, so Muhammad was the prophet to the unbooked people.

Those who claim that this means that the prophet was unlettered go on to claim that the Qur'an was a miracle. However, others argue that even if he could not read or write Muhammad could have used a scribe.

Historians argue that Nabataean merchants were literate as they had to write out bills of sale. Most Nabataean merchants could speak several languages. Nabataean shepherds even left graffiti on rocks and stones. Besides this, Muhammad's cousin Ali was one of the foremost literary figures of his time.

Islamic traditions tell us that when the Treaty of Hudaibah was being signed, Muhammad took a pen from Ali, struck out the words in which Ali had designated him as "the apostle of God" and wrote instead with his own hand the words, "son of Abdullah." (Sahih Muslim, Book 019, Number 4403) Also, on his death bed Muhammad asked for a pen to write. (Sahih al-Bukhari, Volume 1, Book 3, Number 114)

The argument that Muhammad was illiterate and so could not be the source of the Qur'an is pointless for there was no need for Muhammad to be literate. His followers always memorized his revelations. As far as anyone can tell, the Qur'an was not committed to writing until much later after Muhammad died.

Death of Muhammad

Muhammad died when he was 63 years old. On his death bed he is supposed to have said: *"Today I have perfected your religion and have chosen for you Islam. I have left for you the Qur'an, and the religion Islam."* (Sahih Muslim Book 043, Number 7155, and Sura 5:9 Malik translation) He then told his followers to hold to these.

He died after a 10 day illness. The people of Medina refused to believe it but Abu Bakr said, "Whoever worshiped Muhammad, know that Muhammad is dead. Whoever worships Allah, know that Allah lives." (Bukhari Volume 2, Book 23, Number 333)

Dissension arose immediately after Muhammad died. When his body was lying on the lap of his wife, a fight broke out over who would be the next leader. Soon after this Islam split into two movements: Shite and Sunni.

Muhammad was a great military and political leader but power seemed to 'go to his head.' From a Christian point of view several things seem questionable. When Muhammad needed financial support he raided caravans going to Mecca. When there were no caravans his men raided the tribes and villages around Arabia, especially attacking Jews and Christians. When Muslim men began dying in battle, Muhammad announced that whoever died in a holy war would be forgiven and go straight to the Gardens of Paradise. When his wealthy and influential wife died, he entered into a series of marriages, including one child of nine years old. When people complained about his marriage to his son's wife, he received a convenient revelation that allowed it. Muhammad led 27 battles and gave orders for another 39. The historian, Sa'id Muslim records that he ordered the beheading of 900 Jewish men and directed at least 27 assassinations or massacres.

Responding to Muslims

Muslims commonly ask Christian visitors to their lands three questions. 1. Where are you from? 2. Are you a Muslim? 3. What do you think of Muhammad?

Christians usually say they are Christians, and they often wisely say that they do not know much of Muhammad, but they know about Jesus, and would be happy to tell the Muslim about him. However, in their own hearts, most Christians wonder about Muhammad. What should they think of Muhammad?

Ever since New Testament times people have said that they were prophets of God. I John 2:18-23 tells us:

> *"Little children, it is the last time: and as ye have heard that antichrist shall come, even now are there many antichrists; whereby we know that it is the last time. They went out from us, but they were not of us; for if they had been of us, they would no doubt have continued with us: but they went*

*out, that they might be made manifest that they were not all of us. But ye
have an unction from the Holy One, and ye know all things. I have not
written unto you because ye know not the truth, but because ye know it,
and that no lie is of the truth. Who is a liar but he that denies that Jesus is
the Christ? He is antichrist, that denies the Father and the Son. Whosoever
denies the Son, the same hath not the Father: (but) he that acknowledges
the Son hath the Father also."* (KJV)

The Bible recommends to us to test the spirits and all new messengers.
When Muhammad arrived he brought a religion that denied that Jesus
was the Son of God. The verses we just read clearly tells us, *"Whosoever
denies the Son, the same hath not the Father."* It is clear that Muslims,
who deny the sonship of Jesus, are not true followers of God. However,
Muhammad did bring many positive corrections to the false Christian
teachings of his day. He spoke out against icons and statues that the
Christians were beginning to revere and worship. He spoke out against
the veneration of Mary and the saints, insisting that there was only one
God worthy of worship. However, the message he brought was not in
agreement with the Bible; rather it reflected Muhammad's worldview
and cultural needs.

Testing the Spirits

Do you remember the test that Khadija did to see if Gabriel was really
an angel? As soon as she removed her clothing Gabriel disappeared. The Bible
provides us with other ways of testing the spirits. Do you know where this is
taught in the Bible?

*"Beloved, believe not every spirit, but try the spirits whether they are of God:
because many false prophets are gone out into the world. Hereby know ye
the Spirit of God: Every spirit that confesseth that Jesus Christ is come in
the flesh is of God: And every spirit that confesseth not that Jesus Christ is
come in the flesh is not of God: and this is that spirit of antichrist, whereof
ye have heard that it should come; and even now already is it in the world.
Ye are of God, little children, and have overcome them: because greater is he*

that is in you, than he that is in the world. They are of the world: therefore speak they of the world, and the world heareth them. We are of God: he that knoweth God heareth us; he that is not of God heareth not us. Hereby know we the spirit of truth, and the spirit of error. " (I John 4:1-6 KJV)

Here we are told several ways to test the spirits. First, the spirit must agree that Jesus the Messiah is come in the flesh. Second, if the spirit speaks of worldly things and the world receives them, then it is not of God.

Think of Muhammad. He reacted badly when he saw a cross. He denied that Jesus was anything more than a prophet. He refused to accept him as God incarnate who came in the flesh. His message offered men a life of sexual pleasure. He also offered a paradise of physical pleasures, rather than spiritual ones. And the world readily accepted Islam as their religion.

Questions for Reflection and Group Discussion

1. What are the marks of a true prophet according to the Bible? Use both the Old Testament and New Testament for this. (Think of miracles, fulfilled prophecies, consistent with former revelations, Deuteronomy 18:15-18)

2. Was Muhammad demon possessed or obsessed? Consider spiritually: heard voices, hatred of the cross. Morally: obsessed with sex, loved power, directed battles and assassinations. Materially: sought financial gain, loved money, participated and encouraged looting, killing and raping.

3. How could Muhammad accurately describe Jerusalem even though he had never been there?

4. Is Islam a religion of faith or works or both?

5. Compare Jesus and Muhammad using the temptations of Jesus. How did Jesus react to temptation? How did Muhammad react?

6. Does God abrogate, change, or annul his word? Why or why not? How would you speak to a Muslim who insists that the Old Testament and the New Testament are no longer valid, because God has brought forth a newer revelation?

Chapter Five
Expansion of Islam

So far we have been studying about the founding of Islam. Christians often ask several questions at this point. The first is about the Muslim's name for God: Allah. Where did this name come from, does it refer to the same God that Christians worship and how does a Muslim's understanding of who God is differ from ours?

Did Allah exist before Muhammad?

During the time of the prophet Muhammad, people in Arabia began to use the name "Allah" for God. This is recorded in the Qur'an and the Hadith literature of Islam. Previous to this, very few written accounts exist about what was happening in Arabia. If any existed, they were destroyed in the fighting that took place during the early years of Islam. Today our sources of life in Arabia come from:

1) Outside sources like Byzantine church records in northern Arabia (Jordan, Syria, Lebanon, etc)
2) Graffiti written on rocks and canyon walls throughout Arabia
3) Islamic sources written 300 – 400 years later

Today many Christians have wondered about the name "Allah." Where did it come from? Did Muhammad make up a new name for God, or was the name "Allah" known to others?

In ancient times, one of the names for god was *'El.* It meant "strong one." This name for God was used throughout Canaan, Edom, Israel and Arabia.

Many people had names that incorporated El such as Wadal-'el ("friend or lover of 'El"), Daniel ("judged of 'El"), Micha'el ("one is like El") Waqi'ha'el ("El protects"), and so on. This is found hundreds of times in Nabataean and Safaitic graffiti as well as in the Bible. Think of the name El-Shadda (Exodus 6:3). The name *El* in various forms appears over 40 times in the book of Job, one of the oldest books in the Bible. Later, the Nabataeans used *El* as a name for God. One Nabataean name, Rav'el ("El is Great") is the name of two Nabataean kings. *El* names are found in other Arabian scripts such as Safaitic, Thamudic, Himyarite, Qatabanian, Sabaean, and Palmyrene.

The main word that the Jews used for God was Elohim pronounced *al-o-heem*. When the Jews wanted to emphasize the word, they emphasized the first syllable and elongated the middle vowel to make it Eloah (*al-ow-ah*). There are 123 instances of this in the Old Testament. There were various pronunciations of this word, and in some cases it was pronounced with little emphasis on the middle 'o', thus becoming *ALLoAH*, with the o dropping from the middle. Thus, when the Arabs heard the Jews talking of the God of Abraham, they made it into Allah, pronounced *al-l-ah*. The Arabs held the *al* sound rather than pronounce the *o*. Many really religious Muslim scholars and clerics today still pronounce "Allah" very similar to the Jewish *Eloah*. When the Arabs wrote "Allah" they usually wrote the letters "El" three times. Al-el-lah = Allah.

Interestingly enough, there are ancient inscriptions that mention Allah. This was sometimes written as "Illah." (double *El*). Some of the Nabataean names were: 'Aush'allah ("Allah's faith"), 'Amat-'allahi ("she is a servant of Allah"), Hab-allahi ("beloved of Allah"), Han-allahi ("Allah is gracious"), Abd'allah ("slave of Allah"), and Shalm-lahi ("Allah is peace"). The name Wahab-allah is found throughout the entire Nabataean region and means "gift of Allah." This demonstrates that Allah was accepted as a name for God long before the time of Muhammad, and was often used by Christians.

For many centuries Muslims have used the term, *Bi Ism Allah iRahman iRahiim* ("In the name of Allah, the Merciful and Gracious") whenever they begin a formal talk or write something formal. This term is used several times in the Old Testament:

Exo 34:6	El	The LordGod is merciful and gracious
2Ch 30:9	Elohim	God is gracious and merciful
Neh 9:17	Elowah	God ready to pardon, gracious and merciful
Neh 9:31	El	A gracious and merciful God
Psa 86:15	El	A gracious and merciful God
Joel 2:13	Elohim	God is gracious and merciful
Jonah 4:2	El	A gracious God, and merciful

The term *Bi Ism Allah irRahman irRahiim* was used on many Arab church documents before the coming of Islam. Christians stopped using this when the Muslims began to use it in every document and in everyday speech.

How is Allah different from the Christian God?

For Muslims, Allah is the all powerful creator and sustainer of heaven and earth, the judge and rewarder of mankind at the end of life, who has revealed his word to the prophets of old. For centuries churches in the Middle East have agreed with this and have used the term Allah for God. However, the Muslim understanding of the character of God is quite different from the Christian understanding of the character of God.

When Muhammad introduced Muslims to the God called Allah, he combined the characteristics of the old Nabataean gods along with some concepts taken from Judaism and Christianity. All of these were combined into the idea of Allah.

• Jewish God: incorporated as the creator of the world who revealed his word to prophets all down through history, even though many people rejected the word of the prophets.

• Christian God: incorporated into Islam as the God who will judge men and reward them. Islam teaches that Jesus will return to earth to marry, have children and die a natural death.

• ElUzza: the god of Power was incorporated into the characteristics of Allah who rules the world like a great sultan. His will is always done, and he does whatever he desires, be it for good or evil. Muslim men in their homes imitated this and became the sultans of their homes, ruling over their wives and children.

- El-Dushares: the god of Rock and Mountains was incorporated into Muslim worship by keeping the Black Stone in Mecca as the focus of daily prayers. After all, it was through the placing of this rock that the people accepted Muhammad as chosen of God.
- El-Kutbe: the god of Writing was incorporated into Allah, who revealed himself in books which he wrote and then sent down to his prophets. These books were sent to all of the people groups of the earth.
- El-Manaat: the goddess of Fate who arranges everything through time was incorporated into the Muslim idea of fate where nothing is done without God's will. Muslims often refer to the phrase, "It is written," demonstrating that whatever happens is the will of God.
- El-Qaum: the god of War and Protection was incorporated into the Muslim faith where Allah encourages his followers to fight for the faith and fight to spread the faith, giving Muslims the concept of holy war.
- El-Lat: the goddess of Fertility was particularly attractive to men who desired to have ready access to sexual pleasure. Muhammad allowed men to have up to four wives plus concubines and slaves for their pleasure. He also allowed them to easily divorce their wives and marry others, made the men rulers over the women so that they could demand sexual gratification at will, and promised the men a paradise where beautiful women existed only to satisfy their sexual lust.

By combining key concepts of all of these gods into one, Muhammad created a religion that would appeal to followers of Judaism, Christianity, and Nabataean paganism. This was one of the keys of his early success in spreading his religion in Arabia.

Should we use 'Allah' in our ministry?

This problem seems to face foreign Christians ministering to Muslims. It is not a problem to Middle Eastern Christians who have always used the term 'Allah' for God.

The Bible uses various names for God: El, Yahweh, Jehovah, etc. These names can be spelled in many different ways, in English, Aramaic and Hebrew. All of these are simply labels.

An earthly father is often called by different names. His children may call him "Dad" or "Daddy" and his wife may use other names. All of these are simply labels that are used to address the man. As long as "Daddy" refers to themselves and not some other man, most men are happy with its use. In much the same way, Allah works fine for addressing God. Muslims and Christians in the Middle East understand that you are talking about the creator God of the universe. They may misunderstand many things about his character, but they do understand who you are talking about.

The Black Rock

Integral with Islam is the revering of a meteor that fell from the sky. This black rock was originally in a more square shape, but due to millions of people kissing it over the centuries it has been worn oval and smooth. Today it is broken in several pieces and encased in a silver holder, but for centuries the pagans of Arabia worshiped it as a representative of the god Al-Dushares.

In the second century AD, several centuries before Muhammad was born, the ancient historian Maximus of Tyre commented in his book *Philosophoumena*, *"The Arabs serve a god I know not whom, but I saw this statue which was a square black stone."* The book *Suda Lexicon*, which was compiled at the end of the tenth century, refers to older pre-Islamic sources which have since been lost. It states:

> *"In Arabic Petra they worship the god Dushrara and venerate him above all. His statue is an unworked square black stone. It is four (unclear unit of measurment) high and two (unclear unit of measurment) wide. It rests on a golden base. They make sacrifices to him and before him they anoint the blood of the sacrifice that is their anointment."*

The meaning of the ancient measurements have been lost but the meaning of the passage is clear. The Black Rock resided in ancient Petra and was worshiped by the Nabataeans as the god Dushrara. (Dushares)

The Pre-Islamic Concept of Gods and Holy Locations

In pre-Islamic history, polytheism prevailed. People at that time entertained the idea that gods were attached to locations. For example, Dushares was the God of the Edomite mountains. Whenever people journeyed through those mountains they left an offering for the local gods. It did not mean that they exclusively worshiped Dushares, but rather that they respected him and offered something at his shrine. When traveling farther south in Arabia, they might also leave a tribute to the god Wad (Manawat) or Lat. (Al Lat). People were very aware of local gods, but they were also aware of solar or stellar gods which seemed to have a wider influence. Such gods were often represented by the crescent shape.

People usually did not try and export the worship of a local god to other locations. There were exceptions to this rule. Sometimes a group of people arose that tried to impress others with the power or usefulness of their local deity. Kings who went conquering and merchants who traveled tended to take their gods along with them. While these people would give some tribute to a local deity, they might also insist that their own gods were superior to the local gods.

Sometimes a contest between the gods resulted in order to demonstrate whose god was greatest. In a war situation the victor's gods were generally considered superior. If a natural disaster occurred, enterprising persons might convince others of the superior nature of their god.

Local Nabataean gods were often represented by square blocks or other shapes. Some gods had special shapes, like a star, a crescent, or some human characteristic. Human characteristics became popular as the Roman Empire spread.

Nabataeans believed that a particular god resided in a particular place. Thus temples were erected near or at the residence of the gods. Others believed that the gods would visit the temple once it was built.

The Ka'aba

The Arabs of Mecca were merchants. Over time, these merchants had filled Mecca with temples to various gods. After the great earthquake in 551 AD most of the major cities in Arabia had collapsed. The citizens of Mecca dug through the rubble of their city and brought the idols and sacred objects to a central place where nothing more could fall on them. This collection of deities and religious objects became a "holy place" where all the gods were worshiped. This was very different from the Syrian and the Roman worlds. Most Roman cities had multiple temples, each serving a different god. Mecca on the other hand seems to have had only one holy place active at the time. Here 360 gods or holy objects had been collected. These objects were placed around the outer walls of a compound. If each venerated object took up a space of 1 meter, then the original Ka'aba would have measured 90 meters along each side. This was a large area. Visitors could then walk around the open area passing by each holy object as they prayed. This religious function was called *tawaf* meaning "circumambulation".

The Ka'aba today in Mecca measures only 13 by 9 meters and is obviously not the original Ka'aba. Either the modern Ka'aba is much reduced in size, or it does not exist in the same location as the ancient Ka'aba.

Jahaliya: Times of Ignorance

Muslims consider the time before Muhammad to have been the time of ignorance. This has a special term in Islam, known as *Jahaliya*. Originally it meant that people were ignorant of Muhammad and his message, but today many Muslims consider all preIslamic history a time of ignorance and unworthy of any attention. As a result most Muslims know little about ancient history. For them history begins with Muhammad, and everything before him is unworthy of effort.

The Last Years of Muhammad

Muhammad's final years were filled with wars and fighting. The Muslims in Medina fought with the people of Mecca. In effect, the Muslims in Medina were fighting with Muhammad's family and tribal relatives.

AD 624   Muslims raid caravans which leads to the successful Battle of
                Badr (324 Muslims vs. 950 Meccans)

AD 625	Muslims defeated in the battle of Uhud
AD 627	Meccans repelled at the battle of Ahzab (Battle of the Trench)
AD 628	The Treaty of Hudaibya allows Muhammad to return to Mecca the next year
AD 629	Muhammad returns to Mecca on his 1st pilgrimage with 2,000 Muslims
AD 630	Muhammad and 10,000 Muslims take Mecca on Jan 11th general amnesty declared. Ka'aba cleansed. Muslims in control of Mecca
AD 632	Muhammad dies

The Four Rightly Guided Caliphs

1st Caliph—Abu Bakr (632-634 AD)

After Muhammad's death Abu Bakr the prayer leader who had been a faithful companion of Muhammad, was elected as the leader of the Muslims. He was an uncle by marriage to Muhammad and was respected as a leader.

Abu Bakr's first task was to move through Arabia uniting the Arab tribes. After the death of Muhammad, a number of tribes turned from the faith back to paganism, so Abu Bakr sent a large number of faithful Muslims to subdue the revolt forcibly. This resulted in the Battle of Yamama, and sixty of Muhammad's close companions who had memorized his revelations were killed. Under Abu Bakr's military leadership Yemen and Arabia were united under Islam. Then Islam expanded into Syria and Iraq.

2nd Caliph – Umar (634 – 644AD)

Umar was a powerful and harsh member of the Quraish tribe and a new convert to Islam. He was a great military leader, however, and the Muslim armies looked up to him. Under his leadership the Muslim armies captured Damascus (636 AD) and then Jerusalem (638 AD). They gained control of Egypt (641 AD) and then expanded into part of Persia.

Umar also made an important change in Arabia. As many of the Arabian men were away at war there was a dearth of Muslim men in Arabia. Many of the men had taken their wives with them and had moved to the fringes of the empire, where they made their living looting, raiding and furthering the Muslim Empire. Under Umar's leadership most of the Jews and Christians were forcibly moved out of Arabia. This massive moving of people created much unrest, but Umar, rich with the wealth of conquest, paid compensation to those who were moved. Now the Holy city of Medina was surrounded by a solid Muslim population.

3rd Caliph—Uthman (644-656 AD)

Uthman continued to solidify Islam. The empire had expanded so rapidly at the expense of religious development. Now with hundreds of thousands of new followers, the religion of Islam needed to be reinforced. Uthman began by commissioning a group of religious men to gather up the fragments of the Qur'an that had been written on bits of rock, bone and skins. Then they gathered some of those who had been present when Muhammad gave his revelations and they worked out an official text of the Qur'an. This reduced the number and frequency of disagreements over dogma, but many devout believers at the time accused Uthman of tampering with the sacred book.

On the military front, Uthman defeated a Byzantine attempt to retake the city of Alexandria in Egypt in 645 AD, and two years later he started conducting raids west of Egypt into Byzantine North Africa. He then commissioned the construction of a Muslim fleet to guard the Mediterranean against Byzantine naval attacks. Uthman moved on to conquer the island of Cyprus in 649 AD, and he continued with the conquest of Persia.

However, a climate of discontent spread throughout the new Islamic empire, and in June 656 AD a group of Egyptian rebels assassinated Uthman in his home. From that point on, the position of caliphate ceased to be a sacred position of leadership for the entire Muslim community, and became instead a prize to fight over.

4th Caliph – Ali (656 – 661 AD)

Ali was the son-in-law of Muhammad by marriage to Fatima, the daughter of Khadija, Muhammad's first wife. His followers felt that the succession should be in the family of the prophet. He was an early and faithful follower of Islam, and he had tried to curtail the corruption of the Quraish tribe who were awash in loot taken in conquest. Also, Ali had not given his allegiance to the other caliphs.

Not everyone accepted Ali as the next caliph. Aisha, who had been married to the prophet before she was nine years old, and who was the daughter of Abu Bakr, the first Caliph, accused Ali of being lax in bringing Uthman's killers to justice. She raised her own army to try and defeat Ali in what was called the Battle of the Camel. It took place in 656 AD a mere 24 years after the death of Muhammad.

Ali's army defeated Aisha's forces, so she apologized to Ali and was allowed to return to her home in Medina where she withdrew from public life. However, Ali was not able to overcome the forces of Mu'awiya, Uthman's cousin and governor of Damascus, who also refused to recognize him until Uthman's killers had been apprehended. At the Battle of Suffin, Mu'awiya's soldiers stuck verses of the Qur'an onto the ends of their spears, with the result that Ali's pious supporters refused to fight them. Ali was forced to seek a compromise with Mu'awiya, but this so shocked some of his die-hard supporters, who regarded it as a betrayal, that one of his own men struck him down in 661 AD.

On Ali's death, Mu'awiya declared himself caliph. Ali's elder son Hassan accepted a pension in return for not pursuing his claim to the caliphate. He died within a year, allegedly poisoned. Ali's younger son Hussein agreed to put his claim to the caliphate on hold until Mu'awiya's death. However, when Mu'awiya finally died in 680 AD, his son Yazid inherited the caliphate.

Hussein led an army against Yazid but, hopelessly outnumbered, he and his men were slaughtered at the Battle of Karbala (in modern day Iraq). Hussein's infant son, Ali, survived to carry on the line. Yazid then formed the Sunni Umayyad dynasty, cementing the division between the Shi'a (Ali's supporters) and what came to be known as the Sunni.

Early Expansion

Things were slowly changing in the Islamic Empire. Original followers had been attracted by Muhammad's personality. Later, people joined in order to advance themselves personally. As the Empire expanded, land, possessions and prestige could be obtained. All over the empire, Muslim traditions replaced the old Byzantine court system. Muslim troops were well compensated, and Islamic taxes were often less than those exacted by the Byzantines.

Under Muslim law, Christians and Jews became protected subjects. They paid special taxes called *zakat* and they received protection known as *jizyah*. In effect this was a tax on all non-Muslims, and it is still considered fair by many Muslims. They run the country, and non-Muslims pay for the privilege of living in their country.

The Umayyad Period (660-750)

Under Muawiyah I, Muslims advanced across North Africa with unity and zeal. Their forces seemed unstoppable. In the Mediterranean they captured the island of Rhodes and entered the island of Sicily. In the northeast, Muslims crossed the Oxus on the far side of Persia. In the west they laid siege to Constantinople, the capital of the Byzantine Empire.

The years 711-713 AD brought victories in Spain, and Muslim armies crossed into France. In the east they moved along the old Silk Road, crossing into central Asia. Under the Umayyad rulers the Muslim dominion constituted the largest empire in the world, spanning from present day Spain to Afghanistan.

The Umayyad rulers set up their center of rule in Damascus and organized the administration of the empire. They constructed many beautiful buildings, new cities, and administration posts. Due to the taxes on booty from conquest, they enjoyed economic prosperity. They used this money to build the infrastructure of the empire, building impressive buildings, promoting learning, research and translation, and establishing numerous centers of learning. This was the beginning of a time of intellectual advancement. In 750 AD the Abbasid's took control of the eastern part of the empire but the Umayyads maintained control of the west, especially Spain.

The Umayyads in Spain (756-1031 AD)

While the eastern part of the Muslim empire fell under the control of the Abbasids, the Umayyads continued to maintain control in Spain. During this time agriculture was modernized and massive irrigation projects increased the cultivated land. The Umayyads undertook building roads, bridges, and buildings. Trade and industry flourished, especially textile and leather works. The Umayyads continued to patronize art and learning. Their city of Cordova came to be known as the "Jewel of the World". Among its many wonders were the first public street lights, and universities known for advanced learning.

Jewish historians have called this period the Golden Age of Spain. Ambassadors were received from all over the Arabian world, and many of their students flocked to the Muslim university in Cordova. Phillip Hitti, author of *The History of the Arabs* writes of this period:

> *"Muslim Spain wrote one of the brightest chapters in the intellectual history of medieval Europe. Between the middle of the 8th and the beginning of the 13th centuries the Arabic speaking peoples were the main bearers of the torch of culture and civilization throughout the world. They were the medium through which ancient science and philosophy were recovered, supplemented, and transmitted in such a way as to make possible the renaissance of Western Europe."*

Compare

The chart on the next page compares the first 40 years of Christianity (as found in the Book of Acts) with the first 40 years of Islam. Consider how these two religions spread. Christianity was spread by numerous means such as preaching to crowds in Jerusalem, persecution causing believers to move away from Jerusalem further spreading the word, missionaries being sent out (eg. Peter, Paul, Timothy, Silas), Paul witnessing to authorities while in jail, and so on. Christianity spread by peaceful means until it became the major religion in the Roman Empire. Islam was spread by several means such as incorporating pagan ideas into Islam so people would feel like it was their old religion, fighting for leadership, Muslim armies against Muslim armies until a strong man was recognized by all, and last, by forcing people to join Islam. First the Muslims forced the Arabs of the Arabian Peninsula to submit, and then they moved against Egypt, the Byzantine Empire, Persia and so on. They also put pressure on conquered people, giving better rights to Muslims and levying taxes on non-Muslims.

Acts of the Apostles	Spread of Islam
120 gather for prayer in an upper room	Abu Bakr reminds them of the oath of allegiance they took to him.
Matthias chosen as a disciple (Acts 1)	Abu Bakr warns them of others who want to usurp the leadership
The Holy Spirit is poured out	A number of tribes leave Islam
Peter preaches, about 3000 follow (Acts 2)	Abu Bakr sends a large number of faithful Muslims to subdue the revolt forcibly. This resulted in the Battle of Yamama
People sell their possessions (Acts 3)	A number of Muhammad's close companions who had memorized his revelations were killed at Yamama
The lame man is healed in the temple. Peter preaches, 5000 believe. (Acts 3 - 4:4)	Abu Bakr forces all pagans in Arabia to become Muslims
Steven stoned, church scatters. (Acts 8:1)	Muslims under Umar capture Damascus
Peter baptizes first gentile (Acts 8:26)	Muslims under Umar capture Jerusalem
Conversion of Saul of Tarsus (Acts 9)	Muslims under Umar capture Egypt
Saul in Arabia, Peter's vision (Acts 11)	Thousands of non-Muslims forced out of Arabia in an ethnic cleansing
Herod's persecution, Peter in jail (Acts 12)	Uthman builds navy and takes Cyprus
Paul's 1st missionary journey (Acts 13)	Uthman invades Persia

Paul 2nd missionary journey (Acts 15)	Uthman is assassinated
Macadonian call (Acts 16:9)	Ali claims the caliphat
Paul's third missionary journey (Acts 18)	Aisha attacks Ali at the Battle of the Camel
Jerusalem conference (Acts 21:17)	Uthman's cousin attacks Ali at the Battle of Suffin
Paul before Felix (Acts 24)	Ali killed by his own men
Paul before Agrippa (Acts 25 & 26)	Ali's son, Hussein, fights in the Battle of Karbala
Paul in Rome (Acts 28)	Islam splits into two factions: Shi'a & Sunni 680 AD
Christians scatter through the entire Roman Empire	

Questions for Reflection and Group Discussion

1. Is it right to pressure people to become Christians? After all, if they are going to go to hell shouldn't we do everything we can to get them to convert?
2. What motivates us to share Christ? What Bible verses support your ideas?
3. Should people be free to choose their religion? If a Muslim government says that religion is not a personal choice, how will you witness and spread the faith?
4. How would you answer a Muslim who accuses Christians of being weak? They will not fight for their faith!

Chapter Six
Codification of Islam

The Abbasid Early Period (750-945 AD)

The rapid expansion of Islam produced a huge empire with a weak core. Arab armies had reached Spain but could penetrate no further. They had reached Constantinople, but could not take the city. Damascus was poorly situated as a capital city as much of the rapid growth was now taking place in the far east. Damascus was an old city, with old traditions, while the cities in Iraq and Spain were blossoming and growing with new ideas. Thousands of Persians were converting to the faith and emigrating to eastern Iraq where there were lush fields and fertile lands. The new cities of Iraq were more Arab in make-up than the old cities of the Middle East, which had sizable Christian, Jewish and other elements.

Much of the court activity of the Umayyads seemed to revolve around the constant struggle between competing parties who wanted political power. Discontent grew in the east, and eventually civil war broke out. The Shi'as in the east claimed that the right of succession had passed from Ali through Abbas, and down to the present. They claimed that they were acting in the name of a member of the prophet's family, but no one was named directly. An army was formed and the Umayyads were defeated in 750 AD.

Abu Abbas was proclaimed caliph in 750 AD. Shortly after, he moved the capital to Baghdad, where he could better control the empire and where there was less infighting from those who claimed heritage through Muhammad.

Many Shi'a revolts were suppressed, and many members of the family of the prophet were killed. Cycles of stiff tension between Arabs and Persians resulted. Internal revolts affected the conquest at the frontiers, and the expansion of the empire slowed considerably. An Abbasid army did reach Constantinople and threatened to take the city, whereupon the Christians agreed to pay a yearly tribute to keep the Arab armies away. This helped fund the Abbasid family and greatly increased their prestige.

Since Baghdad was a new city, it was planned to express the glory of Islam. The caliph's residence was kept separate so that he could lead a secluded life. The city surrounded the royal palaces and gardens. The caliph had absolute rule and did whatever he wanted, but there were frequent revolts and uprisings among the soldiers. A few years later the capital was moved to Samara, further north from Baghdad, so that the caliph could live away from the hostilities of the city of Baghdad.

Even when the caliph's power was at its height, his power was limited to the cities and productive areas. In order to rule the far flung provinces of the empire, the caliph had to give sweeping powers to his governors and a grant them large part of the taxes they collected. The caliph tried to control his governors by developing a system of intelligence and spies, but many governors built up their own positions so that they were able to rule their own kingdoms.

The caliphs faced another challenge. A secret society movement began spreading among the Muslims, known as the Isma'ilis. They supported their claim to power through the sixth Shi'a imam. The Isma'ilis organized a large scale missionary service, and many Muslims in eastern Arabia and North Africa joined them.

While the Muslim empire was divided by political disunity, it was held together by a system of communication based on messengers rapidly riding from station to station. The empire was also strengthened by a common language (Arabic) and a common religion (Islam). Since the religion was new to many, there were zealous promoters of the religion everywhere. For many people, their allegiance was to Islam, not necessarily to any one political ruler or system.

Most of the areas that Islam conquered had strong and colorful histories, while the Arabians had a rather stark history, so the new Muslim empire desperately needed a culture of its own. Damascus was too preoccupied with its own culture and history, so the new cities in Iraq led the way in the development of Islamic culture. Pre-Islamic Arabian literature had focused on poetry about ancient heroes and erotic love. These poems and the poets were highly acclaimed because poetic expression in Arabic was seen as a great art form. The Bedouin tribes of Arabia had no other art forms. They did not build great buildings, produce painters or sculptors and did not have music other than chants. Instead, storytelling and poetic expression were the most appreciated forms of art. This preoccupation with language spilled over into the larger Muslim world. Now the Muslim world was caught up in recording the teachings and deeds of Muhammad, memorizing the Qur'an, and compiling genealogies so that people could demonstrate how closely they were linked to the family of the prophet. The Qur'an was held as the greatest writing ever created, and thus the Arabic language became an art form across the whole empire. Since the Qur'an forbade paintings and images because Christians worshiped them, Muslim art was restricted to architecture, poetry, prose, war, and the newly adopted Persian art of music. While the fringes of the empire were still caught up in military struggles, Iraq started to emerge as the cultural center of the empire.

The early caliphs had lived in tents because their lives were taken up with fighting, but when the Abbasids arrived they settled in houses in the lush fields of Iraq beside the Euphrates River. A royal city was planned and built where no city had been before. It was an excellent location, with nearby fields of produce and a river that connected it to the sea. The city was built on a grand scale, continuing the Muslims' fascination with architecture and geometrical shapes.

Life in Iraq

At the founding of Islam, education of children was important. Everyone learned to read and recite the Qur'an and parts of the Hadith. Schools were also set up to teach the art of war. Eventually a school was founded in Medina to teach girls to sing and perform other acts of pleasure for men. These girls, often purchased as slaves, became very popular throughout Arabia, some of them being sold for very high prices and eventually ending up in the harem of the caliphs and wealthy men. The harem was simply those women and children who were under the protection of the Caliph. Usually men never entered the harem unless they were eunuchs. In this way they could be trusted to enter the harem without the ability to defile the women. In time, poets and storytellers would enhance the reputation of the harem, especially the caliph's harem, so that people would imagine all sorts of sexual exploits happening there. In actuality, Arab men lived separate lives from the women, focusing their attention on war and business. In many cases the world of men and women never mixed except when the women (wives and concubines) were called out of the harem to separate rooms at the wish of their husbands or owners.

Many of the wealthy men led a life of comfort and ease. For them, hunting, war games, and even chess and backgammon became popular. The scenes painted on the walls of several desert hunting lodges dating from this time tell the story of a life of ease and comfort, focused on the physical pleasures of eating, drinking and sex.

The Rise of Islamic Culture and Science

For the masses of people in Baghdad, Islamic culture focused on religion, music and literature. Since Arabic was the language of the Qur'an and ultimately of God, Arab scholars set about to translate foreign books into Arabic. As fresh streams of thought poured in from Byzantium, Persia, India and Spain, learning became a new passion in the Islamic empire.

Eventually learned teachers gathered students around themselves and started small schools. The Muslim practice of focusing learning around a specific teacher continues on to this day. Many people consider themselves the students of a particular teacher rather than a particular school. In time teachers of philosophy and science arose.

In the Arabic language the word *hakiim* (person of wisdom or doctor) was equally applied to a physician, philosopher, story teller or worker of magic or the occult. Since a *hakiim* was highly honored, study and learning became a popular pursuit. This led to a burst of learning and the advancement of science. Books written in Greek, Latin, Aramaic, Nabataean, Persian and Sanskrit were all translated into Arabic. Many of the translators were also writers, and the books they produced were often mixtures of what they translated as well as their own ideas. Many of the later Arabs were master collectors of knowledge, often seeking out and collecting everything that was known on a specific title, then writing a book under their own name. As the pursuit of wisdom intensified, many Arabs became inventors and intellectual pioneers in their own right.

It is interesting to note that the first 130 years of Islam includedv military conquest but very little cultural advancement. The following outline demonstrates this:

Date	Military Conquests
570 AD	Muhammad born
632 AD	Death of Muhammad 62 years later
638 AD	Syria and Palestine conquered in six years
644 AD	Iraq taken and Persia entered during the following six years
661 AD	Iran and North Africa taken during the following 17 years
718 AD	Siege of Constantinople
747 AD	Abbasid Revolt
751 AD	Battle against Chinese in Central Asia
756 AD	Umayyad Dynasty in Spain at its height
762 AD	Baghdad established as city of peace.

As Baghdad and later Samara developed during the next 150 years, very little military conquest took place, other than the fighting of civil wars and rebellions, but great cultural and scientific advancements were made:

800 AD	Yaqub al-Kindi known for collecting and writing on philosophy, mathematics, physics, astronomy, medicine, music, and geography
803 AD	Jabir Ibn Haiyan, father of chemistry
813 AD	Khawarizmi born, he became a great mathematician in Baghdad
830 AD	The House of Wisdom established in Baghdad to translate Greek, Syriac, Persian and Sanskrit into Arabic
836 AD	Thabit Ibn Qurra As-Sabi al-Harrani born, known for mathematics and astronomy
838 AD	Ali ibn Rabban al-Tabari, noted physician, born
840 AD	Al-Khawarizmi solves algebra equations
861 AD	Al-Farghani, a great astronomer

870 AD	Al-Bukhari, who collected the hadiths or sayings about Muhammad, dies. Note that this is 300 years after Muhammad.
912 AD	Ibn Wahshiya known for agriculture, biology, physics
929 AD	Abu Abdullah al-Battani, a Sabian known for astronomy, math and astrology.
959 AD	Abul Wafa al-Buzjani teaches mathematics and develops geometry and trigonometry
965 AD	Abu Hasan ibn al-Haitham known for optics and physics

For the next 500 years there were virtually no further military conquests and few cultural advances.

Around 1000 AD Europe was in a state of alarm. Muslim armies were in Spain as well as slowly expanding into Eastern Europe. There was little that the Europeans could do, as Europe at that time was divided into hundreds of small states each ruled by a feudal lord. The only unifying power at that time was the Catholic Church which encouraged the European lords to unite against a common enemy, the Muslim; initiating the crusades.

1095 AD	Crusaders from Europe attack the Muslims. Many years of fighting follow
1258 AD	Mongols from the east attack the Middle East and sack Baghdad. The Muslim empire begins to fragment
1291 AD	Acre Castle falls, and the last Crusade is over
1299 AD	The Ottoman Empire begins, based in Turkey
1453 AD	Fall of Constantinople, it becomes a Muslim city
1492 AD	Muslims expelled from Spain
1683 AD	Ottomans defeated at Vienna

From this point on significant military and cultural advances began to take place in Europe, while the Islamic world was left in decline.

The Development of Shari'a Law

As the Arabs translated great works from the west and the east, they came across the Roman and Byzantine books on law. This created some issues for them, as their own system known as '*fiqh*,' was based on the Qur'an and the hadith or traditions of what Muhammad said and did. For them right and wrong were not based on any set of human standards but rather on what was revealed through Allah and his prophet. Most of the Qur'an dealt with issues that faced Muhammad. Only two chapters contained much of anything about legal matters, much of these given while Muhammad ruled Medina. It soon became evident that these were not enough to cover civil, criminal, political and financial situations, especially when ruling such a large empire.

Eventually two schools of thought arose. The Madinah school attached special importance to the Hadiths, or collection of sayings about Muhammad. For them all matters should be settled by the Qur'an and the accounts of what the prophet said and did.

In Iraq, a leading merchant who was often called upon to settle legal cases used the principle of analogical deduction as well as the Qur'an. His name was Abu Hanifah and his approach was considered very liberal at the time. The jurists in Medina set about compiling a book containing 1700 legal traditions, carefully corresponding to the Qur'an and also using a consensus of opinion among jurists in difficult cases. This eventually became the Malikite legal tradition.

Soon after this Ahmad Ibn Hanbal began another school of legal thought in Iraq, which was much more traditional and based on the Qur'an alone and not on analogical deductions. These legalists were much more fanatical, and are often thought of as the founders of today's Muslim fundamentalists. A third school of law developed in Palestine.

By 970 AD the construction of al-Azher mosque and school in Egypt began. This mosque and school would eventually contain four sections, each teaching one of the four legal systems. By 974 AD the caliphs had lost most of their power, and local leaders began rising to prominence.

What Triggered the Golden Age?

This is something that Muslim scholars have never agreed on. Many Muslim scholars have simply assumed that when Islam is practiced as it should be, the result is a burst of knowledge and culture. Historians argue otherwise.

Islam under the caliphs was mediocre at best. Wine, forbidden to Muslims, was consumed by the wealthy who also indulged in many immoral activities, frowned upon by most Muslims.

Many historians believe that the uniting of many empires and lands under one language and religion was the key element in developing a golden age. Added to this was the desire to translate all the great books of the world into Arabic. This provided rich intellectual resources to the Arab scholars. Previous to this, a scholar had to learn many languages in order to access the learning of the world. Now this learning was made available in one common language.

Added to this was the wisdom that had been locked away in hiding for many centuries. Much of this had been preserved in Christian monasteries, pagan temples, and distant lands. One Islamic writer, Ibn Wahsiyah (904 AD), claimed that the Nabataeans were the source of 90% of all of the scientific knowledge known during his time. (*Al-Filiaheh an-Nabatiyah*, by Ibn Wahsiyah) This is because the Nabataeans had collected knowledge but had never used it. Now, with the Nabataean empire united under one language and religion, this knowledge was available to everyone.

Why did the Golden Age die?

This question has also been argued by historians, but many believe the decline began in 833 AD. At this time an argument arose over the origin of the Qur'an. One school of thought believed that the Qur'an on earth is an identical copy of the Qur'an in heaven. Another school of thought believed in the creation of the Qur'an. In 833 AD the caliph issued a decree that every Muslim authority must hold to the belief of the creation of the Qur'an. He began the *mihnah* or a tribunal and trial to convict everyone who denied his new dogma. Thus, the movement that had stood for free thought became a deadly instrument for suppressing thought. Many were imprisoned, and many died. Then in 848 AD, the new caliph restored the old teaching that the Qur'an was not created but revealed.

As science and investigative thinking grew in importance they began to clash with Islam. Many of the great Muslim scientists were skeptics, and some turned to mysticism (Sufism) to find meaning in Islam. The term *Sufi* first appears in Arabic literature in the middle of the ninth century, but mysticism was mixed with Islam as soon as the Muslims met with other religions. The occult practices of Africa, the pagan practices of the Greeks, and the mysticism of India all began to mix with Islam in one form or another. They emerged in the form of a secret society that claimed special knowledge and ability to experience God. This society, known as the Isma'ilis, spread quickly among fringe Muslims who had many occult or mystical practices of their own.

The backlash against this mystical movement was orthodox Islam's inquisition to wipe out everything that was not orthodox. Free thinking and innovation were severely restricted. Within a few years Islam focused on rigid control of the faith and faithful rather than culture and science. The Islamic empire was suddenly plunged into a religious revolution that completely stopped all cultural evolution. Within a few years, the far flung reaches of the Empire began to collapse.

The Crusades

The Crusades began for many reasons. Perhaps they were a response to the Muslims' challenge on Constantinople. Perhaps the Muslims entrance into Eastern Europe provoked them. Perhaps the Catholic Pope's desire to have a military force at this command played a part. But on November 26, 1096 AD, Pope Urban delivered a speech at the Council of Clermont, in which he urged the faithful to "enter upon the road to the Holy Sepulcher, wrest it from the wicked race and subject it" to themselves. (Krey, August, C., *Gesta Francorum* [The Deeds of the Franks], The First Crusade: The Accounts of Eyewitnesses and Participants, Princeton: 1921) The response was overwhelming. In Europe many people lived in poverty, ruled by wealthy lords. The crusades provided a way of escape for them. Petty thieves and highway robbers suddenly found a way to make themselves honorable. By 1097 over a hundred and fifty thousand men arrived at Constantinople. Many of these men were interested in war and loot, some were interested in obtaining new lands, but very few were interested in anything spiritual. After the first battles several groups of crusaders settled in the invaded lands and created states that they ruled over.

Some historians refer to seven Crusades, but in effect there was a continual flow of people from Europe to the Middle East, with different waves appearing to historians as different crusades. For many people, especially Muslims, the Crusades appeared to be a religious invasion, but many men fighting in the

Crusades were simply thugs, thieves and robbers in their own lands. These men butchered, raped and pillaged their way through the Middle East, leaving the defeated Muslims in shock. The Abbasid Empire was now divided, with authority residing in the many states and provinces. As the Crusaders advanced they met resistance from every state, but little widely organized resistance. By 1100 AD Bethlehem had fallen and the crusaders had taken much of the Middle East from the Muslims.

The first clash between the Muslims and Christians left both sides puzzled. The Christians had assumed that they were far superior to the Muslims, and that the Muslims worshiped Muhammad as a god. The Muslims had thought that the Christians were "people of the book" and close to the Muslims in religion and culture. The barbaric acts of the crusaders left them convinced that they were "animals possessing the virtues of courage and fighting, but nothing else." (Usmah Ibn Munqidh, 1095-1188)

By 1140 AD the Muslims began to organize themselves under the leadership of a man known as Nur'al'Din (*light of the faith*). He rallied the divided Muslim states into one group and in 1154 took back Damascus, Antioch, and Tripoli. In Egypt another Muslim man by the name of Salah'Din set out to accomplish two things. He wanted to substitute Sunni Islam for Shi'a Islam in Egypt, and he wanted to win back the Holy Land from the Crusaders. Salah'Din made the change to Sunni Islam very quickly without opposition from the people, and then he set about gathering a large army. Victory followed victory, and in 1187 the Muslims retook Jerusalem, only to lose it again several years later. Eventually peace ensued and the Crusaders controlled the coast, but the Muslims controlled the interior. Christian pilgrims were allowed to visit the Holy sites in Jerusalem and Bethlehem.

Around 1260 AD a slave revolt in Egypt left the Mamluks (slaves) in power. Baybars, a Mamluk slave ruler, began resisting the Crusaders, and eventually gathered an army that marched through the Middle East destroying Crusader strongholds. By May 1291 the last Crusader stronghold fell, and the Middle East was once again under Muslim domination.

History

Muslims claim that the coming of Islam ushered in a great era of scientific knowledge and achievements. This seems obvious to them when they consider their history and the great achievements of Muslim scientists up until the time previous to the crusades. Europe had slipped back into a time of relative ignorance while Middle Eastern culture and life surged forward. Europe had forgotten much of what was learned during the time of the Romans and Byzantines. Instead, life was focused around warlords living in strongholds.

It is true that the west was in a state of decline during this time, but this is not true about Asia. In China, this was the time of the T'ang Dynasty (618 AD - 907 AD). During this period China became the most powerful and largest empire on earth. Art and poetry flourished, and gunpowder and printing were invented. Industry was at an all-time high, and in 806 AD it was recorded that 13,500 tons of iron were produced in China. Trade and contact occurred beyond the borders of China, but eventually Muslim armies encroached from the West and the power of China waned. Foreign religions were eventually banned and there was gradual disintegration and war.

The Sung Dynasty (960 AD - 1223 AD) also took place during the time of Muslim greatness. During this time rule and order were re-established in China. Gunpowder was used for military rockets, making the Chinese armies strong again. Sea trade was helped by the widespread adoption of the compass. Large ocean-going junks traveled to the East Indies, Africa, and India. Records indicate that in 1078 AD, 125,000 tons of iron was produced per year, demonstrating their growing economic power. Then in 1012 AD, a new strain of rice was introduced from Vietnam that doubled or tripled the yield of traditional rice. While China was growing in economic power the Mongols rose to military power in the north and by 1223 AD the Mongol ruler, Genghis Khan had conquered most of Northern China. Kublai Khan then ruled after him, (known as the Yüan Dynasty) from 1264 AD - 1356 AD. During this period Chinese maritime trade was still expanding.

While Muslims claim to have been the greatest civilization at this time, the Ming Dynasty (starting 1368 AD) rose to greatness in China. Between 1405 and 1430 AD the fleets of admiral Zheng-He journeyed to Africa, India, Ceylon, Sumatra and possibly even Australia. His ships were massive, five times the size of contemporary European caravels. They could carry several hundred men and a year's provision. These ships also had watertight bulkheads and sternpost rudders, making them the most advanced ships of the time.

90

With the knowledge of compasses and the ability to navigate by the stars these fleets crossed the Indian Ocean to Africa. Their task was to bring tribute from foreign countries to the Ming emperors. In the early 15th Century a fleet of 60 ships carrying 40,000 troops ventured to the East coast of Africa but found little wealth.

Around 1433 this exploration suddenly ceased. The emperor banned all merchants from going abroad and he claimed that there was little use for foreign goods. Revenue from foreign trade suddenly dropped from 20% in the earlier Sung dynasty to less than 1% in this part of the Ming dynasty. Since the Ming emperors came from an agrarian background they focused on agriculture. This was due to reunification and better land use, opening internal canals, rather than trade overseas. Overseas trade was forbidden under punishment of death.

Thus we can see that while the Muslim Middle East did experience a time of great scientific and cultural advancement, it was not out of line with what was happening in other parts of the world. Only Christianized Europe was experiencing a cultural recession.

Science

Today many Muslim preachers claim that true science is based on Islam. They claim that the Qur'an contains great scientific statements and that true science comes from studying the Qur'an. Unfortunately, in the west, some Christians have made similar claims about the Bible. Therefore it is important for us to understand the relationship between Science and Christianity.

Science and Christianity

The Bible is a record of God's dealing with mankind. It is not a history book, nor is it a scientific book. The Bible makes no claims to be a complete record of history, nor does it claim to be a textbook for science or even culture.

However, even though the Bible is not a science book, if it is true then it should not contradict true science. The Bible should be scientifically sound. However, all through history there have been some scientists whose theories have contradicted the Bible. Today, scientists in the west are split into two groups. The largest group of scientists believe in evolution. They are the most vocal and have convinced many western governments to present only evolution in the class rooms. A second group of scientists in the west believe in creation. Their thinking is known as Intelligent Design. Not all scientists who believe in Intelligent Design believe in the God of the Bible.

Among the people who believe in Intelligent Design are also creationists who believe that God created the world. Evolutionists on the other hand believe that: given enough time, time can do anything. These scientists speak in terms of millions of years. Creationists on the other hand believe that God can do anything, and that time does not matter to him as it matters to us.

Interestingly enough, in the west, Muslims and Christians speak out together against the teachings of evolution. While it may sound like we both have the same message, one needs to listen carefully to distinguish between the two, for the Muslim view of creation is quite different from the Christian view. The most important point is that Muslims do not believe in the fall of man. They believe that Adam and Eve lived normal lives just like all of us, and that God created good and evil, and that life from the beginning of creation until now is much the same.

Science and the Bible

The Bible is not a science book, yet it is scientifically accurate. Christians are not aware of any scientific evidence that contradicts the Bible. Below are listed several statements that are consistent with known scientific facts. Many of these were listed in the Bible hundreds or even thousands of years before being recorded elsewhere.

1. Several books in the Bible refer to dinosaurs. The book of Job describes two dinosaurs. One is described in chapter 40 starting at verse 15, and the other in chapter 41 starting at verse 1. One and a half chapters about dinosaurs is a lot—since most people do not even realize that they are mentioned in the Bible.

2. The Bible frequently refers to the great number of stars in the heavens. Here are two examples: *"I will bless you, and in multiplying I will multiply your descendants as the stars of the heaven and as the sand which is on the seashore; and your descendants shall possess the gate of their enemies."* (Genesis 22:17 NKJV) *"As the host of heaven cannot be numbered, nor the sand of the sea measured, so will I multiply the descendants of David My servant and the Levites who minister to*

me." (Jeremiah 33:22) Today, scientists admit that they do not know how many stars there are. Only about 3,000 are visible to the naked eye. The Australian National University suggests that there are 70,000 million million million. This is a 7 followed by 22 zeros —which is a lot of stars.

3. The Bible also says that each star is unique. *"There is one glory of the sun, another glory of the moon, and another glory of the stars; for one star differs from another star in glory."* (1 Corinthians 15:41) Most stars look alike to the naked eye. Even when seen through a telescope, they seem to be just points of light. However, analysis of their light spectra reveals that each is unique and different from all others. How could a writer of the Bible during the first century claim that the stars were different from one another? Truly God inspired them to write this.

4. The Bible describes the suspension of the Earth in space. *"He stretches out the north over empty space; He hangs the earth on nothing."* (Job 26:7)

5. The Bible includes some principles of fluid dynamics. *"To establish a weight for the wind, and apportion the waters by measure."* (Job 28:25) The fact that air has weight was proven scientifically only about 300 years ago. The relative weights of air and water are needed for the efficient functioning of the world's hydrologic cycle, which in turn sustains life on the earth.

6. We have cave paintings and other evidence that people inhabited caves. The Bible also describes cave dwellers: *"They were driven out from among men. They shouted at them as at a thief. They had to live in the clefts of the valleys, in caves of the earth and the rocks."* (Job 30:5,6)

7. The Bible describes several phases of the hydrologic cycle—the worldwide processes of evaporation, translation aloft by atmospheric circulation, condensation with electrical discharges, and precipitation. *"For He draws up drops of water, Which distill as rain from the mist, Which the clouds drop down And pour abundantly on man. Indeed, can anyone understand the spreading of clouds, The thunder from His canopy?"* (Job 36:27-29) This simple verse has remarkable scientific insight. The drops of water which eventually pour down as rain first become vapor and then condense to tiny liquid water droplets in the clouds. These finally coalesce into drops large enough to overcome the updrafts that suspend them in the air.

8. The Bible describes the recirculation of water. *"All the rivers run into the sea, Yet the sea is not full; To the place from which the rivers come, There they return again."* (Ecclesiastes 1:7) *"For as the rain comes down, and the snow from heaven, And do not return there, But water the earth, And make it bring forth and bud, That it may give seed to the sower And bread to the eater."* (Isaiah 55:10)

9. The Bible describes the Earth's crust along with a comment on astronomy. *"Thus says the LORD: If heaven above can be measured, And the foundations of the earth searched out beneath, I will also cast off all the seed of Israel For all that they have done, says the LORD."* Jeremiah 31:37 Although some scientists claim that they have now measured the size of the universe, it is interesting to note that every human attempt to drill through the earth's crust to the mantle beneath has, thus far, ended in failure.

9. The Bible described the shape of the earth as spherical. *"It is He who sits above the circle of the earth, and its inhabitants are like grasshoppers, Who stretches out the heavens like a curtain, And spreads them out like a tent to dwell in."* (Isaiah 40:22) The word translated "circle" here is the Hebrew word *chuwg* which is also translated "circuit," or "compass" (depending on the context). That is, it indicates something spherical, rounded, or arched—not something that is flat or square.

As we can see, the Bible has many things in it that are scientifically correct, and were written hundreds if not thousands of years before scientists "discovered" them. In all aspects of science, the Bible has always proven correct. When faced with a new theory that seems to contradict the Bible, believers should keep their faith in the word of God, and wait until science catches up with what the Bible teaches.

The Qur'an on the other hand teaches that the sun sets in a muddy pool: *Until, when he reached the setting of the sun, he found it set in a spring of murky water: Near it he found a people: We said: "O Zul-qarnain! (thou hast authority,) either to punish them, or to treat them with kindness."* (Sura 18:86)

It also teaches that sperm comes from the backbone: *"He is created from a drop emitted. Proceeding from between the backbone and the ribs."* Sura 86:6-7

While some Muslims try and claim that the Qur'an is scientifically accurate, it is clear from the above two statements that it is not.

Questions for Reflection and Group Discussion

1. Does the rise of science from 800 – 1100 AD prove Islam was right? Why or why not?
2. In what ways is Shari'a law a good thing, and in what ways a bad thing? How did it affect Islam?
3. How should Christians respond to those we disagree with? Is there a case for physical struggle in the Bible?
4. Were the Crusades effective in any way?
5. What were the results of the Crusades on the Christian presence in the Middle East?
6. How should we respond to Muslims who are upset about the Crusades?

Chapter Seven
The Spread of Islam

How did Islam Spread?

Was Islam spread by the sword? This is a common idea held by many, but does it hold true?

During Islam's first 100 years, Muslim armies conquered from North Africa to Afghanistan. After defeating the local armies, a few Muslims were left as the occupiers of the land and the armies moved on. Those that occupied the conquered lands were faced with tremendous problems of control and administration. In most of the conquered lands people continued following their own religions. Non-Muslims were called *Dhimmi*, or *protected ones*. This protection was really a tax levied on non-Muslims. Those that converted to Islam no longer had to pay the tax.

As Muslim armies marched across North Africa they came in contact with many Arabs from the old Southern Arabian kingdom of Sheba. Around a hundred years before the Muslim armies marched out of Arabia into North Africa, the ancient dam at Marib, Yemen, had broken and their civilization had dispersed across much of North Africa. The original Sheba civilization dated back to the time of King Solomon and the Queen of Sheba. Their civilization, at the edge of the desert, was made possible by a large dam that was built across the end of a valley. As rain fell in the mountains it ran into streams and then into a river that flowed into the desert. The people of Sheba dammed the river and irrigated more than 25,000 acres of land. Thousands of people lived around the dam, and a successful civilization was born. The first warnings of pending doom came in 450 AD when the dam broke. The technology that was used to build the dam thousands of years before had been lost. The people of Sheba did their best to fix the dam, but it broke again in 542 AD. The second set of repairs lasted until 570 AD, the year that Muhammad was born. That year the dam burst, and the people of Sheba gave up hope and moved *en masse* away from Southern Arabia. Thousands moved across North Africa, and others flooded into the towns and villages in Northern Arabia.

When the Muslim armies first marched across North Arabia and North Africa, it was these people from the old Kingdom of Sheba that readily converted to Islam. The conquering Muslim armies made good use of these new Muslim converts, placing them into administrative positions in the conquered lands. As news of this spread, the people from the old kingdom of Sheba readily converted to Islam as soon as the Muslim armies arrived, and then they quickly moved into positions of power and authority in the lands they had come to a mere one hundred years earlier as refugees.

As the Muslim empire grew, life for non-Muslims was never easy. Non-Muslims could not hold government office or be civil servants. Non-Muslims were second-class citizens, ruled over by Muslim overlords who decided the laws and customs of the land. Non-Muslims had to pay a tax for every non-Muslim member of their family. Some families were reduced to poverty through this. Christians and pagans who refused to pay the tax were dealt with very harshly, and this harsh treatment earned Islam the reputation of trying to spread their religion with violence and the sword. In the Muslim mind, however, non-Muslims were going to hell, and so it was out of mercy that Muslims pressured non-Muslims to convert. If a non-Muslim refused and died, it was only the fate that he or she had chosen for him or her self by refusing the glorious religion of Islam.

On the other hand, Muslims were given privileges in society. Muslim businesses flourished and had the favor of the government. Muslim men could have up to four wives, while those from a Christian background could only have one. The church at that time did not allow for divorce, but Muslim men could freely divorce their wives and re-marry. Over time, many nominal Christians gave up their faith and became Muslims. They were warmly welcomed by the Muslims and made a part of the Muslim community. Christian men who couldn't find wives among the shrinking Christian population could always count on getting married if they converted to Islam.

The Christian church reacted strongly. Christians were persecuted by Christians if they converted to Islam, and some were killed. Many Christian churches began to tattoo small crosses onto the wrists of Christian babies and children, so that they would be forever marked as Christians. Despite this, the realities of life in a Muslim setting continued to cause Christians to convert to Islam. This has continued down to the present time, when Christians continue to convert to Islam in many Muslim countries.

A missionary recently related this story: *One day a group of angry people stood on our street corner shouting at each other. They were very angry, and it appeared as if violence might begin at any moment. I asked my neighbor what had happened, and he explained to me that the night before a Christian girl had run away from home and married a Muslim boy that she had met at the government school. In doing so she had said the Muslim creed and had accepted Islam. The Muslims were rejoicing and taunting the Christians "We got one of yours!" The Christians were angry and threatening to kill a Muslim girl in revenge. In the end the police were called, and the mob dispersed. The situation was rectified several weeks later when the Christian girl who had converted to Islam was killed by her own family. Peace slowly returned to our community after this.*

In much the same way, the Christian and pagan populations were slowly won over to Islam, until everyone in many of the lands that the Muslims occupied submitted to Islam. In many cases, those that truly wanted to follow Christ emigrated away from their countries to more tolerant lands.

The Golden Age of Islam

During the Golden Age of Islam that followed the military expansion of Islam, many people became enamored with Islam, believing it to be the cause behind the growth of science and culture. Muslim missionaries began to move among people trying to convince them of the greatness of Islam. These missionaries found response from many of the poor and less educated. By converting to Islam these people immediately gained status and many doors of opportunity opened to them.

98

The writings of Muslim scholars impressed even western scholars during the time of the Middle Ages, wheere knowledge and study were limited to only a few. During this time, Europe had fallen into a state where thousands of small warlords controlled small areas of Europe. These warlords fought with each other, and only united together under a larger king if there was some gain for themselves. The Roman Catholic church was interested in power and prestige rather than ministering to people. In this time of confusion and struggle, Islam stood out as a shining light of hope. Most leading Muslim men were gentlemen who had been well trained in schools. They were polite, spoke several languages, and were often men of means and culture. Western scholars therefore held them in great respect. As a result, western kings and warlords were frightened by Muslim advances, and so the idea of a military crusade against Islam grew in popularity.

For two hundred years, between 800 AD and 1000 AD, Muslim culture and knowledge advanced much faster than those of the nations around them. As centers of learning were developed in Baghdad, thinking men were attracted to the city. By 830 AD the Mamuns House of Wisdom was established, and European, Syrian, Nabataean, Persian and Indian writings were all translated into Arabic. These were carefully studied, and much of the old scientific knowledge of the Greeks and Romans came to light. Arab scholars then worked through this material and further developed this thinking. A host of great scholars emerged, but we will only look at three of them.

Mohammad al-Khawarizmi was born at Khawarizm (Kheva), south of the Aral Sea. Very little is known about his early life, except for the fact that his parents had migrated to a place south of Baghdad. The exact dates of his birth and death are not known, but it is established that he lived at Baghdad from 813 to 833 AD and probably died around 840 AD.

Khawarizmi was a mathematician, astronomer and geographer. He was perhaps one of the greatest mathematicians who ever lived. He was the founder of several branches and concepts of mathematics and influenced mathematical thought to a greater extent than any other Islamic writer. His work on algebra was outstanding, and he became known as the founder of Algebra. The very name Algebra has been derived from his famous book Al-Jabr wa-al-Muqabilah. His arithmetic combined Greek and Hindu knowledge and also contained his own contributions. He explained the use of the Hindi concept of zero and developed the decimal system so that the overall system of numerals: 'algorithm' or 'algorizm' is named after him. He also introduced the Indian system of numerals (now generally known as Arabic numerals) that are presently used in the west, and he developed several arithmetical procedures, including operations on fractions. He also made progress in the science of geometry and calculus and was involved in a project that tried to measure the volume and circumference of the earth.

Khawarizmi also contributed to the science of astronomy, on which he wrote a book. In the area of geography he revised early Greek views and produced a map of the world. He also worked on clocks, sundials and astrolabes used for navigation.

Ibn Sina (980 - 1037 AD) was born near Bukhara, Uzbeckistan on the Silk Road. As a young boy be became well versed in religion and science. He studied philosophy by reading various Greek books on this subject and learnd logic and other subjects from Natili, a famous philosopher of the time. While still a young man, he attained such a degree of expertise in medicine that his renown spread far and wide. At the age of 17, he was fortunate in curing the King of Bukhara of an illness when all the well-known physicians had given up hope. On his recovery, the King wished to reward him, but the young physician only desired permission to use his uniquely stocked library.

After his father's death Ibn Sina began traveling and studying under several famous men. He wrote a book on medicine, and was instrumental in curing several leading men of the time from their ill health, causing him to gain more fame as a great healer.

It is estimated that he was the most well-known physician, philosopher, astronomer and medical writer of his time. His major contribution to medical science was his famous book *al-Qanun*, known as the *Canon* in the West. The *Qanun fi al-Tibb* is an immense encyclopedia of medicine with over a million words. It surveyed the entire medical knowledge available from ancient and Muslim sources. Due to its systematic approach, it remained supreme for six centuries as the primary work on medicine. In his book Ibn Sina gathered and published all the known knowledge on medicine and drugs. The book described 760 drugs and became the most widely used reference for medicine for several centuries afterwards.

Ibn Sina also wrote an encyclopedia *Kitab al-Shifa* which covered a vast field of knowledge from philosophy to science and made several contributions to mathematics, physics, geology and music.

Al-Idrisi (1099 - 1166 AD) was born in Spain and later traveled far and wide in connection with his studies. Not a lot is written about him because the Arab writers of the time considered him to be a renegade, since he was closely associated with the court of a Christian king and had written in praise of him.

Al-Idrisi wrote several books, including *Kitab al-Jami-li-Sifat Ashtat al-Nabatat* which was on medicinal plants. He studied and reviewed all the literature on the subject of medicinal plants and formed the opinion that very little original material had been added to this branch of knowledge since the early Greek work. He therefore collected plants and data not reported earlier and added this to the subject of botany, with special reference to medicinal plants. Thus, a large number of new medicinal plants together with their evaluation became available to the medical practitioners. He gave the names of the drugs in six languages: Syriac, Greek, Persian, Hindi, Latin and Berber.

Al-Idrisi also loved geography and he made a silver globe for King Roger II and an accompanying book *Al-Kitab al-Rujari* (*Roger's Book*) which was a geographical encyclopedia of Asia, Africa and European countries. The globe weighted 400 kilograms. Maps made from this globe were widely used for several centuries. Christopher Columbus used a map originally taken from Al-Idrisi's work to guide him across the Atlantic.

Fragmentation of Islam

The Mongols began their push into Central Asia and Persia in the early 13th century under Genghis Khan. The cities of Bukhara and Samarkand fell to Genghis Khan's armies in 1220. From there it was not difficult for them to raid into Persia, and by 1221 the Persian cities of Merv, Nishapur, and Balkh had fallen. In the inevitable pillaging that followed Mongol attacks, the invaders decimated the population of these regions, sparing only those they deemed useful. The Mongols also uprooted many Muslim graves and defiled their holy sites.

The Great Khan Möngke decided to attack the Muslim Abbasids in

Baghdad at the same time as his election in 1251. The Great Khan disliked the fact that his new Muslim subjects revered the caliph, who they deemed to be in a higher position than the Great Khan. Möngke decided to send his brother, Hulegu, into Iraq at the head of the invading Mongol army, with the goal of sacking Baghdad and destroying the Abbasid rulers. Hulegu set out in 1253 and by 1255 reached the walls of Baghdad.

The Muslim Abbasids were at a disadvantage. While they theoretically had a large enough army, their troops had been neglected and were poorly trained. Some of their army were Sunni Muslims and some were Shi'ite. Many of the Shi'ite secretly welcomed the Mongols, hoping that they would destroy the Sunnis and allow Shi'ites freedom of worship. (Much the same way that Shi'ite Iraqis recently welcomed American troops because they wanted to be free from Sunni rule. Once free, they turned against the Americans so that they could exercise Shi'ite dominion over the Sunnis).

The Mongols also had the support of non-Muslims who lived in the Muslim empire. Many Christians in the region saw the Mongols as saviors, hoping that by destroying the leaders of Islam the faith itself would also be destroyed. Indeed, in return for Christian support, the Mongols (some of whom were Nestorian Christians themselves) spared Christian churches and communities from pillaging.

The city of Baghdad fell to the Monguls in 1258 AD, and the Muslim caliph was captured and killed. Thus 500 years of Abbasid rule came to an abrupt and violent end.

The rest of the Middle East lay open to the Mongols. Muslim attention had long been directed towards the Crusaders from the West, so the Mongols from the east quickly moved forward, occupying city after city.

The Mamluks or slave rulers of Egypt presented a serious challenge to the Mongols as they began launching attacks on Syria. The Mamlukes were experienced soldiers, having fought many battles with the Crusaders. Now they turned towards the invading Mongols and defeated them. Some historians have suggested that the Mamluks' success was because they had been using horseshoes for their horses since 1244. The Mongols did not use horseshoes, and the rocky terrain of Syria reportedly injured the Mongol horses' hooves to the extent that they were unable to fight effectively. Additionally, the Mamluks realized that grasslands were needed to pasture the Mongols' horses. Therefore, the Mamluks burned the grasslands in Syria in their wake, to prevent the Mongol horses from grazing.

The Mamluk victories over the Mongols in 1260 were a turning point for the Mongols. Möngke's death signaled an end to a united Mongol Empire, as the struggle over his successor split the realm and broke the momentum of the Mongol advance. Infighting followed, and by 1263 alliances and peace treaties were signed.

The Mongol invasion was not entirely negative for the Islamic world. Perhaps the most significant achievement of the Muslims under Mongol rule was their ability to absorb the Mongols into their Islamic culture, rather than allowing its destruction at Mongol hands. This feat can be seen in the triumph of the Islamic faith over Mongol shamanism and Buddhism. It occurred so quickly, in fact, that only 40 years after the fall of the Iraq in 1258, the Mongols had themselves adopted Islam as the official religion of their empire. This amazing conversion from Buddhism to Islam is one of Islam's greatest accomplishments. It was not done through the use of force or threats. We will examine why this took place below.

The Black Plague

The first outbreak of the plague may have been in Central Asia but it was first reported in China in the early 1330s, and it spread to eight areas of China and throughout the Mongol Empire: Hubei, Jiangxi, Shanxi, Hunan, Guangdong, Guangxi, Henan and Suiyuan.

Many Mongols and Muslims fell to the plague, and by 1347 it was reported in Turkey. In that same year, the great trade center of Caffa on the Crimean peninsula came under siege by an army of Mongol warriors. After a long siege the Mongol army was reportedly very sick from the disease, so they catapulted their corpses over the city walls, infecting the inhabitants of the city. The merchants then fled by boat, transferring the plague via their ships into the south of Europe, where it rapidly spread. According to accounts, so many died in Caffa that the survivors had little time to bury them, and bodies were stacked like firewood against the city walls.

In October 1347, a fleet of Genovese trading ships fleeing Caffa reached the port of Messina in Sicily. By the time the fleet reached Messina, all the crew members were either infected or dead. Presumably the ships also carried infected rats or fleas. Some ships were found grounded on shorelines, with no one aboard remaining alive. Looting of these lost ships also helped spread the disease.

From Italy the disease spread northwest across Europe, striking France, Spain, Portugal and England by June 1348, then turned and spread east through Germany and Scandinavia from 1348 to 1350. It was introduced to Norway in 1349 when a ship landed at Askøy, then proceeded to spread to Bjørgvin (modern Bergen). Finally it spread to northwestern Russia in 1351; however, the plague largely spared some parts of Europe, including the Kingdom of Poland and isolated parts of Belgium and the Netherlands. The plague also struck various countries in the Middle East, leading to serious depopulation and permanent changes in both economic and social structures. It is estimated that the total number of deaths worldwide was 75 million. Some historians think that nearly one third of the population of Europe died.

The Islamic world suffered at least five major plague epidemics before the major Black Death in the 14th century. In 639 AD one of these outbreaks killed 25,000 Muslim soldiers in the army of Umar, the second Muslim caliph.

People in both the Middle East and Europe believed that the plague was an airborne disease. It was not until an outbreak of the plague in Hong Kong in 1894 that scientists determined that the disease was spread primarily through fleas who carried it from rats – the original hosts to humans. In the medieval period, however, with no scientific explanation for the disease available, both Christians and Muslims believed that the plague was of divine origin.

In Christian Europe, people believed that the plague was punishment from God for the sins of all Christians. The Christian doctrine of original sin also factored into the European view of the plague, because they believed that the disease was God's punishment to humans for having been born in sin. Also, death was always treated as punishment in Christian Europe, and the idea that the widespread death caused by the plague might be due to something other than God's wrath was not considered.

Islamic theology held different views about the plague. Muslims agreed with Christians that the disease was the work of God, but they did not necessarily view it as a punishment. Muslims preserved their belief in a compassionate and merciful God, and thus they believed that death from the plague was an offer of martyrdom from God. They formed three basic tenets for coping with the plague:

1. The plague was a mercy and a martyrdom from God for the faithful Muslim, and a punishment for the infidel.
2. A Muslim should neither enter nor flee a plague-stricken land.
3. There was no escape or solution to the plague because diseases came directly from God.

Muslim doctors and scientists often had a difficult time in reconciling these tenets, particularly the third one, with growing evidence that it was contagious. As well, doctors often felt obliged to try to treat people infected with the plague in any way they could, which conflicted with the Islamic theological view that the disease had been sent by God and therefore must simply be endured. Theologians also encountered problems when the plague hit the holy city of Mecca in 1349, likely the result of pilgrimage traffic during the Hajj. They believed that the prophet had promised that no disease would ever come to either Mecca or Medina. Some Muslims explained the plague's presence in Mecca as the result of unbelievers living there, while others rejoiced in the miracle that it never spread to Medina. (The Islamic World, 1998, Univ. Calgary)

Regardless of its theological interpretations, the Black Death wreaked havoc on the communities of many different religions, causing widespread death wherever it went. In the Islamic world, it had a particularly devastating effect militarily and economically. The rapid spread of the plague through armies affected the outcome of several minor wars throughout the Islamic world. Even the strong Mamluk army in Egypt was so devastated by the plague that the decline in its military capabilities led to their eventual defeat by the Ottoman Empire in the early 16th century.

Muslim Expansion

The Arabs of Arabia have always been merchants and traders. For centuries

Arab merchants traveled the globe with their goods. Several major trade routes linked the Arab world with the east. The greatest of these was known as the "Silk Road." It passed from Damascus through Iraq, Iran and Central Asia, all the way to China. All along this trade route, Muslim merchants built caravan stopping places. Many of these turned into towns and eventually cities. Since these cities were filled with Arab merchants, Islam spread as these Arabs converted to Islam. In this way, many cities along the Silk Road became centers for propagating Islam to the surrounding countryside long before the Mongol invasion.

While the Silk Road was an important overland link that helped the expansion of Islam, Arab Muslims were also mariners, traveling the seas in their small ships known as dhows. These merchants visited the coastal cities of Iran, Pakistan, India, and through-out Asia, even reaching to China. When Marco Polo, the western explorer, entered Canton China around 1200 AD, he discovered more than 100,000 Arab and Iranian merchants living in the city. The life of these Muslim merchants centered around the port. They received cargos brought by Arab or Persian ships, and sold them locally. They also bought local goods which the same ships then took away to other lands. Thus Islam was introduced into the many great sea-ports all around Asia. Here the Muslims were successful businessmen with prestige and power. They built mosques and schools, and contributed to the local society. Eventually these Muslim businessmen became the means of introducing Islam into many of these cities.

Mongol Conversion to Islam

While the Mongols were an important military force, they were not unified in the area of religion. Overall, the Mongols were highly tolerant of most religions, and typically sponsored several religions at the same time. Though many people believe that the Mongols were primarily Buddhist, during the early Mongol Empire they had a substantial number of Christians, many of whom were in positions of considerable power. Many Mongols had been converted by Christian Nestorian missionaries from the Assyrian Church of the East, since the seventh century. When Genghis Khan, then a young man known as Temüjin, swore allegiance with his men at the Baljuna Covenant, there were representatives of nine tribes among the 20 men. Temüjin was a shamanist, and the others included several Christians, three Muslims, and several Buddhists.

Many Mongol tribes, such as the Kerait, the Naiman, the Merkit, and to a large extent the Kara Khitan, were Nestorian Christian. Under the Mongul ruler Möngke, the main religious influence was that of the Nestorians.

Some of the major Christian figures among the Mongols were: the daughter-in-law of Genghis Khan and the mothers of the Great Khans: Möngke, Kublai, Hülagü and Ariq Böke. Each of these rulers were also married to Christian princesses. Many of the lesser rulers also Christians or had Christian mothers or wives. A Mongol was the highest authority (Patriarch) of the Nestorian church from 1281 to 1317 under the name Mar Yaballaha III.

Genghis Khan, though himself a shamanist, had many Christians among his relatives but was tolerant of other faiths. His sons were married to Christian princesses who held considerable influence at his court.

As the Mongols had primarily a nomadic culture, their practice of Christianity was different from what might have been recognized by other Christians. The Mongols had no churches or monasteries, but claimed a set of beliefs that descended from the Apostle Thomas. Their religious practice relied on wandering monks. Further, their style was based more on practice than belief. Since Christian Mongols were converted from shamanism, they originally had a great deal of interest in how Jesus healed the sick, so the practice of Christianity became interwoven with the care of the sick. Jesus was considered to be a powerful shaman. The Mongols also adapted the Christian cross to their own belief system, making it sacred because it pointed to the four directions of the world. They had varied readings of the Scriptures, and had a special feeling of affinity to the wandering Hebrew tribes. Christianity also allowed the eating of meat, which was different from the vegetarianism of the Buddhists. And of particular interest to the hard-drinking Mongols, they liked the fact that alcohol was allowed in Christianity. Another attraction was that the name Jesus sounded like *Yesu* the Mongol number "9". It was a sacred number to the Mongols, and was also the name of Genghis Khan's father.

Marco Polo and his brothers Niccolo and Matteo were European explorers to China. They returned to Europe in 1271 with an invitation from Kublai Khan to the western church imploring that they send a hundred teachers of science and religion to reinforce the Nestorian Church among the Mongols demonstrating that Christianity was well established in this vast empire.

Eighteen years later John of Monte Corvino set out for China. Although the great Khan had already died by the time John arrived (1294), the court at Khanbaliq received him graciously and encouraged him to settle there. John was China's first western missionary, and he was significantly successful. He labored largely in the Mongol tongue, translating the New Testament and Psalms. He built a central church, and within a few years (by 1305) could report six thousand baptized converts.

But John of Monte Carvino's mission was of relatively short duration. Two massive political catastrophes hastened the extinction of this missionary effort to China. First, the Black Death during the latter half of the 14th century in Europe so depleted the missionaries and their supporting churches that they were unable to sustain the mission to China. Second, the Yuan Dynasty began to decline. In 1362 the Chinese expelled the Mongols from their territory, launching the Ming Dynasty (1368). Since the missionaries had been identified with the Mongols, they were all expelled.

In the end, the Christian presence in Mongolia became very mixed with shamanism and lost most of its message and power. As the Muslim presence continued to grow in the empire, Muslim merchants and businessmen gained much influence. Kublai Khan, the last true Great Khan was a strong warrior, but his critics still accused him of being too closely tied to Chinese culture. When he moved his headquarters to Beijing, there was an uprising in the old capital that he barely staunched. He focused mostly on foreign alliances and opened trade routes. He dined with a large court every day, and met with many ambassadors and foreign merchants. Kublai Khan even offered to convert to Christianity if this religion was proved to be correct by 100 priests. At this time the plague was ravaging much of Asia and Europe. Although the priests prayed for the suffering, they could heal no one. As the plague advanced, it became obvious that Christians had no special protection from the plague and that they were powerless before it. As the Muslims grew in economic power, there were advantages to becoming Muslim.

After Kublai died in 1294, his heirs began fighting, and the Silk Road closed. As the Mongol Empire broke up, it divided into four parts, with three of the four becoming Muslim. The fourth group adopted Tibetan Buddhism as the official religion, but the majority of the ordinary Mongols, especially those who continued living in Mongolia, remained shamanists. After the decline of the Yuan Dynasty, shamanism once again became the dominant religion. To this day, Islam and shamanism have existed side by side in Central Asia.

What Makes Islam Attractive?

Many Christians today are puzzled when they meet people who have converted to Islam. What is it that makes Islam attractive? Here are some of the things that attract people to Islam:

First, most Muslims are completely convinced that their religion is true. When they speak to others they sound completely sure of themselves and their faith. They know their Islamic history, and they know how to practice their religion, and they are convinced that only they are going to paradise and that all others are going to hell.

Second, Muslims freely talk of their religion with others. They openly pray before others, and their dress and manners depict that they are pious followers of Islam. This often speaks to those who are unsure of what to believe in life.

In many countries, Muslims are in a majority. If you become a Muslim you can be included in the majority rather than being a part of a minority. This usually opens opportunities for work and marriage. Non-Muslims have difficulty doing business in a Muslim country, so converting to Islam means that they are better accepted in the business community.

Some men are attracted to Islam because men are in a place of power over women. Women exist to serve and please men. Men seek sexual fulfillment through multiple wives and concubines.

Another thing that makes Islam attractive is that vices, such as prostitution, alcohol and drugs are better controlled in Muslim countries. It is often safer to raise children in a Muslim city than in a western one. Last, wealth, power, honor and influence are all highly esteemed in Islam.

Christianity on the other hand has few things that make it appealing, but there are a few. In most Muslim countries, Christians can more easily emigrate to the west. Christians can drink alcoholic drinks and they are not 'controlled' by the state in western countries.

Most Muslims consider western countries to be Christian countries; therefore, the problems that western countries face are usually considered "Christian problems." Thus, Christianity and Judaism are considered the source of most of the evils in the world today.

So, to the Muslim, Christianity does not look very attractive. All over the world, Christians are the minority, never the majority. They are often struggling, divided into competing groups, and are usually more associated with the poor than the rich and powerful. All around the world the media speaks poorly of Christians. Even Christian history is filled with difficulties and persecution.

In Muslim eyes, Jesus, the founder of Christianity, was a failure. While he did great miracles and taught great things, he never amounted to much. After only three years he was killed and his followers scattered. From the very beginning of the church, Christians were persecuted. They did not take up arms and fight for themselves. In fact, Christians were often servants or even slaves. Nevertheless, when given an opportunity, Christian people and nations exploited others. The Crusades demonstrated how barbaric they could be. Slavery demonstrated how they exploited others. Lastly, modern economic exploitation demonstrates how they care only for themselves and not for others.

Questions for Reflection and Group Discussion
1. Compare the spread of Christianity to the spread of Islam. What was similar, what was different?
2. Why would people choose Islam over Christianity? Why would you choose Christ over Muhammad?
3. Should missionaries compare Islam and Christianity and try to demonstrate how Christianity is better? Why or why not?

Chapter Eight
Islam Today

In this lesson we will continue to learn about how Islam expanded around the world.

African Expansion

Islam expanded into Africa in a slightly different way. First, the Muslim armies crossed through the deserts of North Africa, eventually reaching Morocco. They then turned northward, conquering through Spain into southern France.

The Sahara desert was a great barrier to the lands in the south where there were dry plains and swampy valleys, so Islam did spread south of the desert, but at a very slow rate. Muslim armies never penetrated south of the Sahara, because there was little wealth to loot and few civilizations to conquer. Bush, jungles, swamps, rivers, mountains, and most of all swarms of biting flies and insects kept them away. The presence of sickness and disease sapped the Muslim armies of whatever enthusiasm they may have had about moving south.

So, once again merchants pioneered the way, this time into Africa, although at a much slower rate than in Asia. There was little in Africa for the merchants to profit from, other than selling goods to Africans. However, one resource in Africa immediately caught the attention of the Muslim Arab merchants. It was that of slaves.

Contrary to what many Muslims claim, the Arabs of Arabia were proud of their white skin, and they looked down upon the black people of Africa as second class. Ibn Khaldun, the great Arab historian and geographer of the 14th century wrote: " ... *the Negro nations are, as a rule, submissive to slavery, because they have little that is human and possess attributes that are quite similar to those of dumb animals.*" (Ibn Khaldun as quoted in Bernard Lewis, *Race and Color in Islam,* Harper and Row, 1970, quote on page 38.) So Black Africans were imported into the Islamic world as slaves for the wealthy.

Slavery was also practiced in Europe through the Middle Ages. It is recorded in the history of many nations that their rulers tried to limit the export of slaves to other places, which were depleting their own workforce. From 800 AD – 1200 AD Viking raiders captured white females in Europe and sold them to the Arabs in the Middle East, mainly as sexual slaves or concubines. During this same period, black female slaves were imported into the Middle East from Africa. Many of the young black men who were sold as slaves to the Arab world were operated on, and their entire sexual organs were removed. This was usually done on boys, ages 8 – 12 years old. Hundreds of thousands of black boys were mutilated. The survival rate was only around one in ten, so the price of black eunuchs was high, and usually only the wealthy could afford them as guards for the women's side of the house. White slaves were also in demand. In Spain, in a Muslim raid against Lisbon in 1189, the caliph Yacoub al-Mansur took 3,000 female and child captives. The governor of Cordoba in 1191 took 3,000 Christians as slaves after his attack on the city of Silves in southern Portugal.

By the end of the 14th century, black slaves were introduced into Europe and after that the demand for black slaves rose sharply. By the 1700's black slavery was common in much of the western world as well.

The Qur'an does not speak against the practice of slavery. Slavery is mentioned twenty-nine times in the Qur'an, giving instruction about the legal status of slaves. Most of the material deals with releasing slaves or with sexual relations with slaves:

> *Never should a believer kill a believer; but if by mistake one kills a believer it is ordained that he should free a believing slave and pay compensation to the deceased's family unless they remit it freely. If the deceased belonged to a people at war with you and he was a believer the freeing of a believing slave is enough. If he belonged to a people with whom you have a treaty of mutual alliance compensation should be paid to his family and a believing*

slave be freed. For those who find this beyond their means a fast for two months running is required as a way of repentance to Allah: for Allah hath all knowledge and all wisdom. (Sura 4:92)

But those who divorce their wives and then wish to go back on the words they uttered should free a slave before they touch each other: this are you admonished to perform: and Allah is well-acquainted with (all) that ye do. (Sura 58:3)

Force not your slave girls to whoredom to seek enjoyment of the life of the world, if they want to preserve their chastity. But if one force them, then after their compulsion Allah will be forgiving and merciful. (Sura 24: 23)

Eventually Islam spread through parts of central Africa, but it was only in the last 200 years as travel became easier in Africa that Islam began to spread again, this time accompanied with money from oil rich Muslim countries.

The Ottomans

While Islam had spread east and west, it had made little initial progress to the north. That changed when a Muslim leader, Osman, began to expand his area of rule in modern day Turkey. He was a strong ruler who began uniting Muslim areas under his leadership. The Christian Byzantine Empire was much weakened by this time, and, soon after Osman's death, Mehmed II led a Muslim army that captured the Christian city of Constantinople in 1453. The Ottomans continued their expansion into Europe, pushing right up to the city of Venice in northern Italy. The Ottomans enlarged their influence in Muslim lands expanding through the Middle East and across parts of North Africa.

For many years the Ottoman Empire was the greatest Muslim empire both militarily and scientifically. As an example, in 1513 an Ottoman admiral known as Piri Ibn Haji Memmed began to collect maps in order to construct a map of the whole world. His Piri Reis map, drawn just a few years after Columbus 'discovered' America, clearly shows Antarctica, all of South America and parts of North America. By 1521 the Ottoman Turkish admiral had relatively accurate maps of the entire world. This is only 29 years after the Spanish began their journeys to the new world.

In time, however, European nations developed naval powers, and with the development of alternate sea routes from Europe to Asia and the New World the Ottoman economy was severely damaged. Before this the Ottomans had controlled the land routes to Asia, but now the Europeans began sailing around Africa and on to Asia. On land, the Ottoman armies were defeated at Vienna, and from this point on the empire slowly began to shrink.

In the years that followed the Ottoman Empire began to collapse financially. For many years it was known as the "Sick man of Europe." World War I brought about the complete collapse of the empire. As the British advanced against the Turkish army, many Arabs rose up in what is known today as the Arab Revolt. At the end of the revolt, many of the modern Arab nations of today were founded.

East Asia

As Muslim expansion in Europe and Africa slowed, Islam began making gains in East Asia. Muslim merchants regularly traveled through Indonesian waters on their way between Arabia and China. The first Muslim populations emerged in Indonesia in the 13th century in northern Sumatra. Other Indonesians slowly accepted Islam. By the 16th century it was the major religion. In most cases Islam was mixed with the existing animistic culture and religion. The result is something known as *kebatinan* which is a mixture of animism, Hinduism, Buddhism, and Sufi Islam. *Kebatinan* worship includes sacrifices and devotions to local and ancestral spirits. These spirits are believed to inhabit natural objects, human beings, artifacts, and gravesites of important Muslim saints. Illness and other misfortunes are traced to such spirits, and if sacrifices or pilgrimages fail to calm the angry demons, the advice of a *dukun* or healer is sought.

Most Indonesian Muslims are Sunni, although some follow other branches of Islam, including 100,000 Shi'as. In general, Muslims are considered either "modernists" (who closely adhere to scriptural orthodox theology while embracing modern learning and modern concepts) or "traditionalists" (who often follow charismatic religious scholars organized around Islamic boarding schools). Today Islam is Indonesia's dominant religion with approximately 88% of its population identifying themselves as Muslims, making it the most populous Muslim-majority nation in the world.

The West

The growth of Islam in the western word has been very slow. While some Muslims emigrated to Europe and America over the centuries, it is only during the last 100 years that Muslims in larger and larger numbers have emigrated to the west. In most cases, Muslims were ignored and allowed to build mosques and practice their religion as long as it didn't interfere with the lives of people around them. However, changes in population have caused the numbers of Muslims in the west to rise significantly. First, many western families have only one or two children while Muslim families are having six or seven or more children. Also, since western families have been small, many countries such as Canada, Australia and New Zealand have opened their doors for immigrants from other countries. There have been many Muslims among the people that flocked to the west. As a result, Muslims have started to make an impact on western society, although few western people have converted to Islam. However, as Muslim men take western women for their wives, all of these women convert to Islam in order to marry. Usually they are agnostics or non-practicing Christians. For them, religion is not important, and they love their husbands and want to belong to their families.

Islam Around the World

Today Muslims can be found in almost every country of the world. They are a fast growing religion, with their numbers increasing both from having large families and also from gaining new converts. Below are a series of stories that illustrate some of the situations around the world.

Africa: The People of the Sacred Forest were always cautious and often lived with fear. They believed that once they were initiated into the group that they were "born again" through the devil's mouth. They received special powers, but most of this power was reserved for the chief leader of the cult. Whenever he came to town, everyone would run and hide.

There were also many Muslims in the town. They were not part of the People of the Sacred Forest. They believed in Allah, and that he was the ruler of the world. However, they also respected and feared the leader of the People of the Sacred Forest and recognized that he has powers. Sometimes when they wanted to cast a spell on someone, either for good or evil, they would approach the leader of the People of the Sacred Forest and pay him to cast the spell for them.

There were also a few Christians in the town, but most people ignoredthem. They seem powerless. They had no witchdoctor or shaman like the People of the Sacred Forest, and they were few in number, unlike the many wealthy and successful Muslims. However, everyone started talking when the village chief's son announced that he was now a Christian.

Soon after this, an event happened that changed the thinking of many people. Just after the noon meal, several people rushed down the main street telling people that the leader of the Sacred Forest People was coming. The village leader's son was on the street just then and he refused to rush inside. His father was very afraid of what would happen and became very angry when his son refused to move. "I belong to Jesus now," his son said, "and he has set me free from the devil's power. He will keep me safe." The chief was amazed when nothing happened to his son. "It must be true that this Jesus is really more powerful than all the spirits we fear," he exclaimed. The Muslims however were still antagonistic and demanded that the village leader be a Muslim. Obviously the power of the leader of the People of the Sacred Forest had been challenged. But the Muslims were quick to step into his place. (Taken from *Unafraid Of The Sacred Forest*, Ronaldo Lidorio, 2007)

Turkey

Murat grew up in a Muslim home. Everyone he knew was a Muslim. All of the other children in the school were Muslims. In Turkey, people take pride in being western. They have freedom of religion, and a secular government. But none of this mattered to Murat. His world was made up of only Muslims.

Then, when Murat was seven years old, something terrible happened. A terrible earthquake destroyed his city. Murat was caught in the middle of the earthquake. As walls and rocks began falling around him, Murat crawled into a small space where he was safe. Tons of rock and cement crashed down on top of him, killing his entire family.

After the earthquake, people came from all over to help. A small group of Christians came from the capital city to help provide food and do whatever they could. During the following days, rescuers frantically pulled people from the rubble. At last they gave up hope of finding any more people alive. As people left, the Christians stood near the pile of rubble that had buried Murat and prayed for those who might remain that God would be merciful to them.

Several days later the bulldozers arrived and started clearing away the rubble. It was then that the workmen discovered seven-year old Murat under a huge pile of bricks and concrete. He had been buried alive for nine days.

"It's a miracle," said the doctors who examined Murat. "It's so hot here in August, we don't know how anyone could live so long in this heat without water."

"But I did have water," Murat insisted. "Every evening, a nice man came to visit me and brought me bread and water." Everyone was puzzled. Since his family were dead, they knew of no one who could have visited him, and how could he have anyway, since Murat was buried deep under the rubble?

Was this a miracle? Did God send an angel to visit Murat? The Christians in Turkey believe in miracles. Every Turkish believer is a miracle. There are 66 million Turks, and only very few have become followers of Jesus.

Europe

Jamiyla seemed to be a typical French girl, except for her black hair and tan-colored skin. All of her friends thought of her as a typical French girl, but Jamiyla was different. All of her friends were Catholics, although most of them were only very nominally Catholic. But Jamiyla was a Muslim. Her mother was a French woman who had married an Arab Muslim. That is what gave Jamiyla her slightly dark color and black hair.

One day while they were on a school trip, the girls sat under a tree during the lunch break. Gina noticed that Jamiyla was very quiet. "What's the problem?" she asked. "You look like you've lost your best friend. But you couldn't have, because I'm right here."

Jamiyla smiled, but her eyes were sad. "It's my father," she said. "He's a Muslim, you know." Gina nodded. She had visited Jamiyla's family many times. "My father is insisting that we are all Muslims because he is a Muslim."

"Yeah," Gina added. "I'm a Catholic because my parents are Catholics. But we've never been to the church, except to get me baptized when I was born."

"I know. That would be fine with me. I don't mind being a Muslim. But my father came home last week and had a big fight with my mother."

"What about?"

He is insisting that she wear the *Hijab*. The Muslim dress.

"Oh my God," Gina gasped. "Your mother is a classy looking woman. She would look absolutely wretched in one of those black things. A black blob!"

Jamiyla started to cry. "And he wants me to wear one too."

Gina was stunned. She swore under her breath.

Jamiyla dabbed at the tears under her eyes. "Today is my last day to wear western clothing. I insisted that I could dress like everyone else on this trip. But tomorrow I must wear a scarf and Muslim dress."

Gina stared at her friend. "That's terrible!"

Jamiyla started crying again. "A black blob," she wailed.

"What if you refuse?"

"My father will beat me," she cried. "My mother refused, and he hit her."

Gina swore again. "You should run away."

"I don't have anywhere to go. My father will track me down. He is insisting that I wear the hijab and learn how to honor and respect my religion." Gina put her arm around Jamiyla and tried to console her on her last day of freedom.

America

Jason was a black young man living in Los Angeles, America. Many years ago his ancestors were slaves, brought from Africa to work on American sugar plantations. Now that slavery was over, his family struggled with poverty and life in the inner city. While his parents both worked, they never seemed to have much money after the rent, utilities and food were paid for. Jason had always wondered about his history. Where had his family come from? What sort of life had they lived in Africa? Would he have fit in better in Africa than he did in America? During his years in school he thought about searching for his roots, but he never knew how to go about it.

Then one day he met Carman, another young black man. Carman was tough, strong, and bold. All the young men looked up to him, and he always seemed to know what was going on, and how to respond to situations. A short time later Carman told him that he had discovered his African roots. He was from an Islamic tribe in central Africa. His family had been rulers, and he was a prince. Jason was awed by Carman. While many of the other young men seemed to be lost in a daze, struggling with inner-city life and addictions, Carman was sure of himself and what he believed and who he was. One day, when Carman was going to the mosque, Jason went along with him. It proved to be a turning point in his life. When they arrived at the mosque, several men at the door recognized Carman and welcomed him. Jason shook their hand, and felt accepted and special. Carman told him to simply watch while he went through the Muslim prayers with the others in the mosque. Jason was attracted to the way that the men all prayed together, moving in a strange harmony as they stood, kneeled and bowed. The sound of the Arabic language was unfamiliar and yet strangely attractive as the leader chanted from the Qur'an. "Yes," Jason thought to himself. "This is my religion. My roots are here in Islam." When one of the men asked Jason if he would like to attend a small class to learn about Islam he readily accepted.

Questions for Reflection and Group Discussion
1. How would you explain the Christian position on slavery? What is your Biblical basis?
2. Spend a few moments praying for the Muslim world.
3. Spend a few moments praying against the spread of Islam around the world.

Understanding Islam
(Through theology)

Chapter Nine
Islamic Authorities

The Qur'an

The Qur'an is the sacred book of Muslims, written in the Arabic language, and considered by them to be the inspired Word of God. The word "Qur'an" means "the collected things" according to some authorities. Others say that it means "The Reading." The word itself is used several times in the book. The Qur'an contains 114 chapters or *suras* of varying length which were received piece by piece by Muhammad. Sura 25:32, the first revelation, was given in the month of Ramadan, now the Muslim month of fasting. This is indicated in Sura 2:185. Muhammad related the Qur'an verbally to his followers who memorized it. The Qur'an is written in poetic style. Every chapter other than the ninth, which some say was once part of the eighth, commences with the words: "*In the Name of God the Merciful and the Compassionate.*" Tradition says that some parts were written on scraps of palm leaves, stones, and on shoulder blades of animals, as well as in the memory of a number of men who memorized the chapters that they had heard Muhammad speak. Some of them memorized chapters learned from others who had memorized.

The Abu Bakr Collection

A number of versions of the revelations were in circulation, but when several of those who had memorized the revelations were killed in the "Battle of the Garden" (Yamama), Abu Bakr, the new caliph, said to Zaid bin Thabit:

> "You are a wise young man and we do not have any suspicion about
> you, and you used to write the Divine Inspirations for Allah's apostle.

So you should search for the fragmentary scripts of the Qur'an and collect them."

"By Allah!" Zaid said "If they had ordered me to shift one of the mountains it would not have been heavier for me than this ordering me to collect the Qur'an. Then I said to Abu Bakr, "How will you do something which Allah's apostle did not do? Abu Bakr replied "By Allah, it is a good project." (*Sahih al-Bukhari*, Vol 6:477)

From this we learn several things: The Qur'an was not collected as a single writing during the lifetime of Muhammad. Muhammad had not been interested in collecting the revelations. It was not going to be an easy project. If any one person had memorized the entire Qur'an then it would have been easy, recording the memorized material and checking it with others who had memorized it.

Zaid goes on to say: "So I started looking for the Qur'an and collecting it from palm-leaf stalks, thin white stones and also from the men who knew some of it by heart, till I found the last verse of *Surat at-Tauba* (repentance) with Abu Khuzaima al-Ansari, and I did not find it with anybody other than him." (*Sahih al-Bukhari*, Vol 6: 478)

From this we learn several things: The records of the revelations to Muhammad were scattered, some being memorized and some written. He checked with many people and many sources, demonstrating that he could not rely on any one scribe or source. Some of the sources were unique; in other-words, they were added to the Qur'an on the authority of one man's recollection of what Muhammad had said.

Some of Muhammad's revelations were lost however. Ibn Abu Dawud records:

"Many suras of the Qur'an that were sent down were known by those who died on the day of Yamama... but they were not known by those who survived them, nor were they written down nor had Abu Bakr, Umar or Uthman collected the Qur'an, nor were they found with even one person after them. (Ibn Abu Dawud, *Kitab–al Masahif,* p 23)

Despite all of these records, many Muslims today believe that the Qur'an was written down during Muhammad's time and that today we have a perfectly preserved copy of what Muhammad uttered. But as we see, Islamic historians themselves tell us that the Qur'an had to be collected, and even then not everything was preserved.

Uthman's Collection

By the time Uthman became the third caliph, several versions of the Qur'an were being circulated in the provinces. Zaid's compilation was kept as the personal property of Caliph Abu Bakr, then Caliph Umar, and then it passed to Umar's daughter Hafsa. (*Sahih al-Bukhari* 6:478) This left Uthman without a written copy of the Qur'an. By this time, Abdullah ibn Mad'ud, Ubay ibn Ka'b, Mu'adh ibn Jabal and others were also circulating copies of their own rendition of the Qur'an.

A dispute arose in the armies led by General Hudhaifa over the reading of the Qur'an. Troops had joined from various areas of Arabia, and each area had its own version of how the Qur'an should be recited. The general appealed to Caliph Uthman, who then ordered that all the manuscripts be sent to him so that they could compile one main authority, which would then be sent back to them. Uthman then chose three men to rewrite the Qur'an. He instructed them:

> "If any of you disagree with Zaid on any point, then write it in the dialect of the Quraish tribe as the Qur'an was revealed in their tongue..."

> "... Uthman sent to every Muslim province one copy of what they had written, and ordered that all the other Qur'anic materials, whether written in fragmentary manuscripts or whole copies, be burnt. (*Al Mukhari*, Vol 6:479)

When the soldiers moved through Arabia collecting variant readings of the Qur'an and destroying them, Abdullah Ibn Mas'ud refused to give his copy over. He was one of those who had memorized what he had personally heard Muhammad speak. He and many others around him in Iraq claimed that their copy was more accurate than the one that Uthman was propagating. The same happened in Busra, Syria, where Muslims had copies of Abu Musa's version of the Qur'an. These copies did not have the first chapter nor the last two chapters of the Qur'an in it, and Abu Musa argued against including them. (*Sahih al-Bukhari*, Vol 6:510, *Al-Itqan* by Jalal al-Din and *Kitab al-Masahif* by Ibn Abu Da'ud)

In the end the will of the caliph prevailed, and all variant versions of the

Qur'an were destroyed, and only one official version was recognized by Muslims everywhere. However, Uthman's version of the Qur'an did not have any vowels. It was written only with consonants. Because of this, variant readings still existed across the Muslim world, with people from different areas reading the Qur'an with their own dialect. During the time of Caliph Abd al-Malik of Iraq, eleven direct changes were made to the Qur'an, and these are still in use today.

More than 300 years after Muhammad, Ibn Mujahid wrote a book outlining seven different variant readings (*ahruf*) that were in common usage based on Arabic dialects. While most Muslims assume that all early versions of the Qur'an were destroyed, many in fact have survived. Manuscript 1605 (which is held in the Vatican) is an early Qur'an. In recent years dozens of early manuscripts and fragments were discovered in the great mosque in Sana'a, Yemen. These early versions contain hundreds of differences.

How the Muslims view the Qur'an

Muslim children are taught to memorize the Qur'an, or at least its most relevant verses. Therefore, Muslims can always bring these memorized passages to their defense.

Here are some of the things they believe:

1. Abraham is said to have been a Muslim, his son Ishmael is said to have founded the Arab race, and so, therefore, Muhammad is in apostolic succession from Abraham and Ishmael, just as the Jews were in apostolic succession through Isaac.
2. The Qur'an claims to confirm the books of the former prophets and to complete them. Muhammad is the final prophet.
3. The Qur'an is a revelation from the Lord of the World (Sura 26:192) and from Allah, the mighty, the wise. (Sura 39:1)
4. The Qur'an was revealed to Muhammad (Sura 47: 2): "*Believe in that which has been revealed to Muhammad.*"
5. It was revealed to Muhammad by the Holy Spirit (Sura 26:194): "*The Faithful Spirit has brought it on thy heart.*" Some Muslim commentators consider this to be the angel Gabriel, who is said to have brought the revelations from heaven to Muhammad.
6. It was brought down from the highest to the lowest heaven on the Night

of Power or the Night of Majesty, about the 27th day of the month of Ramadan, a night known to Muslims as *Lailat al-Qadr*, or literally, "night of majesty, grandeur, greatness or power." This night is said to be better than a thousand months (Sura 97:3). The Angel Gabriel is said to have revealed the first part of the Qur'an to Muhammad on this night.

7. The Qur'an is eternal and uncreated, having existed in Heaven from the beginning of time. It was revealed to Muhammad at the appointed time. It is to be read and believed. Sura 17:106-108: "*And it is a Qur'an we have made distinct, so that thou mayest read it by slow degrees. Surely those who are given the knowledge before it, fall down prostrate on their faces when it is recited to them.*"

8. The Qur'an is a miracle from God. When Muhammad was challenged to produce a miracle to prove his apostleship, he pointed to a chapter of the Qur'an demanding that his opponents produce one like it. Sura 10:37-38: "*And this Qur'an is not such as could be forged by those besides Allah, but it is a verification of that which is before it and a clear explanation of the Book, there is no doubt in it, from the Lord of the Worlds. If they say: He has forged it? Say: Then bring a chapter like it, and invite who you can besides Allah, if you are truthful.*"

9. The Qur'an was originally revealed in Arabic because Arabic is the language of heaven. Sura 12:2: "*Surely we have revealed it--an Arabic Qur'an.*" Sura 26:193: "*...in plain Arabic language.*" Sura 41:44: "*And if We had made it a Qur'an in a foreign tongue, would they have said: Why have not its messages been made clear? What a foreign (tongue) and an Arab! Say: it is to those who believe a guidance and a healing, and those who believe not, there is a deafness in their ears and it is obscure to them. These are called to from a place afar.*" From these quotations we see the arguments that Muslims raise. They say that, whereas we have to translate our Bible always from Hebrew and Greek causing inevitable differences, the Qur'an came in Arabic and remains in Arabic. Many Muslim teachers therefore say that the Qur'an is untranslatable.

10. The pages of the Qur'an are pure and its directions are right. Sura 98:2-3: "*A messenger from Allah, reciting pure pages...wherein are (all) right books.*"

The Law of Abrogation

In the Qur'an, later verses abrogate or cancel out the earlier verses or books they contradict. Muslims believe that the original copy of the Qur'an (*Umm al-Kitab* meaning, "origin or mother of the book") remains with God in heaven. God has power to alter and confirm as He will. Sura 13:39: *"Allah effaces (destroys) what He pleases and establishes what He pleases, and with Him is the basis of the book."* Sura 2:106: *"Whatever message We abrogate or cause to be forgotten, We bring no better than it or one like it. Knowest thou not that Allah is possessor of power over all things?"*

Some Muslim scholars deny that any verse, book or teaching in the Qur'an has ever been abrogated. They claim that when sufficient meditation is given to any apparently irreconcilable statements, further meditation will reconcile them. They base this on the following verse in Sura 4:82: *"Will they not then meditate on the Qur'an? And if it were from any other than Allah, they would have found in it many a discrepancy."*

Their argument is that although God has the power to abrogate, he does not in fact do so. Everything in the Qur'an would agree if more time were given to meditation. This seems to be a very weak, insupportable argument, and this continues to be a theological argument among Muslims.

Who May Touch the Qur'an?

The Qur'an is treated with reverence by Muslims. They dare not touch it until they have washed and purified themselves, nor do they hold it below waist level. Sura 56:77-79: *"Surely it is a bounteous book that is protected, which none touches save the purified ones."* In most homes, the Qur'an is placed on a very high shelf, so that nothing in the room is above it.

Dates of the Giving of the Qur'an

It is impossible to state with accuracy the dates when various sections of the Qur'an were revealed, but approximately 92 chapters were revealed in Mecca and 22 chapters were revealed in Medina. These chapters, however, are all jumbled together, so it is impossible with detailed study to tell which came before the other.

The Qur'an and Chronology

The Qur'an gives no outline of history ... in fact many Muslims are confused about history because of the Qur'an. For example, in some places, Miriam the sister of Moses is confused with Mary the mother of Jesus. This is because the Qur'an is not written in chronological order. The first chapter is a short prayer exalting God. It has become an essential part of all Islamic liturgy and prayer. The rest of the chapters are graded generally by length, from longest to shortest. It is thus impossible to tell from the book the chronological order of the revelations.

Most Muslims therefore have no concept of history, who came before who, the order of the prophets, or the history of the Jews and Christians. The Bible, on the other hand, is rich with chronological materials, providing us with a broad outline of the history of God's revelation from the beginning of the world until Jesus Christ.

The Qur'an and Geography

The Qur'an is a very poor geographical reference book, as it refers to only a dozen or so geographical locations. There is only one mention of the city of Mecca. It also mentions the People of 'Ad but archaeologists today have yet to confirm who and where these people were. Greek and Roman historians, as well as the Bible are rich in geography, mentioning many places that are only now coming to light as having actually existed.

How the Qur'an was Received

When receiving his revelations, Muhammad would often go into a trance. Sometimes he closed his eyes, sometimes he shook, and sometimes he foamed at the mouth. On occasion he roared like an animal. Those who saw him said it seemed as if "his soul was being taken from him," or he was intoxicated. After the trance, Muhammad would then speak, giving the revelation that God had revealed to him. Every revelation was spoken as if God were speaking to mankind, or even to Muhammad. The followers of Muhammad were awed that he would receive direct revelations from God.

Proof that the Qur'an is from God

What proof is there that the Qur'an is truly from God? When Muslims are asked this question they point to Sura 17:85-88 which reads:

> When question you about the Spirit of inspiration tell them: "The Spirit is at the Lord's command and I am not given any knowledge of it but a little.". If We want, We can definitely take away all that which We have revealed to you: then you will find none to help you in getting it back from Us. But your Lord has blessed you with this knowledge; surely His goodness to you has been great indeed. Declare: "Even if all human beings and Jinns combined their resources to produce the like of this Qur'an, they would never be able to compose the like thereof, even if they helped each other as best as they could."

For the Muslim, the presence of the Qur'an is proof enough. They believe that it is greater than any other book written, and this alone is proof enough for them that it comes from God.

The Bible

Christians do not believe that God ever dictated his revelation directly to men, who then wrote it down. Rather, Christians have always believed in inspiration, where the Holy Spirit of God supervised or oversaw human writers as they wrote or spoke. In this way, they wrote precisely what God wanted written. The word "inspiration" literally means "God-breathed" in the Greek. Because Scripture is breathed out by a God who always speaks the truth, then it is true and inerrant.

Second Peter 1:21 tells us that *prophecy came not in old time by the will of man: but holy men of God spoke as they were moved by the Holy Ghost.* The word moved is translated from the Greek word *phero* this verse literally means to be driven by the wind. The Greek word *pharo* is also used in Acts 27:15-17. The experienced sailors could not navigate the ship because the wind was so strong. The ship was being driven, directed, and carried about by the wind. This is similar to the Spirit's driving, directing, and carrying the human authors of the Bible as he wished. The word is a strong one, indicating the Spirit's complete direction of the human authors. Yet, just as the sailors were active on the ship (though the wind, not the sailors, controlled the ship's movement), so the human authors were active in writing as the Spirit directed.

All down through history, God has worked out his perfect will through imperfect people, and inspiration is no different. God moved in the hearts of men and directed their thoughts as they wrote. What was written was not so much God speaking directly to mankind; rather, the Bible is a record of God's revelation of himself and his will to mankind all down through history. Since God never changes, and he always speaks the truth, Christians believe that all Scripture is relevant and applicable today.

Most Christians also believe that the inspiration of the Bible refers to the original documents only and not to the copies. Christians hold that the original writings were without error in everything they said. But the copies are not inspired. What we have today are copies of inspired documents. Christians readily admit that some copying errors have woven themselves into some of the Bible. However, this does not mean that the Bible is not trustworthy.

Only 1/1000th of the Bible has any textual variation in the copies. That means that the Bible as a whole is around 98.5% textually pure. The New Testament is about 99.5% textually pure. (Geisler, Norman, *Christian Apologetics,* 1976, p. 307; and Mcdowel, Josh, *A Ready Defense*, 1993, p. 45) Furthermore, enough copies have been unearthed by archaeologists that we can reconstruct the Bible to almost 100% accuracy. The errors that we find are copying errors, usually to do with numbers, word order, spelling, and punctuation.

Evidences that the Bible is True

The most important evidence is that of prophecy. There are two kinds of prophecy in the Bible. The first kind are prophecies dealing with secular nations. The second kind are messianic prophecies about the coming Messiah.

For instance, in Daniel chapter two, four kingdoms are described in the dream of Nebuchadnezzar who was the king of Babylon. The four were the Babylonian Empire, the Persian Empire, the Greek Empire and the Roman Empire. (Dan. 2:39-43). These four kingdoms occurred just as prophesied.

The Bible also prophecies that three famous cities would be destroyed and never rebuilt. This is still true today of Nineveh (Nahum 1:10; 3:7,15; Zepheniah 2:13-14), Babylon (Isaiah 13:1-22), and Tyre (Ezek. 26:).

Another example is Daniel's prophesy in chapter 12:4 that in the last days knowledge would increase as well as the ability to travel great distances. This is now true today.

The second type of prophecies are Messianic prophecies. Listen to what was written about the Messiah, hundreds of years before he was born:

Isaiah 7:14 tells us that the Messiah would be born of a virgin, *"Therefore the Lord himself will give you a sign: The virgin will be with child and will give birth to a son, and will call him Immanuel."* This was fulfilled in Matt. 1:18,25, *"This is how the birth of Jesus Christ came about: His mother Mary ... was found to be with child through the Holy Spirit... But he (Joseph) had no union with her until she gave birth to a son. And he gave him the name Jesus."*

Micah 5:2 tells us that the Messiah would be born in Bethlehem, *"But you, Bethlehem Ephrathah, though you are small among the clans of Judah, out of you will come for me one who will be ruler over Israel, whose origins are from of old, from ancient times."* This was fulfilled in Matt. 2:1, *"After Jesus was born in Bethlehem in Judea, during the time of King Herod, Magi from the east came to Jerusalem."*

Isaiah 40:3 tells us that Jesus would be preceded by a messenger, *"A voice of one calling: 'In the desert prepare the way for the LORD; make straight in the wilderness a highway for our God.'"* This was fulfilled in Matt. 3:1-2, *"In those days John the Baptist came, preaching in the desert of Judea and saying, 'Repent, for the kingdom of heaven is near.'"*

Isaiah 53:3 tells us that the Messiah would be rejected by His own people: *"He was despised and rejected by men, a man of sorrows, and familiar with suffering. Like one from whom men hide their faces he was despised, and we esteemed him not."* This was fulfilled in John 7:5, *"For even his own brothers did not believe in him,"* and John 7:48, *"Have any of the rulers or the Pharisees believed in Him?"*

Zechariah 12:10 tells us that the Messiah's side would be pierced. *"And I will pour out on the house of David and the inhabitants of Jerusalem a spirit of grace and supplication. They will look on me, the one they have pierced, and they will mourn for him as one mourns for an only child, and grieve bitterly for him as* one mourns for an only son." This was fulfilled in John 19:34, "Instead, one of the soldiers pierced Jesus' side with a spear, bringing a sudden flow of blood and water."

Psalm 21:1,11-18 tell us that the Messiah would be crucified "For the director of music. To the tune of "The Doe of the Morning." A psalm of David. My God, my God, why have you forsaken me?... Do not be far from me, for trouble is near and there is no one to help. Many bulls surround me; strong bulls of Bashan. Dogs have surrounded me; a band of evil men has encircled me, they have pierced my hands and my feet. I can count all my bones; people stare and gloat over me. They divide my garments among them and cast lots for my clothing." This was fulfilled in John 19:23-24. For instance, the other two men had their bones broken, but Jesus had all of his bones intact: "When the soldiers crucified Jesus, they took his clothes, dividing them into four shares, one for each of them, with the undergarment remaining. This garment was seamless, woven in one piece from top to bottom. "Let's not tear it," they said to one another. "Let's decide by lot who will get it." This happened that the scripture might be fulfilled which said, "They divided my garments among them and cast lots for my clothing." So this is what the soldiers did."

Although these prophecies do not "prove" biblical inspiration, they are strong evidence that it is indeed inspired. Another evidence of the inspiration of the Bible is that the Bible refers to itself as inspired. Hebrews 3:7-8 tells us that the Holy Spirit says "Today, if you hear his voice, do not harden your hearts as you did in the rebellion, during the time of testing in the desert" This is a quotation from Psalm 95:7. The writer of Hebrews accepts that the Holy Spirit inspired the writer of the psalms.

Matthew's gospel tells us in chapter 1:22-23, "All this took place to fulfill what the Lord had said through the prophet: 'The virgin will be with child and will give birth to a son, and they will call him Immanuel' -which means, "God with us." This is a direct quote from Isaiah 7:14. So Matthew understood that when Isaiah spoke and wrote this, God was speaking.

There are many examples of this in the Bible. For instance, in Acts 1:16 we read: "Men and brethren, this Scripture must needs have been fulfilled, which the Holy Ghost by the mouth of David spoke before, concerning Judas who was a guide to them that took Jesus."

In Acts 4:24-25 we read, *"And when they heard that, they lifted up their voice to God with one accord, and said, "Lord, thou art God, which hast made heaven, and earth, and the sea, and all that in them is: Who by the mouth of thy servant David hast said, "Why did the heathen rage, and the people imagine vain things?""*

Added to this, Jesus promised His followers that it would be the work of the Holy Spirit to provide an accurate recounting of the events of his life (John 14:26). *"the Holy Spirit, whom the Father will send in my name, will teach you all things and will remind you of everything I have said to you."* Because of this, you and I can trust the Bible as the Word of God. The Holy Spirit supervised the process from the beginning to the end.

Second Timothy 3:16 tells us, *"All scripture is given by inspiration of God, and is profitable for doctrine, for reproof, for correction, for instruction in righteousness."* When Paul said that "all Scripture" is inspired, he did not have in mind just the Old Testament. Paul had already quoted from the Gospel of Luke 10:7 as "Scripture" in his first letter to Timothy when he said: *"The worker deserves his wages."* This phrase is not found in the Old Testament, but it is found in the Gospel of Luke.

The apostle Peter also describes Paul's letters as being scripture in 2 Peter 3:15 - 16:

> *Bear in mind that our Lord's patience means salvation, just as our dear brother Paul also wrote you with the wisdom that God gave him. He writes the same way in all his letters, speaking in them of these matters. His letters contain some things that are hard to understand, which ignorant and unstable people distort, as they do the other Scriptures, to their own destruction.*

Jesus' View of the Bible

In Matthew 5:17-18 Jesus taught us that he had not come to abolish the law but to fulfill them.

> *I tell you the truth, until heaven and earth disappear, not the smallest letter, not the least stroke of a pen, will by any means disappear from the Law until everything is accomplished.*

In John 10:35 he taught us that *"The Scriptures cannot be broken."* The Greek word here means destroyed, dissolved or broken in pieces. When battling with the temptations of Satan Jesus used Scripture each time as his final authority. You can read about this in Matthew 3. He also used it as the authority for his teachings when he argued with the Sadducees in Matthew 22:29 stating, *"You are in error because you do not know the Scriptures or the power of God."*

When debating with the Jews, Jesus made a bold statement about prophecy in John 5:39 *"You diligently study the Scriptures because you think that by them you possess eternal life. These are the Scriptures that testify about me."*

Even the apostle Paul recognized that when he wrote, he was writing the words of God. In 1 Corinthians 2:13 Paul said he spoke *"not in the words which man's wisdom teaches, but which the Holy Ghost teaches; interpreting spiritual things with those that are spiritual."* In 1 Corinthians 14:37 Paul says, *"If any man think himself to be a prophet, or spiritual, let him acknowledge that the things that I write unto you are the commandments of the Lord."* In 1 Thessalonians 2:13 he adds, *"For this cause also thank we God without ceasing, because, when you received the word of God which you heard from us, you received it not as the word of men, but as it is in truth, the word of God, which effectually works also in you that believe."*

It is clear from these verses that Paul did not receive his gospel message from other men but rather he received it (as he says in Galatians 1:12) *"through revelations of Jesus Christ,"* and also according to 2 Corinthians 12:7, some of these revelations were *"exceeding great."*

Can we Trust our Bibles?

When investigators are trying to determine if someone's story is true or not, they concentrate on several main ideas. First, does the story make sense? And does its time frame make sense? When examining the Bible, there is a clear progression of time, starting with creation to the life of the early church. The dates make sense. There are no major conflicts with the dates of historians that Bible scholars cannot answer. However, when one comes to the Qur'an little makes sense historically. There is no sense of chronology, no sense of how the stories fit into history. As a result many Muslims are confused about history.

Second, investigators look for details. The Bible is rich with details about locations and customs of people. There are thousands upon thousands of geographical references in the Bible. These are places that archaeologists have found and verified. The Qur'an is different. There are few geographical references, and many vague terms. This is also true of the Gnostic writings and others who tried to add to Scripture. If the writers were actually present when the events took place, they would include many correct details. If they were not, they would simply tell a basic tale, with as few details as possible.

Based on this evidence, be it the prophecies of the Bible, the internal witness of the Bible, the historical proofs, or the incredible geographical and cultural details in the Bible, we as Christians can be assured that our Bible is trustworthy. We have ancient manuscripts that date very close to the time of writing. God has preserved his word, from its writing down to the book we hold in our hands. While Muslims claim this is true for their Qur'an, it does not hold up under close examination. Ancient Qur'anic manuscripts have significant differences between them. However, rather than admit their weakness, they attack the Bible, drawing the attention away from the weaknesses in their own book, refusing to admit that there is any problem with their own Qur'an.

Questions for Discussion and Reflection
1. Compare how Muslims view the Qur'an's inspiration with how Christians view the inspiration of the Bible.
2. Do you think the Qur'an is really the final authority for Muslims? Do they have other authorities? If so, what are they?
3. Compare how Muslims treat their Qur'an to how Christians treat their Bible.

Chapter Ten
Islamic Authorities: Hadith

During Muhammad's lifetime, whenever people had a problem or wanted to know how to act, they approached Muhammad, and he gave them instruction. If Muhammad did not know what to do, he waited until a new revelation came. After Muhammad's death the revelations ceased. With the rapid expansion of Islam, however, the need for rules and regulations was urgent in order that the vast and diverse groups of people could be effectively governed. The Qur'an was very specific in some areas, such as words to be spoken in worship and very vague in others, such as matters of state finance and commerce.

The Qur'an was revered above all as the uncreated word of Allah. It was the final source of authority where it applied, being called the "written revelation," or "the writings that are inspired." In addition to the Qur'an, people referred to what they remembered Muhammad as saying or doing. These sayings were known as the *hadith,* and the customs that Muhammad did were known as *sunna.* Many people used these as a guide in their daily lives and conduct. Some of the hadith were regarded as the actual word of God and were held in reverence next to the Qur'an.

Muslims did not begin collecting the traditions associated with Muhammad until more than two centuries after his death. When Muslim lawyers began to find the Qur'an inadequate to help them with new problems, they began searching for the actual sayings and practices of the prophet to help them. A group of men arose known as the *"Searchers After Knowledge"* whose task it was to collect the true sayings of Muhammad. As time passed, the number of traditions multiplied, including some that others questioned.

Eventually three different types or categories of laws were established based on the traditions of what Muhammad said or did. These categories were:

1. Laws based on the actual words of the Prophet (e.g. a man told Muhammad that he had anal intercourse with his wife, Muhammad said that a man's wife was his "property (*tilth*) to do with as he pleased.")

2. Laws based on Muhammad's acts (e.g. he was careful never to use the toilet in a way to expose his naked bottom towards the Holy City of Mecca. Hence, today many Muslim builders and architects are careful not to place toilets in a way that people will bare their bottoms towards Mecca.)

3. Laws based on those things done in the presence of Muhammad which he did not forbid.

The first problem that the Searchers after Knowledge faced was that there were hundreds of thousands of reported sayings of Muhammad. Since it was several hundred years after Muhammad's death, no one was left alive that had actually seen Muhammad, so they had to sift through all of the reported sayings of Muhammad and choose the ones that were actually true.

In order to do this, they considered two things. First, there was the tradition itself. Did it fit into what was known of Muhammad and the teachings of the Qur'an? Second, and perhaps more important, was the chain of narrators relating the tradition? Could the tradition be traced back from person to person to a reliable source?

In the end they came up with three categories of traditions, depending on their supposed accuracy. These were:

1. Sound Hadiths. Those that were considered to be genuine traditions handed down by a pious person of integrity which did not contradict any prevalent belief.

2. Beautiful Hadiths. These were traditions where the narrators did not possess the moral qualities of sound Hadiths, or there may not be perfect agreement as to the reliability of the tradition.

3. Weak Hadiths. These are traditions where the narrator was of a questionable authority or where serious doubts could be raised because of the unorthodoxy of its contents because it contradicted what the compilers considered to be true.

Traditions were placed in categories based on the chain of narrators. The weakness of Hadiths lay in the fact that the collectors of the traditions placed more reliance on the chain of narrators than on the authenticity of the tradition itself. If the chain of narrators was unbroken, it was accepted as a valid tradition.

Eventually three types of Hadiths developed, based on how far back they could be traced. A *"Connected Hadith"* had an unbroken chain of transmitters all the way back to Muhammad. *"Disconnected Hadiths"* could be traced back to the second generation from Muhammad. And *"Uncertain Hadiths"* could be only traced back to a third or forth generation from Muhammad.

The first systematic collection of traditions was compiled by Imam Malik, who died 180 years after the Hijra, though some say that his collection is not reliable. The most authoritative one still in use today came from Imam Bukhari. (AH 256/AD 870) He claimed to have examined over 600,000 traditions, retaining about 7,000 of them. Of 40,000 narrators, he rejected 38,000. His collection is known as-*Sahih Bukhari*. His traditions are considered both sound and connected.

Five years later, another collection appeared, written by Muslim Ibn al-Hajjaj. These two books, together with four following ones (*Sahih Abu Da'ud, Sahih al-Tirmidhi ,Sahih al-Sughra,* and *Sahih Ibn Maja*), are regarded by most orthodox Sunni Muslims as the Hadith, and are known as the "six correct books."

Alongside these are other collections of hadiths by different compilers that are not considered so correct. In many cases, the correctness of the writings depended on the political correctness of officials at the time, mostly during the Abbasid dynasty. Anything that did not agree with Islam as it was seen by the Abbasid rulers was not accepted. For this reason, the earlier writings of Ibn Ishaq on the *Life of Muhammad* were edited and corrected to reflect the popular view of Islam at the time.

By solidifying the texts of the Qur'an and Hadiths, and making them the supreme authority for Muslims the Abbasids strengthened their rule and the religion of Islam. The Shi'a Muslims on the other hand, accept only the hadiths that can be traced back through Ali and the family of the prophet and Ali's adherents.

Islamic Authorities: Shari'a Law

Besides the Qur'an and the Hadiths, most Muslims look to Shari'a law for guidance. As we mentioned earlier, four Orthodox schools of law were originally established by four different Muslim doctors or imams. In Cairo, the al-Azhar mosque has four schools in separate sections. Though these four schools of interpretation agree on general matters, they differ on minor points. In addition to the Qur'an and Hadith, two other authorities are accepted as a basis of law. These are the:

1. *Ijma'* (the agreement of the highest qualified imams or learned doctors)
2. *Qiyas* (the analogical reasoning of the learned with regard to the teaching of the Qur'an, Hadith and the *Ijma'*)

While some Muslims believe that changes in the law could be made only by the original Ijma', others, including the Shi'as, say that wise doctors from any period of time can be included in the Ijma'. The four different Islamic legal schools are as follows.

The Hanafiyah

Founded by Imam Abu Hanifa, who died 150 years AH, this school was centered in the city of Baghdad. Hanifa ignored the Hadith and tried to use mainly the Qur'an and *Qiyas* (analogical deduction). Today most of the followers of his school of interpretation are found in Turkey, Central Asia and North India, as well as Egypt where it is the officially recognized school of law.

Malakiyah

Imam Malik Ibn Anas, who died 179 AH founded the Malikite School in Medina. He based his system of law on the traditions and customs of how law was practiced in Medina. Most of the followers of his school of interpretation today are found in West Africa, the Sudan, Upper Egypt, all of North Africa, and in Arab countries on the Persian Gulf.

Shafi'iyah

The founder, Imam Ash-Shafi'i, who died in 204 AH is regarded as one of the greatest of Muslim lawyers of all time. He was born in Palestine, of the

Quraysh tribe. He later moved to Mecca and also lived in the Yemen, Syria and Egypt. He built the Shafi'ite school, with Cairo and Baghdad as its main centers. The mosque of Al-Azhar in Cairo expounds his system. His interpretations of law are accepted by Muslims living in Lower Egypt, South Arabia, Syria, East Africa, South India, Palestine, the Hejaz, the Malay Archipelago and parts of Central Asia. He attempted to reconcile the differences between the systems of Hanifa and Malik, and laid down definite rules for Qiyas or legal reasoning.

Hanbaliyah

Ahmad Ibn Hanbal (who died 241 years after the Hijra) was born in Baghdad and founded his own legal school. This school was very powerful and had numerous adherents for the first century after Hanbal's death. Hanbal was a conservative and a traditionalist who discarded *Qiyas*. His followers became very fanatical and gradually diminished in numbers. It is said that the Wahabbis of Saudi Arabia have arisen out of the followers of Hanbal. Apart from the Wahabbis, there are few adherents of this school of law today. Hanbal wrote the *Musnad* which contains over 30,000 traditions. Isma'il al-Bukhari was one of his pupils.

The Differences between Shi'a and Sunni Interpretation of Law

The Shi'as reject *Ijma'* which are agreements made when highly trained doctors and Imams discuss the law. They claim that their imams are the infallible interpreters of the Qur'an because they possess superhuman knowledge. Second, the Shi'as maintain that the imams are divinely appointed having descended from Adam, down through Abraham and Muhammad, whereas the Sunnis believe that the caliphs or imams were to be elected.

How Muslim Law is Classified

The Islamic religion is a religion of works, but it is different from many other religions in this aspect. Most other religions have a prescribed set of religious duties that people should follow and the rest of the time they are free to live their lives. Shari'a law, on the other hand, prescribes everything that a man should do and covers every detail of human life: religious, political, social, domestic and private.

Muslim law divides all of man's actions into the following groups:

1. Actions that are obligatory to all believers
2. Actions that are not obligatory but desirable
3. Actions that are indifferent
4. Actions that are objectionable but not forbidden
5. Actions that are prohibited

The lawful actions are known as *Mashru* They include :

1. Those actions which are obligatory and enjoined by God himself; disobedience of these is positive infidelity and punishable
2. Those actions which are a duty but, when neglected and constituting sin, do not amount to infidelity to the faith
3. Those actions which were practiced by Muhammad
4. Those actions that are considered commendable, sometimes practiced by Muhammad and his followers, and sometimes not
5. Those actions which are permitted; they are indifferent and can be omitted without fear of sin

There are three classifications of unlawful actions. These include actions that are considered mortal sin and are most corrupting. These are known as *mufsid*. Then there are actions that are strictly forbidden, such as the eating of pork. These are called *haram*. Lastly, there are actions that are considered as unclean. These are called *makruh*. Muslim religious experts spend many hours debating different actions, trying to decide where they fit. Topics such as watching secular films, prostitution, colonialism, economic exploitation, racism, breaking covenants, polluting, and so forth are all carefully classified. This demonstrates the extent to which Shari'a law has gone, as it classifies and judges all of man's actions.

Teachers

Most Muslims follow their favorite religious teachers. These teachers are much looked up to, trusted and revered by their followers. For most common people, religious teachers are the primary source of authority. Some of these teachers have become famous in the Muslim world and are widely recognized.

Very often, these teachers simply give their opinions, but express them in a very eloquent way, using the Qur'an and Hadiths when they can be used to support them. There is no concept in Islam of systematic theology or systematic study of the Qur'an. If fact, most Muslims would be very uncomfortable with a study of the Qur'an, for it would assume that mere humans could question the Qur'an. Rather, the approach that Muslims take is that of memorization and submission. The only ones who can interpret are well trained religious scholars. Shari'a law is debated, but never the meaning of the Qur'an.

One of the problems that western scholars face is that Muslim scholars usually do not have to give proof of what they say. They may say things as if they are facts, but their statements are not based on earlier facts. Some teachers have taught about the 12 sons of Muhammad, even though there is no historical evidence that any of his sons lived for more than a few years. For many Muslims, the fact that a Muslim teacher said something is proof enough. Therefore, when a Muslim teacher says that astronauts in space have heard the call to prayer, it is immediately accepted and told to others until everyone believes it, but no one can trace the source. This can prove very difficult to Christians who are trying to establish facts so that they can argue logically against them.

Christian Authorities

Just as the Muslims have Hadith to add to the authority of the Qur'an, Christians have often wanted to add more to the authority of the Bible. In some settings, Christians add the teachings of the church. Many established traditional churches put equal weight on the authority of the church and the authority of the Bible. Thus, when a church leader or theologian states something, it is taken as an authority.

In the years that followed the spread of Christianity, false teachers began teaching other doctrines. Two types of false teachers plagued the early church: those that wished to include some aspect of Mosaic Law in Christian teaching and those who wished to add more to what Christians taught.

The Gnostics

First we will examine those that wished to add more to what the Bible contained. These were called the Gnostics. The term "Gnostic" comes from a Greek word that means "knowledge." The Gnostics believed that they were privy to secret knowledge about the divine.

Numerous references to the Gnostics appear in second century Christian literature, as the early church fathers wrote about them and against them. The Gnostics are also alluded to in the Bible in such places as 1 Timothy 1:4, 1 Timothy 6:20, and the entire book of Jude. Some Bible scholars have theorized that Gnosticism has its roots in pre-Christian religions that brought their ideas into Christianity.

There are many Gnostic writings, including: The Gospel of Thomas, The Secret Book of James, The Naassene Fragment, the Gospel of Mary, The Dialogue of the Savior, The Gospel of the Savior, The Gospel of Truth, Excerpts of Theodotus, The Acts of Peter, The Acts of Thomas and many more. As time progressed, Gnosticism became its own religion.

A short definition of Gnosticism is:

> *A religion that differentiates the evil god of this world (who is identified with the god of the Old Testament) from a higher more abstract God revealed by Jesus Christ, a religion that regards this world as the creation of a series of evil powers who wish to keep the human soul trapped in an evil physical body, a religion that preaches a hidden wisdom or knowledge only to a select group as necessary for salvation or escape from this world.* (Kirby, Peter. "Gnostics, Gnostic Gospels, & Gnosticism." *Early Christian Writings*. 2012)

Christians and the Law

The second type of false teachers were those that wanted to mix some part of the Old Testament law with the new Christian faith.

In the Old Testament, the Jews followed the laws of Moses. When Jesus the Messiah arrived, he spoke much about the Law and those who tried to carefully follow it. Many good Muslims are trying to keep the Muslim laws, just as many good Pharisees were trying to keep the Jewish laws. Therefore it is important to understand what Jesus wanted us to believe about the Old Testament law. In order to do this, we need to study Matthew 5:17-20:

> *Do not think that I have come to abolish the Law or the Prophets; I have not come to abolish them but to fulfill them. I tell you the truth, until heaven and earth disappear, not the smallest letter, not the least stroke of a pen, will by any means disappear from the Law until everything is*

accomplished. Anyone who breaks one of the least of these commandments and teaches others to do the same will be called least in the kingdom of heaven, but whoever practices and teaches these commands will be called great in the kingdom of heaven. For I tell you that unless your righteousness surpasses that of the Pharisees and the teachers of the law, you will certainly not enter the kingdom of heaven.

In these verses the "law and the prophets" refer to the holy books that God gave to the Jews. Jesus didn't come to replace, abolish or correct these Scriptures. He completes what the others had started, and He accomplishes the things that the prophets had predicted would happen. This is contrary to what most Muslims expect. They hold the idea that one revelation cancels and replaces the previous one; therefore, it is important to explain to Muslims about fulfilment and completing, but never cancelling. The Lord Jesus also affirms that the Scriptures will be neither lost nor corrupted in the future. This is contrary to what Muslims have been told about books being lost or changed.

Notice Matthew 5:20. At that time the Pharisees and the Sadducees were considered to be the most pious of believers. They tried to do all that was in the law of God, but Jesus teaches us that the law is only the beginning:

"You have heard that it was said to the people long ago, 'Do not murder, and anyone who murders will be subject to judgment.' But I tell you that anyone who is angry with his brother will be subject to judgment. Again, anyone who says to his brother, 'Raca,' is answerable to the Sanhedrin. But anyone who says, 'You fool!' will be in danger of the fire of hell. Therefore, if you are offering your gift at the altar and there remember that your brother has something against you, leave your gift there in front of the altar. First go and be reconciled to your brother; then come and offer your gift. Settle matters quickly with your adversary who is taking you to court. Do it while you are still with him on the way, or he may hand you over to the judge, and the judge may hand you over to the officer, and you may be thrown into prison. I tell you the truth, you will not get out until you have paid the last penny." (Matthew 5:21 - 26)

Everyone knows that God's commandments say, "Do not kill." But Jesus teaches us that any hostility expressed against someone is a sin. The heart of someone who is angry with another or who despises another person is not much different than the heart of someone who would kill another. God looks on the heart, not just at the actions of man, and judges him for his heart attitude and not just his actions.

In Jesus' time, when the believers wanted to worship God they still went to the temple with an animal to sacrifice in order to be able to approach God. Jesus said that it was useless to approach God in prayer, worship, or any other religious act if the person's heart was guilty of committing a fault against someone else. He must first reconcile himself with this other person before reconciling himself with God. Sin is an obstacle in the relationship between the believer and God.

Now look at Matthew 5:27 - 30:

> You have heard that it was said, 'Do not commit adultery.' But I tell you that anyone who looks at a woman lustfully has already committed adultery with her in his heart. If your right eye causes you to sin, gouge it out and throw it away. It is better for you to lose one part of your body than for your whole body to be thrown into hell. And if your right hand causes you to sin, cut it off and throw it away. It is better for you to lose one part of your body than for your whole body to go into hell.

Everyone knows that God's commandment says: "Do not commit adultery." Here Jesus gives a new commandment; he explains the true sense of the old one. The heart of the one who looks at a woman that is not his wife and commits adultery with her in his thoughts is no different in his heart than the person who seizes the opportunity to commit the act itself. Because of what is found in our hearts we are sinners.

The Bible teaches us that the Law reveals to us the condition of our hearts. Galatians 2:23 - 24 tells us: "*But before faith came, we were kept under the law, locked up unto the faith which should afterwards be revealed. Wherefore the law was our schoolmaster to bring us unto Christ, that we might be justified by faith.*"

The Law is there to reveal to us who we really are. It is like a teacher who guides us. Without the Law we would not know right from wrong.

So why did God give the Law in the first place? The Scriptures give several reasons. First, the Law was given to show God's standards of conduct. Those who measure up through obedience to these standards are said to be righteous, while those who do not measure up because of disobedience to the Law are

144

said to be unrighteous, as Deuteronomy 6:25 notes: *"If we diligently observe this entire commandment before the LORD our God, as he has commanded us, we will be in the right."* Second, the Law was given to make us aware of sin. In Romans 3:20b, Paul wrote, *"...for through the law comes the knowledge of sin."* Paul repeats this idea in Romans 7:7 *"...Yet, if it had not been for the law, I would not have known sin. I would not have known what it is to covet if the law had not said, 'You shall not covet.'"'* Third, the Law was given to lead us to Christ. *So the law was put in charge to lead us to Christ that we might be justified by faith.* (Galatians 3:24, NASB) Given the knowledge of sin in our lives, and given the power of sin in our lives, the only hope for us is not more Law, but the destruction of sin through the Lord Jesus Christ.

So can a person be declared righteous through obedience to the Law? In theory, yes. The Law details God's standard for righteous conduct. In fact, the righteousness of Jesus Christ is the righteousness which comes through obedience to the Law. That righteousness through obedience is possible is shown both in Deuteronomy and Romans:

> *"If we diligently observe this entire commandment before the LORD our God, as he has commanded us, we will be in the right,"* (Deuteronomy 6:25)

> *"For he will repay according to each one's deeds: to those who by patiently doing good seek for glory and honor and immortality, he will give eternal life; while for those who are self-seeking and who obey not the truth but wickedness, there will be wrath and fury. There will be anguish and distress for everyone who does evil, the Jew first and also the Greek, but glory and honor and peace for everyone who does good, the Jew first and also the Greek."* (Romans 2:6-10)

Whether or not an individual other than Jesus Christ will be declared righteous on the basis of obedience to the Law will be examined in the question concerning our standing before the Law.

Is the Law still in effect? Yes. Matthew 5:17-18 is quite clear. Jesus said:

> *"Do not think that I have come to abolish the Law or the Prophets; I have not come to abolish them but to fulfill them. I tell you the truth, until heaven and earth disappear, not the smallest letter, not the least stroke of a pen, will by any means disappear from the Law until everything is accomplished.*

145

It is therefore clear that the Law will remain until God remakes heaven and earth. And it is easy to see why. We know that while Christ has defeated sin, Christ has not yet eradicated sin. As long as sin is still in the universe, the Law will remain as a witness against it.

Since the Law of Moses is still in effect, what is our standing before it? The answer is simple: We are guilty. There is not one person who has ever lived, who is alive today, or who will live (except for Jesus Christ) who can be judged by this law and still be declared "not guilty." Romans 3:9-20 is emphatic on this:

> "*What shall we conclude then? Are we any better? Not at all! We have already made the charge that Jews and Gentiles alike are all under sin*". (3:9)

All are guilty under the Law before God. This is evident in both the New Testament and the Old Testament, as Paul teaches on this subject in Romans.

> *As it is written: "There is no one righteous, not even one; there is no one who understands, no one who seeks God. All have turned away, they have together become worthless; there is no one who does good, not even one." "Their throats are open graves; their tongues practice deceit." "The poison of vipers is on their lips." "Their mouths are full of cursing and bitterness." "Their feet are swift to shed blood; ruin and misery mark their ways, and the way of peace they do not know." "There is no fear of God before their eyes."* (Romans 3:10-18)

This is God's judgment on mankind, and His judgment is both just (in that He shows no favoritism) and true. There is no defense for us if we are judged by our deeds:

> *Now we know that whatever the law says, it says to those who are under the law, so that every mouth may be silenced and the whole world held accountable to God.* (Romans 3:19)

When we stand before a Holy God and see Him in all of His splendor and glory there will be nothing that we can say in our own defense.

> *Therefore no one will be declared righteous in his sight by observing the law; rather, through the law we become conscious of sin.* (Romans 3:20)

The verdict, based on law? Guilty. No exceptions. No excuses. No second chances.

Is there any possibility that our good deeds will be weighed against our bad, and perhaps, in the balance, we come out ahead? What will God say to us if we try to keep the law with a sincere heart, yet make the occasional mistake? He will still say "Guilty!"

> *For whoever keeps the whole law and yet stumbles at just one point is guilty of breaking all of it."* James 2:10

Paul repeats this idea in Galatians 3:10.

> *For all who rely on the works of the law are under a curse; for it is written, "Cursed is everyone who does not observe and obey all the things written in the book of the law.*

God's standard of righteousness under Law is absolute fidelity to the Law. How, then, can sinful man stand before a Holy and Just God? Romans 3:21-28 addresses this matter: *But now a righteousness from God, apart from law, has been made known, to which the Law and the Prophets testify.*

That is, this righteousness is as evident in the Old Testament as it is in the New. It should not come as a surprise to anyone.

> *This righteousness from God comes through faith in Jesus Christ to all who believe. There is no difference, for all have sinned and fall short of the glory of God, and are justified freely by his grace through the redemption that came by Christ Jesus.*

The righteousness that comes by faith in Jesus Christ is the only way that man can stand before God.

> *God presented him as a sacrifice of atonement, through faith in his blood. He did this to demonstrate his justice, because in his forbearance he had left the sins committed beforehand unpunished--he did it to demonstrate his justice at the present time, so as to be just and the one who justifies those who have faith in Jesus. Where, then, is boasting? It is excluded. On what principle? On that of observing the law? No, but on that of faith. For we maintain that a man is justified by faith apart from observing the law. (3:25-28)*

So, then we are justified by faith in the shed blood of Jesus Christ. One might argue we are saved by faith in Jesus; but, because the Law is still in effect, can it not still judge us? This is the key point that is missed by so many people, but the answer is emphatically no, and the reason is given in Romans 7:1-4.

Do you not know, brothers for I am speaking to men who know the law -that the law has authority over a man only as long as he lives? For example, by law a married woman is bound to her husband as long as he is alive, but if her husband dies, she is released from the law of marriage. So then, if she marries another man while her husband is still alive, she is called an adulteress. But if her husband dies, she is released from that law and is not an adulteress, even though she marries another man. So, my brothers you also died to the law through the body of Christ, that you might belong to another, to him who was raised from the dead, in order that we might bear fruit to God.

Jesus Christ did not abolish the Law, nor has the Law ever been set aside. But in Jesus Christ, we have died to the law, and it therefore has no jurisdiction over us. Jesus did not change the Law; Jesus changed us. This principle is restated in Colossians 3:1-4.

Since, then, you have been raised with Christ, set your hearts on things above, where Christ is seated at the right hand of God. Set your minds on things above, not on earthly things for you died, and your life is now hidden with Christ in God. When Christ, who is your life, appears, then you also will appear with him in glory.

How salvation works is really quite simple, just as a husband and wife are joined together in marriage, a believer in Christ is joined to Christ. The blood that Christ shed covers all our sin; the death that Christ died is our death; and the life that Christ lives becomes our life.

God can and does say to us, *"Their sins and iniquities I will remember no more"* (Hebrews 10:17), because we are joined to the blood of Christ which is the payment for our sins.

Likewise, when Christ died, we died. And the Law has no jurisdiction over the dead. Can you imagine some court bringing a dead body before a judge and jury? Carry this one step further and imagine that the dead corpse has a notarized, signed, witnessed, utterly unassailable death certificate. Imagine if the corpse comes back to life and carries that death certificate, around with him. Imagine if that person is then brought before trial for some reason; when the corpse produces, as his defense, his death certificate he must be released. Dead men can't be tried under the Law. This is our relation to the Old Testament Law. We are dead in Christ. We have nothing to do with law. It simply doesn't apply to us. When Christ died, we died.

So what is our relationship to the law? Can it still be a guide for us? This is a common notion held by many Christians. It is common ... but wrong. What usually happens is that people divide the Mosaic Law into pieces -- usually the Ten Commandments are in one group and the remaining 603 are in the other. Then it is said that Christ fulfilled the 603, but it is up to us to fulfil (or live) the ten. But the Law is not divisible as was previously shown. Remember, in Gal. 3:10 Paul wrote, "*For all who rely on the works of the law are under a curse; for it is written, Cursed is everyone who does not observe and obey all the things written in the book of the law.*" The Christian who wants to keep or be guided by part of the Law must keep or be guided by all of the Law. But just as the Law has no authority to condemn those who are in Christ, it likewise has no jurisdiction to guide those who are in Christ.

Rather, the Christian must live by the power of God and by walking with the Holy Spirit. The life that God wants each Christian to live is really quite simple. Our life is to be a life of love. A life of rejoicing. A life of peace between men in all circumstances. A life marked by patience, kindness, and goodness. A life which is gentle and faithful. A life of self-control. When our life is filled with these things, then we are living the true Christian life. And the source of our Christian life is the Holy Spirit: Galatians 5:22-23 tells us, "*... the fruit of the Spirit is love, joy, peace, patience, kindness, goodness, faithfulness, gentleness, and self-control.*"

This is what will speak to a Muslim's heart. Muslims are trying to live good lives by keeping the Laws of Islam. These laws are much like the laws of Moses. They tell man how to act, but they don't give him the power to actually act that way. When Muslims see the good lives of Christians, they assume that we are good at keeping the law. This is why we must add words to our actions, and explain to them that any good we do, is through the power of God working in us. Otherwise, we would be terrible people like many others. It is the Holy Spirit of God that transforms us. Keeping the law never changes man; only God can do this.

Gospel of Barnabas

Muslims sometimes refer to something known as *The Gospel of Barnabas*. This is a well known book in the Muslim world, and many Muslim writers make reference to it, claiming that it is the only known surviving gospel written by a disciple of Jesus, and that it was accepted by the early church. Others say that no other gospel can come close to it in historical accuracy and authenticity.

Western scholars, however, have long accepted that the *Gospel of Barnabas* is a fake. First, there are no early copies of this gospel. While the accepted New Testament books are verified by over 3,500 early manuscripts, there is not a single early manuscript for the Gospel of Barnabas. The earliest copy is an Italian manuscript from either the 15th or 16th century. Before this it was unknown, and no one made any reference to it, not even Muslim writers who were attacking Christianity. It is especially interesting to note that no church teacher between the first and 15th century ever quoted from it or disputed it. It is like it never existed. Some Muslims disagree, but they are usually confused with a first century writing known as the *Epistle of Barnabas*, which is an entirely different book of Gnostic origin.

In the *Gospel of Barnabas*, we find teaching that is completely different from everything found in the accepted gospels. For instance, in the *Gospel of Barnabas* Jesus did not claim to be the messiah and he did not die on the cross. The book also contains figures of speech and descriptions of medieval life common to Western Europe, proving that it was not written before the 14th century. It also contains numerous mistakes, including references to the year of Jubilee being every 100 years instead of every 50 as the Bible states. It also claims that Jesus was born when Pilate was governor, which is 25 years too soon for Pilate. And of course, it makes geographical mistakes, like mentioning that Jesus sailed to Nazareth. This could not be possible because Nazareth is neither on the seashore nor on a river.

The *Gospel of Barnabas* also quotes directly from the Latin Vulgate translation of the Bible, even though it was supposedly written in the first century. It mentions a vassal who owes a share of his crop to his lord (this was practiced in Medieval Europe) and it mentions wooden wine casks rather than the wine skins that were used in Bible times. It also has several Muslim influences, using the Arabic word *dikka* which is a platform used in a mosque, and saying that Jesus will return for Israel, and Muhammad will stand for the salvation of the whole world. Finally, Jesus preaches a sermon that begins with the Muslim *butba*, or praising Allah and his holy prophet, and contains a denial that he is the son of God.

Some Christians have been fooled or confused when Muslims quote from the *Gospel of Barnabas*. They should not. The *Gospel of Barnabas* is a complete forgery written almost a millennium after Muhammad started Islam.

Questions for Reflection and Group Discussion
1. What sort of false teachers are affecting the church today?
2. How would you witness to a Muslim who claims that by following Islamic law he can make himself acceptable to God?

Chapter Eleven
Islamic Beliefs (*Iman*)
God, Angels, Prophets, Judgment

Islamic theology centers on five basic beliefs: God, Man, Angels, Hell, Jinn. In this lesson we will look at God, man, prophets and judgment in order to better understand how Muslims view the relationship between God and mankind.

God

We will start with God, whom the Muslims call "Allah." The name "Allah" refers to God's essential being and is known in Arabic as the *Ism adh dhat* the "essential name of God." Muslims have 98 other names given to God but they are really attributes of the divine being. Muslims do not acknowledge any of the names used for God in the Old Testament, claiming that God was known as Allah since the time of Adam and that Adam and all the Jewish prophets were all Muslims.

Sura 7:10 says Allah's names are the best names. According to the Hadith, there are 99 names for God and whoever recites them, shall enter Paradise. So it is common to see Muslims holding a string of beads which is used to help them recite these names. There are usually 33 beads on the string. Sometimes there are 99 beads, separated into three sections of 33 beads by two different beads with a much larger bead at the end acting as a kind of handle. (Incidentally, there is no bead for the name "God is Love," which shows a serious lack in the foundation of the Muslim's conception of God.) There is a name "Allah Wudud "The Loving One" or "The Beloved One" which occurs twice in the

152

Qur'an. This however is understood as a characteristic of the divine will rather than part of God's nature.

The Hadith state that God has a hundredth name known as the Great Name. Muhammad said that whoever called upon God by that name would receive all his desires. No person knows what this name is, and Muslim scholars and mystics have spent much time searching for it.

The Muslim Attributes of God

There are seven principles attributed to Allah:

1. Life. His existence has neither beginning nor ending. He receives neither profit nor loss from whatever happens.
2. Knowledge. He knows all things visible or invisible, past or future. He never forgets, is never negligent, and never makes an error.
3. Power. Allah is almighty. If he wills he can make stones and trees talk. His power is everlasting.
4. Will. He is able to do what he wills. He need not act. Good and evil exist by his will. If a man is pious it is because of the will of Allah, and if a man is an unbeliever, it is due to the will of Allah.
5. Hearing. God hears every sound, high and low but he hears without ears.
6. Seeing. He sees all things, even the steps "of a black cat on a black stone at night." He is able to see without eyes.
7. Speech. He speaks but without a tongue.

Muslims Emphasis God's Unity

Sura 112:1-4 tells us, "*Say: He Allah is one, Allah is he on whom all depend; He does not beget nor is he begotten; and none is like Him.*" This is one of the verses most commonly quoted to Christians by Muslims to argue against the deity of Christ.

The *Tahlil* is the first part of the Muslim Creed, and it witnesses that "There is no God but God" (*"La ilaha illa Allah"*).

The association of other gods with Allah is known as *shirk* and is the greatest sin possible to a Muslim. Sura 4:48 says: "*Surely Allah forgives not that a partner should be set up with him and forgives all else to whom he pleases. But whoever sets a partner with Allah, he devises indeed a great sin.*"

God's Greatness

The *Takbir* is the name given to the Arabic expression "*Allahu Akbar*" which literally means "Allah is greater." The Muslim repeats this phrase constantly, and it means that no matter what a man can think of, God is greater than that.

God's Revelation of the Divine Will or Law, Known as *Tanzil*

The expression *tanzil* or "sending down" teaches us what the Muslims believe about revelation or the sending down of God's message. It really indicates the object of God's revelation the Qur'an. Christians say that Christ is the object of God's revelation, while Islam says it is His message or the Qur'an. Sura 50:16 tells us, *"And certainly we created man, and we know that his mind suggests to him and we are nearer to him than his life-vein."* By this Muslims believe that the Qur'an speaks to us, as God knows us, and his revelation speaks to us.

God's Transcendence, known as *Tanzih*

The Muslim believes that God is really unknowable. He holds himself aloof from man, and his real self can never be known by any man. Whatever man thinks of Allah, He is something different. He does not exist in anything nor does anything exist in Him. He is completely unknowable and unknown.

Angels

The Qur'an has much to say about angels, as do the Hadiths. First, Muslims believe that God created the devil from fire, men from clay, and angels from light. The angels have life, speech and reason. Muslims also believe that the angels have no carnal desire or anger. It is said that their food is celebrating God's glory, their drink is proclaiming God's greatness, their conversation is commemorating God and their pleasure is worshipping God.

Angels are thought to be inferior to human prophets, because they were commanded to prostrate themselves before the prophets: '*Adore Adam,' they adored him, save only Iblis (Satan) who refused and was too proud."* (Sura 2:34)

Muslims believe that every Muslim believer is attended by two recording angels, one of whom records his good actions, and the other his evil actions. Sura 82:11-12 mentions this: *"Honorable recorders, they know what you do."* Sura 50:14-15 adds to this: *"We are nearer to him than his life vein. When the two receivers receive, sitting on the right and on the left."* See also Sura 17 :14-15.

154

When Muslims pray, they often end their prayer by greeting the angels that sit on either of their shoulders.

Muslims believe that there are four archangels, or super angels. These are:

1. Gabriel, the angel of revelation
2. Mika'il (Mikal) the patron of the Israelites,
3. Israfil who is to sound the trumpet, at the last day
4. Azra'il the angel of death.

The chief angel in charge of hell is called *Malik* (king) and he has 19 subordinates called *Az Zabaniya* (guards). Sura 14:30-31 mentions them: *"Over it are nineteen. we have made none but angels wardens of the fire."*

Muslims believe that there are two angels, Munkar and Nakir who examine the *"dead in their graves on the night after burial and question them as to their faith."* Everyone will be asked: Who is your prophet? And what is your book? (Ahmad Ibn Hanbal, *Musnad, III,* 3, 40 amd Pazdawi, *"Ehl-i Sünnet Akâidi"* Translated by Şerafettin Gölcük, İstanbul 1980, 237)

Muslims believe that there are eight angels who support the throne of God. Sura 69:17 describes them: *"Above them eight will bear that day thy Lord's throne of power."*

Muslims also believe that angels intercede for man and celebrate the praises of the Lord. Sura 42:3-4 adds: *"While the angels celebrate the praise of their Lord."*

To the Muslim, angels also act as guardians to men. Sura 13:11 states: *"For him are angels guarding the consequences of his deeds."*

Prophets

Muslims believe that there are 104 books deemed as sacred having been delivered by God to mankind.

- To Adam - 10 books
- To Seth - 50 books
- To Enoch (Idris) - 30 books
- To Abraham - 10 books
- To Moses - 5 books called the Taurat
- To David - The Psalms, called the Zabur
- To Jesus (known to Muslims as Isa) - The Gospel, called the Injil
- To Muhammad - The Qur'an

The books from Adam to Abraham are said to be lost, but all that is necessary for Muslims to know of these books is to be found in the Qur'an.

Some Christians try and use the Qur'an to prove to Muslims that they should read what was written before. The following are a selection of passages that might be used to direct Muslims to read the books that were delivered before the Qur'an:

- Sura 2:4: *"And those who believe in that which has been revealed to you and that which was revealed before you."*
- Sura 35:24: *"And there is not a people but a warner has gone among them."*
- Sura 10:47: *"And every nation has a messenger."*
- Sura 4:164 and Sura 40:78: *"And certainly we sent messengers before you: there are some of them that we have mentioned to you and there are others whom we have not mentioned to you."*

Many Muslims, however believe in abrogation; that is a later revelation has replaced the earlier ones.

When Muslims approach the Bible they often claim that Christians and Jews have changed their books. By this they attempt to justify some of the statements in the Qur'an that seem to oppose the Bible.

They also claim that the Qur'an corrects and abrogates previous scripture because it was revealed last. In this connection they quote Sura 5:48: *"And we have revealed to you the book with the truth, verifying that which is before it of the book and a guardian over it."*

Muslims assert that because the books of the Prophets (Old Testament) and the Gospels have been altered, the Word of God as given in them contains a mixture of truth and error. The Qur'an was given to correct these errors. Sura 16:63-64 notes: *"Certainly we sent messengers to nations before you... And we have not revealed to you the book except that you may make clear to them about that which they differ."* Sura 5:3 states: *"This day have I perfected for you your religion and completed my favor to you and chosen for you Islam as a religion."*

Muslim Beliefs about the Prophets of God

Muslims distinguish between prophets and messengers. A *nabi* or prophet is anyone directly inspired by God. Muslims accept many of the Old Testament characters as prophets, and they also include the Lord Jesus as a prophet, but nothing more. A *rasul* (messenger) is one to whom a special message has been entrusted. *Rasul* is used in the headings of the Epistles, i.e. *The Epistle of Peter* (known in Arabic as *Butrus*) is "*Rasul Butrus.*"

Tradition states that Muhammad said there were 124,000 prophets and 315 messengers or apostles. Of these, nine are said to be *Ulu al-'Azam* (possessors of power). These nine are Noah, Abraham, David, Jacob, Joseph, Job, Moses, Jesus and Muhammad. Six are given special titles; Christ's being "*Rhuh Allah*" (the Spirit of God).

Three women are said to be prophetesses: Sarah because she received the news of Isaac's birth by revelation, the mother of Moses who also received the news of Moses' birth by revelation and Mary who received the news of Christ's birth from an angel.

Most Muslims believe that prophets and messengers each came with a specific book or message to a particular people. Moses was the prophet to the Jews; Jesus was the prophet to the Christians, etc. The Qur'an is special, because it is a message to everyone everywhere.

Judgment and Hell

The Last Day has many names in the Qur'an. Among them are:

- *Yaum al-Qiyama*   (Day of Uprising or Resurrection)
- *Yaum al-Fasl*   (Day of Separation-or Decision).
- *Yaum al-Hisab*   (Day of Reckoning)
- *Yaum al-Ba'th*   (Day of Sending Forth-Awakening)
- *Yaum ad-Din*   (Day of Judgment)
- *Yaum al-Akhir*   (The Last Day)
- *Al-Yaum al-Muhith*   (The Encompassing Day)
- *As-Safah*   (The Hour or Pouring Out)

Muslims believe that on the resurrection day the body will be raised and united to its soul. One bone of the body will be preserved uncorrupted until the Last Day, at which time the rest of the body will grow from it.

They believe that on the Last Day there will be three blasts of a trumpet. At the first blast all creatures in heaven and earth will be struck with terror. At the second blast all creatures in heaven and earth will die. At the last blast, forty years later, all will be raised again for judgment.

Sura 81 teaches that there will be a general resurrection of men, angels, spirits and animals. Sura 32:5 teaches us that the Day of Judgment will last 1,000 years, but Sura 70:4 says it will be 50,000 years *"A day the measure of which is fifty thousand years."* When all are assembled for judgment the angels will keep them waiting for 40 years (this period varies up to 50,000 years according to differing commentators). After this, God will appear to judge them, and Muhammad will intercede for them after Adam, Noah, Abraham, Moses and Jesus have declined, feeling themselves unworthy of so great a task.

Each Muslim person will be examined from his own "Book of Deeds" which will have all his words and actions recorded. The righteous will receive their book in their right hand, but the unrighteous will be forced to take their books in their left hand which will be bound behind their back.

Muslims believe that all deeds and words (or, according to some, the books containing the records of these deeds and words) will be weighed in a balance scale--one balance being over paradise and the other over hell. Sura 21:47 says: *"And we will set up a just balance on the Day of Resurrection, so no soul will be wronged in the least, and if there be the light of a grain of mustard seed, we will bring it and sufficient are we to take account."*

Islam and the Book of Deeds

There is no way of salvation (or entering Paradise) in Islam other than by works. When a Muslim is asked, "Where are you going when you die?" he will usually reply, "If my works are good I will go to Paradise."

Muslims believe that a Book of Deeds is kept for each person by two recording angels. An angel on man's right side records his good deeds, and an angel on man's left side records his evil deeds (in Arabic these angels are called *Kiram al-katibin*). In this Book of Deeds every spoken word and every action great or small is written down.

Sura 18:49 says: *"And the book shall be placed, then you will see the guilty fearing from what is in it; and they will say: Ah! Woe to us! What a book is this! It omits not a small one nor a great one, but numbers them all."*

Sura 50:18: *"He utters not a word but there is by him a watcher at hand."*

Sura 43:80: *"Or do they think that we hear not what they conceal and know their secret discourses? Yes, our messengers will write them down."*

Sura. 80:10-12: *"And surely there are keepers over you, honorable recorders, they know what you do."*

Sura 21:94: *"So whoever shall do good deeds, and he is a believer, there shall be no denying of his work; and we will write it down for him."*

There are also to be "Books of Nations" read at this time. Sura 45:28 states: *"And you shall see every nation kneeling down; every nation shall be called to its book. Today you shall be rewarded for what you did."*

So it is that all of Islam focuses on man's work, trying to obey Allah's commands so that he or she may enter Paradise. Islam is a religion of works. It cleverly combines concepts from the Bible with the ancient Arabian ideas to present a religion that was not only acceptable to the people in ancient Arabia but continues to hold them today.

Christian View

The Bible teaches us about God. It begins, "In the beginning God..." For the Christian everything begins with God and everything focuses on God. However, the Christian view of God is quite different from the Muslim view. The Muslim believes in a God who is powerful, omnipotent and impersonal. He is completely transcendent and therefore distant and distinct from his creation.

The God of the Bible is also all-powerful, but he is also personal at the same time. We learn from Genesis that God walks and talks with His creation. He is very personal, and the Old Testament record shows him reaching out again and again towards mankind. In the New Testament Jesus refers to him as "Father" and teaches his disciples to use his name for God. Nowhere in any other holy book or philosophy do we find God being portrayed as "Father."

Sura 88:12 tells us, *"If you love Allah, follow me (Muhammad), Allah will love you and forgive your sins. Allah is forgiving; merciful...Allah directs the hearts of those that believe him..."* Allah seems to love only those who love him. The God of the Bible loves all, even those who reject him. He is reaching out to mankind, and sacrificially sent Jesus into the world to die for the sins of mankind.

Muslims reject the loving nature of God, because for them it would place God into a place of need. For the Muslim, God is not bound by any moral obligation, as this would limit him. Therefore God is all powerful, and even the author of evil. Allah does not have to be right or just. He is completely all powerful and can do as he pleases, and is under no obligation to do anything. He is totally free to do good or evil; in fact, for the Muslim the very fact that God is both good and evil proves that he is free and all powerful. Allah is above all laws, so he can create and enforce them, but he is not limited by them.

For the Christian, however, the God of the Bible is not evil and does no evil. The reason why God makes moral decisions is because it comes from his very nature. God is free to do whatever he wants, but he has chosen to limit his choices. The biblical God chose to be in covenant with his creation. Before the foundation of the world, God chose to respect his creation. Psalm 77:13 and 99:9 tell us that God is righteous and holy and is incapable of doing evil, even though he allows evil to exist. Habakkuk 1:13 tells us that *"His eyes are too pure to look on evil."*

The God of the Bible differs from the all powerful Allah of the Muslims. For Christians, God is both all powerful, kind, and a personal father; both the almighty creator and a sacrificial servant, both righteous judge and redeeming priest.

If these characteristics seem to be contradictory, it is because God is not limited as men are. He is beyond our feeble wisdom. For Christians, there is much about God that is beyond our full understanding, such as the Trinity. Yet the Trinity demonstrates to us that God is love. Each person of the Trinity expresses complete love and agreement with the other persons of the Trinity. The best example we have of love is God the Father who loves the world and sends God the Son to earth.

In the same way, mankind is made in the image of God. We are capable of giving and receiving love. We enter into relationships with one another. And thus we can understand why God desires to enter into that same relationship with mankind.

For the Christian, God shares his image with mankind. The all powerful God places Adam in the world and gives him authority over the fish of the sea, the birds of the air, over the livestock and over all the earth (Genesis 1:26). We were never created to be God's slaves, we were created from the beginning to be his children and share in his authority. We were given free choice, because God loved us as his children. The Muslim sees everything as "the will of God," while the Christian sees much that displeases God and grieves God.

The Muslim's view of mankind is also very different than what Christians find in the Bible. Both Islam and Christianity teach that man began in the Garden of Eden. However, Christians believe that man became sinful and was separated from God, thrown out of the garden and under God's judgment. Muslims on the other hand believe that Adam was responsible for his own sin, and once he repented God forgave him and extended to him his mercy and guidance. Outside of this, nothing needed to be repaired because nothing had been broken. Muslims believe that all of us need to repent of things we do wrong and receive God's guidance and try to obey his commands. In this way we try to please God. They have no concept of sin separating us from God, or of the atonement and the need for shedding blood. The gulf between man and God is there because of God's position of power, not man's position of sin. They see no need for the incarnation, as God will always be far from mankind, even after judgment. The prophets were sent, not to call us back to God, but to give mankind guidance in how we should live. Final judgment will only assess us on how well we did and reward us accordingly. It will not bring us any closer to God.

Paradise

The subject of Paradise will be dealt with in detail in another lesson. However, here we would like to emphasize that Paradise is the ultimate place where Muslims want to go. The Qur'an uses two terms: *Al-Jannah* or the garden, and *Al-Firdaus* or paradise.

According to the Qur'an, life after death presents a beginning of progression and advancement far beyond anything conceivable in this world. Sura 17:21 says: *"And certainly the hereafter is much superior in respect of degrees, and much superior in respect of excellence."*

The general descriptions of Paradise are literal and material. Some passages of the Qur'an sound strange and perhaps revolting to Christian ears because of their sensual aspects. Muhammad's paradise can be summed up as a garden in which there are beautiful women, couches covered with rich cloths, flowing cups and luscious fruits, in which God does not appear at all. In the Muslim concept of heaven there is no relationship with the Christian teaching of a saved believer, purified and changed into the likeness of Christ and worshipping a holy God.

Muslims also believe that there are seven divisions to heaven, the highest being Paradise. They believe that man moves from one level to another until he finally attains Paradise. God's throne is above them all because God does not mix with men.

Hell

In the Arabic language the world for hell is literally the word for fire: *Nar.* The Muslim hell also has seven divisions. *Jahannam* refers to the section of hell prepared for Muslims, a type of purgatory meant for purification which will not be everlasting. In this respect it is related to the Roman Catholic concept of Purgatory.

The orthodox Muslim teaching is that all Muslims will go to hell. Sura 19:71 says: *"There is not one of you but shall approach it."*

The degree and duration of punishment in hell is dependent upon the enormity of the sins committed by the person. For Muslims who have not committed great sins, hell will be cool and pleasant. However, infidels who say that God is a plural being will have to remain in hell forever subjected to burning flames and icy cold.

Muslims believe that just as heaven begins on earth, so does hell in the temporal punishment of evil deeds. Sura 7:94 says: *"And we did not send a prophet into a town but We overtook its people with distress and affliction in order that they might humble themselves."*

The following verses in the Qur'an support the belief that hell is not everlasting:

• Sura 6:129: *"He shall say, the Fire is your abode, to abide in it, except as Allah please; for the Lord is knowing, wise."*

• Sura 11:106-107: *"So as for those who are unhappy, they shall be in the fire; for them shall be sighing and groaning in it: Abiding therein as long as the heavens and earth endure, except as thy Lord please: for the Lord is the mighty doer of what He intends."*

The word *abad* is used three times in the Qur'an for "abiding" in hell, but is elsewhere used for "eternal or everlasting" in connection with life.

- According to the hadiths: *"the Kanz al-'Urrenal records: Surely a day will come over hell when it will be like a field of corn that has dried up, after flourishing for a while."*
- A recorded saying of 'Umar is as follows: *"Even if the dwellers in hell may be numberless as the sands of the desert, a day will come when they will be taken out of it."* (*Tafsir Fath-al-Byan*)

The Muslim Belief about Predestination

This is the sixth article of the Muslim Creed, and means that God is absolute in His decree of good and evil. Nothing comes to pass, whether good or bad, except by the Divine Will, according to what God has engraved on a preserved tablet by His pen of fate. Sura 14:4 tells us: *"Allah leaves in error whom He pleases and He guides whom He pleases."* Sura 54:49 adds: *"Surely we have created everything according to measure."*

A Muslim believes that God is not limited by any consideration whatsoever, moral or otherwise. It rests with God whether He forgives or damns. It is *"Kama yasha'u"* ("as he wills"), a phrase constantly used in the Qur'an. A tradition states God's attitude in this way: *"These to heaven and I care not, and these to hell and I care not."* (al-Sayyid al-Murtada, vii. 308) God is the sole decider of a man's deeds and destiny. This is of course pure fatalism as practiced by the followers of the ancient Arabian god Manaat, and it places the responsibility of all that a man does, whether good or evil, upon God entirely.

For the Muslim, man is a mere puppet, devoid of free will, a mechanical being. This is utterly foreign to the teaching of both the Old and New Testaments. This teaching is incompatible with a God of love.

In summary, this doctrine means that no person is responsible for what he does. All responsibility for his actions is laid upon God. It also means that God is unjust, for a man is judged by his deeds for which he is not responsible. Muslims are not entirely agreed upon the doctrine of predestination, some sects believing that man is to a certain extent responsible for his actions. The generally held teaching of predestination, however, is quite contrary to the whole purpose of God for mankind.

Man

Muslims view man as being created by God and placed on this earth. God created both good and evil, angels, spirits, and Satan. Man then does his best, and his actions and words are recorded by the recording angels. However, much of what happens in this life happens because it is the will of God. "It is written" is an often used Muslim phrase. Muslims will actually be judged on only a few things. Has he done something forbidden and worthy of punishment such as?

1. Equating something equal with God
2. Drinking wine
3. Eating pork
4. Eating meat not killed in a Muslim fashion. (*halaal* meat).

In this case the one who kills the animal must simply face Mecca and say, "In the name of God the Merciful and Compassionate" as he slits the throat of the animal. If an animal is shot, it is not considered fit for Muslim consumption.

The works that the Muslim has done will also be considered. This includes such things as:

1. Prayers
2. Almsgiving
3. Pilgrimages
4. Other religious actions such as memorizing and reciting the Qur'an

Some Muslims have visited many honorable mosques, gaining much merit, and therefore feel that they can live lives without much care, as they already have done enough good deeds to cover a life of sin.

What about man's actions while here on earth outside of those things that are forbidden? Man and society is a much discussed topic in some circles. Muslims clearly distinguish between man-made laws and God's demands. In their minds, driving over the speed-limit does not constitute a sin, and will not be punishable by death, as it is not mentioned in the Qur'an. This is often the Muslim view of pornography. It may be a dishonorable thing in their home country where dishonor would be brought to their tribe by viewing it, but when visiting a foreign place where they are not known there is nothing wrong with viewing pornography.

Spirits and Satan

Spirits are known as *jinn*. Muslims are very aware of *jinn*, their activity and their influences in life. Muslims believe several things about the *jinn*.

• They believe that God created the jinn 2,000 years before Adam.

• They understand that there are believers and infidels among *jinn* as among men.

• The Qur'an teaches that *jinn* are created from smokeless fire like the devil.

• Muslims believe that *jinn* are peaceable, that they eat and drink and propagate their species.

• The Qur'an teaches that the chief abode of *jinn* are the mountains of Qaf which encompass the whole earth.

• They are taught that the devil is the father of the *jinn*.

In a later lesson we will cover the spiritual world of Muslims and look more closely at how they view the *jinn*, demon possession and exorcism.

The devil is known as Satan (*Shaitan* or *Iblis*) According to tradition, Muhammad taught that the devil can enter into a man as easily as blood flows in his body. He also taught that every man has an angel and a devil appointed over him. Muslims believe that every child of Adam except Jesus and Mary is touched by the devil at his birth. It is the devil's touch that makes infants cry out at birth. Muslims also believe that the devil was created from fire and had the name *'Azazil.* The Arabic name for the devil is *Iblis*. He is also known as-*sash-Shaitan* or the chief devil. Iblis is said to have possessed authority over the animal and spirit kingdom before the creation of Adam. He was expelled from Eden because he refused to submit to Adam. Sura 7:11 tells us: *"Make submission to Adam, so they (the angels) submitted but not Iblis; he was not of those who submitted."*

Biblical View

The Qur'an teaches us that man is greater than the jinn and that he has dominion over them. They believe that the *jinn* refused to submit to man and that is why they are being punished. The Bible teaches us differently. It does not refer to *jinn* but to evil spirits. It tells us that man is lower than the angels, even though he has dominion over the earth. Psalm 8:3-6 tells us:

When I consider your heavens, the work of your fingers, the moon and the stars, which you have set in place, what is man that you are mindful of him, the son of man that you care for him? You made him a little lower than the heavenly beings and crowned him with glory and honor. You made him ruler over the works of your hands; you put everything under his feet.

These verses are repeated in the New Testament in Hebrews 2: 3-6:

When I consider your heavens, the work of your fingers, the moon and the stars, which you have set in place, what is man that you are mindful of him, the son of man that you care for him? You made him a little lower than the heavenly beings and crowned him with glory and honor. You made him ruler over the works of your hands; you put everything under his feet.

Someday, however, the saved will gather in heaven, and at the Marriage Supper of the Lamb we will enter into a relationship with Christ as joint heirs with him and joint rulers of the universe. Most theologians believe that at this time the saved will be higher than the angels who will continue to be ministering spirits.

The Christian's view of heaven is very different from the Muslim view. For the Christian, heaven is a place where we will worship God and serve God. The image given to us in the Book of Revelations clearly shows mankind, saved and transformed, standing in the very presence of God, worshiping him and rejoicing. In Islam, Muhammad called himself the *slave of God* and the best he could offer his followers was a place of physical rewards. In the Bible, Jesus is called the Son of God, and he offers his followers a place in heaven, in the very presence of God where we will worship him and serve him. This is a fundamental difference between what the Qur'an teaches and what the Bible teaches.

One evangelist loved to tell this story:

Long ago a man wanted to meet a Bedouin sheik to discuss business with him. He was unsure where the sheik's tent was located, because the sheik moved from place to place, wherever he could find grass for his camels. So the man began to walk into the desert in the general direction he believed the sheik to be. As he traveled he would stop by the tents of other Bedouin and ask them directions. As the day went by he wondered if he would ever find the sheik. Eventually he stopped at a tent and the man there said that he knew the sheik. "I am the sheik's slave" the man said. "I look after sheep for him. I know where his tent is and I can take you to him."

Just then another man arrived at the tent. When he heard the story he also offered to take the visitor to the sheik. "I am the sheik's son," he announced. "I can take you to the sheik today." Which of these two should the man choose to introduce him to the sheik? Which is better: the slave or the son?

Sadly, many Muslims choose to be slaves even though Islam offers them only worldly pleasures. They are satisfied with the lust of the flesh, material things and the pride of life. They have never enjoyed a relationship with God, and have no concept or even desire to enter into any kind of relationship with God in the future. They are content with the things they know. One evangelist used to challenge Muslims by asking them, "What is the difference between the life of a very rich man and a life in paradise?" The only answer that the Muslim can give is that in Paradise wine, women, and wanton lust will be allowed, while here it is regulated.

It is important for Christians to be clear on what the Bible teaches about predestination and judgment. In the Garden of Eden, Adam and all his descendants were judged; and that judgment falls on all of mankind. We are all the descendants of a thieving gardener (Adam) and a drunken sea captain (Noah). None of us is worthy of paradise, let alone heaven. We all have bad people in our family heritage. None of us can claim to come from good families where everyone was perfect. All of us must be judged on our own merit. It is often helpful to use Matthew 5 here. These are the direct words of Jesus as he teaches us about what is acceptable to God. Lying, pride and lust are all described as evil. Most Muslims will protest that Matthew 5 is too hard on mankind. If this is the standard, no one will achieve it. We must agree. None of us can please God. We are all doomed to hell. Except for God's mercy and grace, all of us will burn in the fire forever. This is what the Bible teaches.

However, God knew this when he created mankind, and long before we came into being, he provided a way of escape for us. But it is not in our own efforts. It is only when we believe and submit that we will receive eternal life.

It is important to explain to Muslims that the Bible teaches that we are already judged. When we die, we will never be judged if we are fit for heaven or hell. That is already decided. We are all going to hell. Romans 5:12 tells us: *Wherefore, as by one man sin entered into the world, and death by sin; and so death passed upon all men, for that all have sinned."*

Galatians 6:7-9 adds:

> *"Be not deceived; God is not mocked: for whatsoever a man sows, that shall he also reap. For he that sows to his flesh shall of the flesh reap corruption; but he that sows to the Spirit shall of the Spirit reap life everlasting. And let us not be weary in well doing: for in due season we shall reap, if we faint not."*

Hell in the Bible

The Bible teaches us that everyone will exist eternally either in heaven or hell.

• Daniel 12:2-3 says: *"Multitudes who sleep in the dust of the earth will awake: some to everlasting life, others to shame and everlasting contempt. Those who are wise will shine like the brightness of the heavens, and those who lead many to righteousness, like the stars forever and ever."*

• In Matthew 25:46 Jesus says: *"Then they will go away to eternal punishment, but the righteous to eternal life."*

• In John 5:28-29 Jesus adds *"Do not be amazed at this, for a time is coming when all who are in their graves will hear his voice and come out - those who have done good will rise to live, and those who have done evil will rise to be condemned."*

• Revelation 20:14-15 tell us: *"Then death and Hades were thrown into the lake of fire. The lake of fire is the second death. If anyone's name was not found written in the book of life, he was thrown into the lake of fire."*

• Everyone has only one life in which to determine his or her destiny. Hebrews 9:27 says, *"Man is destined to die once, and after that to face judgment."*

Heaven or hell is determined by whether a person believes and puts their trust in Christ alone to save them. John 3:16 says *"For God so loved the world that he gave his one and only Son, that whoever believes in him shall not perish but have eternal life."* Verse 36 adds: *"Whoever believes in the Son has eternal life, but whoever rejects the Son will not see life, for God's wrath remains on him."*

We learn from the Bible that hell was designed originally for Satan and his demons (Matthew 25:41; Revelation 20:10). However hell will also be used to punish those who reject Christ. In Matthew 13:49-50 Jesus says, *"This is how it will be at the end of the age. The angels will come and separate the wicked from the righteous and throw them into the fiery furnace, where there will be weeping and gnashing of teeth."* Revelation 21:8 tells us, *"But the cowardly, the unbelieving, the vile, the murderers, the sexually immoral, those who practice magic arts, the idolaters and all liars - their place will be in the fiery lake of burning sulfur. This is the second death."* The Bible also teaches us that Hell is conscious torment. Matthew 13:50 calls it a *"Furnace of fire…with …weeping and gnashing of teeth"* Mark 9:48 tells us that it is a place *"where their worm does not die, and the fire is not quenched."* Revelation 14:10 adds, *"He will be tormented with fire and brimstone."*

The Bible uses several terms that speak of life after death. Four terms refer to a negative experience. *Sheol* is a Hebrew term simply describing "the grave" or "death," it does not refer to "hell" specifically, but simply going into the grave. *Hades* on the other hand is a Greek term that usually refers to hell, a place of torment (Luke 10:15; 16:23)

The Bible also used the word *Gehenna*, which is a term borrowed from a literal burning dump near Jerusalem that always refers to hell, a place of torment. This is found in Matthew 5:30; and 23:33. Another name for hell in the Bible is the "Lake of fire," the final abode of unbelievers after they are resurrected (Revelation 20:14-15).

On the other hand the Bible also speaks of "Abraham's bosom" (Luke 16:22) as a place of eternal comfort. There is one reference to "Paradise" (Luke 23:43), which seems to be a place of eternal comfort. Paul refers to heaven as being "with the Lord," a key phrase that describes where believers will be after death (Philippians 1:23; 1 Thessalonians 4:17; 2 Corinthians 5:8). The term "New heavens and earth" refers to where believers will be after they are resurrected (Revelation 20:4-6; 21:1-4).

Questions for Reflection and Group Discussion

1. Read Hebrews 1:1-2, John 14:16-26 and 16:7-15. What do these verses teach us about God's revelation and relationship to mankind?

2. Read Genesis 12:1-4, 15:1-6, and 17:1-22 What do we learn about God from his covenant with Abraham?

3. Read Genesis 18:1-33 What do we learn from these verses about God?

4. Read Genesis 22:1-24 What do these verses tell us about God and his relationship with mankind?

5. Read Revelation 21 - 22. Discuss together what these two chapters teach us about the future home for mankind. How is this different from earth now or the Islamic version of paradise?

6. Discuss from the Bible: Will God judge people to determiine if they are going to heaven or hell? Why or why not? Is this already decided? What Bible verses should you memorize so you can share this effectively with unbelievers?

7. Will some people suffer more in hell than others? Read and discuss Matthew 10:15, Matthew 11:24 and Mark 6:11.

8. Should Christians fear God's judgment when they die?

9. Is it possible for a Christian to commit such bad sins that he will lose his opportunity to go to heaven? Why or why not?

Chapter Twelve
The Duties of Islam (*Diin*)
The Five Pillars

The Muslim religion requires that all Muslims perform five rites or duties. These are known as the five Pillars of Islam and they are obligatory to all Muslims.

1. The first pillar is known as the <u>Creed</u> or words of witness. The Muslims call this the *shehada*. Missionaries to Muslim lands will hear this creed many times. It is called the shortest creed in the world, and it is repeated more than any other. In Arabic it consists of only eight words, meaning: "There is no God but Allah, and Muhammad is the Apostle of God." Muslims repeat it in their call to prayer, which is broadcast on speakers from the mosque five times a day, as well as during the prayers and at countless other times during the day. It is used as a cry in battle, as an exclamation of joy at the birth of a baby and as a plea which is repeated over and over again at funerals. Since many Muslims believe that they receive eternal credit every time they say the name of God or the creed, this creed is said many times, even if it doesn't have immediate meaning in the situation.

2. The second duty for all Muslims is <u>Prayer</u>. These prayers are known as *salat*. They are ritual prayers said at set times. Muslims do not vary in the wording nor the actions that they do as they pray. The Muslim is called to perform this ritual prayer five times a day, at dawn, soon after mid-day, two hours before sunset, just after sunset and two hours after sunset. Before praying, a Muslim must remove his shoes, wash his feet, hands, and parts of his face and turn towards the Ka'aba at Mecca.

When he cannot go to a mosque to pray, he will pray wherever he happens to be, whether at work, on a journey or in the midst of other duties. He will carry a bottle of water with him for the ritual washing, and if water is not available he will use sand or soil symbolically. The early morning prayers frequently last up to and sometimes beyond an hour. On Fridays a sermon is preached in the mosque as part of the prayers. A sermon may also be included in the last prayers of the day in larger and more central mosques.

Below are some of the Qur'anic verses that instruct about prayer.

"Oh you who believe, when, you rise up for prayer, wash your faces and your hands to the elbows, and wipe your heads, and wash your feet up to the ankles. And if you are under an obligation, then wash yourselves. And if you are sick or on a journey, or one of you comes from the bathroom or you have had contact with women and you cannot find water, take for yourselves pure earth and wipe your faces and your hands with it. Allah desires not to place a burden on you, but he wishes to purify you, and that He may bestow favor on you, so that you may give thanks." (Sura 5:6)

It is also important for Muslims to face the right direction during their prayers. This is called the *qibla* or direction. The niche on the back wall of each mosque points in the direction of Mecca.

Long ago Muslims originally faced the Black Rock, which was located in northern Arabia. Later, the rock was moved, and Muhammad directed his followers to face the rock at the Ka'aba in Mecca whenever they prayed:

We have seen the turning of your face to heaven and now verily We shall make you turn toward a direction (qiblah) which is dear to you. So turn your face toward the Inviolable Place of Worship, so that where-ever you may be, turn your faces when you pray, toward it. Lo! those who have received the Scripture know that this Revelation is the Truth from their Lord. And Allah is not unaware of what they do. (Sura 2:144)

No one verse in the Qur'an lists the complete five times of prayer, but Sura 30:17 is given by some Muslims to indicate the five periods. *"So glory be to Allah when you enter the evening, and when you enter the morning, and to Him be praise in the heavens and the earth, and in the afternoon, and when the sun declines."* The Arabic term *mughrib* (meaning "evening") is said to cover the last two prayers.

The *rak'ah* are the movements that must accompany all Muslim prayers. There are essentially seven movements and they are performed at set times.

- First is the opening greeting: *Allahu Akbar* (Allah, he is greater).
- Second, the person stands with his hands on his navel, and the opening chapter from the Qur'an is repeated, then *Allahu Akbar*.
- Third, the person bows and says three times: *Glory to my Lord, the great one.*
- Fourth, the person stands and says: *Allah accepts any who are grateful to him, Lord, praise be to you.*
- The fifth movement is prostrating on the ground while saying three times: *Glory to my Lord, the highest,* then: *Allahu Akbar.*
- Then the person sits on his legs and says, *Lord forgive me and have mercy on me, Allahu Akbar.*
- Then the person prostrates himself on the ground and repeats three times: *Glory to my Lord, the highest,* then *Allahu Akbar.*

Afterwards the Muslim can rise and hold out his hands in petition and perform *Du'a*, which is a spontaneous private prayer, but this is less important than the ritual prayers.

3. The third pillar of Islam is giving to the needy, known as Zakat. The Qur'anic foundation for Muslim almsgiving is found in Sura 2:43: *"And keep up prayer and pay the poor rate, and bow down with those who bow down."*

Muhammad taught that each Muslim adult (if he was free and sane) was required to give alms if he possessed property. Property for this purpose included camels, bulls, cows, sheep, goats, buffalo, horses, gold, silver, articles of merchandise, mining products, and the fruit of the earth according to fixed scales of taxes. Household property, weapons, and tools were not included. If a person had debts equal to the value of their property then they were not obliged to pay. The almsgiving or taxation was designed to help the poor, and a collector was duly appointed for this purpose. A person was also free to distribute his own alms. If the alms collector approached a person and he claimed that he had already given away his alms, the collector had to accept his word as truth. The most common time for collectors of taxes was on Fridays, so this became the time when the poor and beggars multiplied on the streets to receive the alms. Today alms are also given during the month of Ramadan.

The following classes of people were entitled to receive help from the officially collected *zakat*:

- People whose property was below taxable value.
- People who have no property at all (these are known as *masakin* or poor).
- Slaves who could not have property.
- People deeply in debt with no way out.
- Alms were also given to people who were in the service of God and also for those engaged in religious warfare.
- Hospitality given to travelers could also be counted for *zakat*.

Lastly, the collectors of the alms themselves could receive the alms. This created problems, as sometimes the collectors secretly became wealthy at the expense of the poor.

Today the general impression is that *zakat* is simply a ritual and not an organized, efficient method of providing for the poor. If you do give money to a poor Muslim or a beggar, they will never say, thank you, for in doing so they would rob you of the reward God might give you in heaven. When giving alms to a person, one usually receives the reply, May God bless you, or May God bless your hands.

4. The fourth Pillar of Islam is that of <u>fasting</u> or *saum*. There are several Muslim fasts. The most important one is during the month of Ramadan which is the ninth month of the Muslim calendar. This is obligatory for all Muslims. Sura 2:163-185 declares: *"Oh you who believe, fasting is prescribed for those before you, so that you may guard against evil."* Verse 185 declares that the Qur'an was revealed in the month of Ramadan.

Based on a reported saying of Muhammad, Muslims believe that during Ramadan the gates of paradise are open and the gates of hell closed, and that all who keep the fast will be pardoned of all their past excusable sins.

A number of regulations govern the fast:

- The fast cannot begin until some Muslim is able to state that he has seen the new moon. This leads to frequent divergences of opinion. In the Middle East the beginning of the Fast appears to depend to some extent on which of the two main political camps the person owes his allegiance, i.e. Egyptian or Saudi Arabian. There is often a difference of 24 hours between the two.

- The fast must be kept by young people from about the age of 10 or 12 years. Certain classes of persons are exempt from fasting such as the sick, the infirm, pregnant women, and travelers on a journey of more than three days. Even these are expected to make up the fast for the days they have missed, as soon as they are able.

- The fast commences at dawn as soon as a white thread is distinguishable from a black thread and it continues until sunset. During this period not even one's own spittle should be swallowed.

- During the month of Ramadan an additional 20 *rak'at* or sets of prayers are said after the night prayer. These are called the *tarawih* meaning "rest," because the congregation sits down and rests after every fourth set of prayers.

- Ramadan lasts for 30 days which is the length of a Muslim month. By western reckoning, Ramadan comes about 10 days earlier each year.

- After sunset and until dawn a Muslim can eat as much as he likes and indulge in any lawful pleasure. It is a common sight to observe Muslims sitting with a bottle of water and a few dates before them waiting for the ending of the daily fast. After this the Muslims can eat as much as they want during the evening hours. Often extended families meet together for a large meal to break the fast.

- It is reported in most Muslim countries that more food is consumed during the month of Ramadan than at any other time of the year. In some places, businesses open at night, and feasting takes place until dawn.

5. The fifth pillar of Islam is the Pilgrimage or *Hajj.* This pilgrimage to Mecca is obligatory to every Muslim at least once in his lifetime if he is an adult, free, sane, healthy, and has sufficient money to provide for his journey and support his family while he is away. Sura 22:27 says: *And proclaim to men the Pilgrimage, they will come to thee on foot and on every lean camel, coming from every remote path."*

The *Hajj* takes place in the month of the *Hajj,* the 12th month of the

Muslim calendar. A person who has completed the pilgrimage takes the title *Hajj* or *Hajji*. This person may wear a small white cap to demonstrate that he has been on the hajj, or he may dye some reddish brown into his beard.

The *Hajj* is highly organized, with many regulations and directions. There are three actions in the pilgrimage that are obligatory and thought to be instituted by God himself. The first is to wear no other garment but the *ihram* which consists of two seamless wrappers each six feet long by three and a half feet wide. One is thrown over the back exposing the right arm and shoulder and knotted on the right side. The other is wrapped around the loins from the waist to the knees and knotted in at the middle. The second action is to stand on the mountain of Arafat. The third is to make a circuit around the Ka'aba seven times in a ritual called the *tawaf.*

There are five duties of the pilgrim which are said to be obligatory, but the omission of which does not constitute an unpardonable sin. The first is to spend the night between the 9th and 10th day of the month at a place halfway between Mina and Arafat. The second is to run the distance between the mountains of Safa and Marwa. The third is to perform the rite of throwing stones at the pillar representing Satan. The fourth is to make an extra circuit around the Kaaba if the pilgrim is a non-Meccan. The fifth is to shave the head after the pilgrimage is over.

A tradition attributed to a saying of Muhammad is: *"He who makes the pilgrimage for God's sake and does not talk loosely nor act wickedly, shall return as pure from sin as the day he was born." "Verily the pilgrimage puts away poverty and sin like the fires of a forge remove the dross."* (Mishkat, book xi. Ch. 1)

Twelve actions that take place during the pilgrimage:

- First, in the vicinity of Mecca the pilgrim bathes himself, performs two prayers and exchanges his clothes for the *ihram*. He must keep his head uncovered, is not to shave, pare his nails, nor wear any garment other than the *ihram*. Sandals are permitted, but not shoes.
- Second, when he arrives in Mecca he must wash himself at the sacred Mosque and then kiss the famous black stone.
- Third, he must circle the Ka'aba seven times, three times quickly and four times slowly; kissing the black stone each time he passes it.
- Fourth, he should proceed to the Place of Abraham and recite: *"And*

we made the house a resort for men and a place of security so take the place of Abraham as a place of prayer. And We enjoined Abraham and Ishmael saying: Purify my house for those who visit it, and those who abide in it, for devotion and those who bow down and those who prostrate themselves" (Sura 2:125). The pilgrim should also perform two sets of prayers.

- The fifth step is going up the hill to Mount Safa reciting: *"Oh you who believe, seek assistance through patience and prayer; surely Allah is with the patient."* (Sura 2:153)

- At the top of Mount Safa he should face the Ka'aba and recite *"There is no God but God. God is greatest. There is no God but God,"* and other quotations.

- The seventh step is to run between Mount Safa and Mount Marwa seven times repeating the above prayers on the top of each hill. This should all take place on the sixth day, and in the evening he must return to Mecca and encompass the Ka'aba once more.

- The ninth step happens on the seventh day when he must listen to a sermon in the mosque.

- On the eighth day he goes to Mina and spends the night there. On the ninth day he should go to Mount Arafat and then on to Al-Muzdalifah to spend the night.

- The last action happens on *Eid al-Adha* (The Feast of Sacrifice) or *Eid al-Kabir* (The Great Feast) which is celebrated throughout the Muslim world. On this day the pilgrims gather stones from Al-Muzdalifah and return to Mina where they cast seven stones at each of three pillars, the largest of which is called the Great Devil. Then they go to the other end of the Valley of Mina and slay a sacrifical sheep, goat, cow, or camel. The pilgrimage is now complete and the new *Hajji* can shave, pare his nails, and resume ordinary dress. He now bears the honored title *Al-Hajj* or *Al-Hajji*.

6. There is a sixth pillar of Islam, known as <u>Holy War</u> or *Jihad*. Today most Muslims consider countries and governments to be associated with some religion. To them China is a Buddhist country, America is Christian, India is Hindu, and Saudi Arabia, Iran, Jordan, Syria and many more are Muslim countries. Thus, when countries go to war, it is always a religious war. In the

west, Americans separate religion and government. For them war seldom has any religious overtone, so non-Muslims often struggle to understand the concept of "Holy War" as understood by Muslims.

A growing number of Muslims regard *Jihad* or Holy War as the sixth pillar of Islam. For them Holy War is a general duty of all male, free, adult Muslims, sane in mind and body and having means enough to reach the Muslim army. This is a duty that is incumbent on Muslims until the whole world is Islamized. The Holy War must be declared by a Muslim Sovereign or Imam, and Muslims from any place can join and fight.

Holy War is regarded as a Divine institution, and its purpose is to advance Islam and repel evil from Muslims. If a Muslim country is attacked by an infidel country, the Imam may summon all Muslims to its aid, including Muslims from the whole Muslim world, depending upon the danger imposed by the invading army.

Thus when America invaded Iraq, several Muslim leaders declared that it was a Holy War. Immediately, bus loads of Muslim volunteers poured into Iraq from all over the Muslim world. They were doing their part to fight on behalf of Muslims against their Evangelical Christian enemies.

According to Islamic teaching, people against whom the *Jihad* is directed are to be invited to accept Islam. Those who accept Islam will be given full citizenship rights of the Muslim country. Those who refuse will be made to pay a tax. They will be able to retain their families and property but will be inferior citizens. Those who will not embrace Islam nor pay the tax but choose to fight may have their families and property taken from them and they may be enslaved. Apostates will be put to death.

Muslims who die fighting in a Holy War are assured of Paradise and special privileges there. This is a great incitement to joining a Jihad. Today there are a number of Muslim organizations that offer financial aid to the family members of those killed in a Holy War. This money is usually paid to the young man's mother. In the case of martyrs who give their lives in a suicide attack, many of the attacker's families receive over $10,000 compensation from these religious organizations. (Meo,Nick, *Taliban recruits suicide bombers*, The Telegraph, 30 May, 2009)

Biblical View

The topic of prayer is addressed in many places in the Bible. Prayer is an important part of the Christian's spiritual life. However, when Muslims and Christians speak together, they often have many misunderstandings about prayer. Therefore it is important that Christians understand what the Bible says about prayer and be able to explain it to their Muslim friends.

First, there is no correct or certain posture for prayer. In the Bible people prayed on their knees (1 Kings 8:45), bowed (Exodus 4:31), fell on their faces before God (2 Chronicles 20:18; Matthew 26:39), and prayed standing up (1 Kings 8:22). Christians are free to pray with their eyes opened or closed, and they may pray quietly or out loud. The important issue is that we concentrate on speaking to God and give him our attention while we speak to him. Christians are also free to address God with their own way of speaking.

- Matthew 6:7 tells us: *When you pray, don't babble on and on as people of other religions do. They think their prayers are answered only by repeating their words again and again.*
- Ecclesiastes 5:2 adds: *Do not be quick with your mouth, do not be hasty in your heart to utter anything before God. God is in heaven and you are on earth, so let your words be few.*
- John 15:7 Jesus tells us: *If you stay joined to me and my words remain in you, you may ask any request you like, and it will be granted.*
- Ephesians 6:18 instructs us to *pray in the Spirit on all occasions with all kinds of prayers and requests. With this in mind, be alert and always keep on praying for all the saints.*

If we do not know what to say, the Bible promises us that the Holy Spirit will help us, and he will take our simple prayers and intercede for us. Romans 8:26-27 puts it this way:

> *In the same way, the Spirit helps us in our weakness. We do not know what we ought to pray for, but the Spirit himself intercedes for us with groans that words cannot express. And he who searches our hearts knows the mind of the Spirit, because the Spirit intercedes for the saints in accordance with God's will."*

In order for our prayers to be successful the Bible requires several things.

- We must have humble hearts. 2 Chronicles 7:14 says: *If my people, who are called by my name, will humble themselves and pray and seek my face and turn from their wicked ways, then will I hear from heaven and will forgive their sin and will heal their land.*

- We must pray wholeheartedly. Jeremiah 29:13 guarantees: *You will seek me and find me when you seek me with all your heart.*

- We must pray in faith. Mark 11:24 declares: *therefore I tell you, whatever you ask for in prayer, believe that you have received it, and it will be yours.*

- We must be righteous. James 5:16 commands: *Therefore confess your sins to each other and pray for each other so that you may be healed. The prayer of a righteous man is powerful and effective.*

- We should make sure that we are walking in a right relationship with God, always obeying him and pleasing him. 1 John 3:22 says: *And we will receive whatever we request because we obey him and do the things that please him.*

Christians can be sure that God does answer us when we pray. There are many promises in the Bible that God does hear and answer our prayers. Here are two examples:

Psalm 34:17 *The righteous cry out, and the LORD hears them; he delivers them from all their troubles.*

Psalm 91:15 *He will call upon me, and I will answer him; I will be with him in trouble, I will deliver him and honor him.*

Even though we have promises that God will hear us and answer us, some of our prayers seem to go unanswered. Why is this? The Bible gives several reasons or causes for failure in prayer:

• Disobedience - Deuteronomy 1:42-45 *But the LORD said to me, "Tell them, 'Do not go up and fight, because I will not be with you. You will be defeated by your enemies.'" So I told you, but you would not listen. You rebelled against the LORD's command and in your arrogance you marched up into the hill country. The Amorites who lived in those hills came out against you; they chased you like a swarm of bees and beat you down from Seir all the way to Hormah. You came* back and wept before the LORD, but he paid no attention to your weeping and turned a deaf ear to you.

- Sin - Psalm 66:18 *If I had cherished sin in my heart, the Lord would not have listened.* Isaiah 59:2 adds *But your iniquities have separated you from your God; your sins have hidden his face from you, so that he will not hear.*

- Indifference - Proverbs 1:28-30 *Then they will call to me but I will not answer; they will look for me but will not find me. Since they hated knowledge and did not choose to fear the LORD, since they would not accept my advice and spurned my rebuke.*

- Neglect of mercy - Proverbs 21:13 *If a man shuts his ears to the cry of the poor, he too will cry out and not be answered.*

- Despising the Law - Proverbs 28:9 *If anyone turns a deaf ear to the law, even his prayers are detestable.*

- Stubbornness - Zechariah 7:11-13 *But they refused to pay attention; stubbornly they turned their backs and stopped up their ears. They made their hearts as hard as flint and would not listen to the law or to the words that the LORD Almighty had sent by his Spirit through the earlier prophets. So the LORD Almighty was very angry. 'When I called, they did not listen; so when they called, I would not listen' says the LORD Almighty.*

- Wrong motives for asking - James 4:3 *When you ask, you do not receive, because you ask with wrong motives, that you may spend what you get on your pleasures.*

Sometimes our prayers are refused. Prayer must be in accord with God's divine will. 1 John 5:14 teaches us: *This is the confidence we have in approaching God: that if we ask anything according to his will, he hears us.*

Christians are instructed to pray in groups and also individually in secret. First, God wants us to pray together with other believers. Matthew 18:19 teaches us: *Again, I tell you that if two of you on earth agree about anything you ask for, it will be done for you by my Father in heaven.* Luke 1:10 adds, *And when the time for the burning of incense came, all the assembled worshipers were praying outside.* We have the example of groups meeting in the early church such as in Acts 1:14, *They all joined together constantly in prayer, along with the women and Mary the mother of Jesus, and with his brothers.*

But God also wants us to pray alone and in secret: Matthew 6:6 tells us: *But when you pray, go into your room, close the door and pray to your Father, who is unseen. Then your Father, who sees what is done in secret, will reward you.* Jesus exemplified this for us in his own life. Mark 1:35 says, *Very early in the morning, while it was still dark, Jesus got up, left the house and went off to a solitary place, where he prayed.* Luke 5:15-16 says, *Yet the news about him spread all the more, so that crowds of people came to hear him and to be healed of their sicknesses. But Jesus often withdrew to lonely places and prayed.* Luke 6:12 also tells us, *Now it came to pass in those days that He went out to the mountain to pray, and continued all night in prayer to God.*

Most Muslims believe that Christians do not pray because they never see them praying. If you would like to be a witness to Muslims, it is important to let them see and hear you praying. This often has a powerful impact on their lives as they compare their own formal prayers with the fervent prayers of righteous Christians.

The Bible also teaches Christians to fast. However, fasting as taught in the Bible is very different from the kind of fasting that Muslims experience. For Muslims, the purpose of fasting is to practice self control and self denial. Christians, however have a different emphasis when they fast.

The Scriptures do not command Christians to fast. It is not something that God requires or demands of Christians. At the same time, the Bible presents fasting as something that is good, profitable, and expected. The Book of Acts records believers fasting before they made important decisions (Acts 13:4; 14:23). Fasting and prayer are often linked together (Luke 2:37; 5:33). Too often, the focus of fasting is on the lack of food. Instead, the purpose of fasting should be to take your eyes off the things of this world, and instead focus on God. Fasting is a way to demonstrate to God, and to yourself, that you are serious about your relationship with Him. Fasting helps you to gain a new perspective and a renewed reliance upon God.

Fasting should be limited to a set time, especially when the fasting is for extended periods of time. Fasting is not intended to punish your flesh, but to help you focus on God. Fasting should not be considered a "dieting method" either. Do not fast to lose weight, but rather to gain deeper fellowship with God. Yes, anyone can fast. Some may not be able to fast from food (diabetics for example), but everyone can temporarily give up something in order to focus on God.

By taking our eyes off the things of this world, we can focus better on Christ. Fasting is not a way to get God to do what we want. Fasting is a means through which God changes us. Fasting is not a way to appear more spiritual than others. Fasting is to be done in a spirit of humility and a joyful attitude.

Matthew 6:16-18 declares,

> *When you fast, do not look somber as the hypocrites do, for they disfigure their faces to show men they are fasting. I tell you the truth, they have received their reward in full. But when you fast, put oil on your head and wash your face, so that it will not be obvious to men that you are fasting, but only to your Father, who is unseen; and your Father, who sees what is done in secret, will reward you.*

Questions for Reflection and Group Discussion

1. Why do you think Muslims do not pray directly to God using their own prayers?
2. Is prayer simply obedience to God or is it communication with God or something else? Why do you think this?
3. If a Muslim asked you how Christians fast, what would you answer? Can you describe fasting from the Bible? Consider the following verses: Joel 2:12, Psalm 35:13, Matthew 9:14-15, Isaiah 58:3-7
4. If a Muslim asked you about how Christians give alms, what would you answer? Consider Ezekiel 7:19 and Mark 12:38-44.

Chapter Thirteen
Varieties of Islam

According to the Hadiths (*Tirmidhi Kitabul Iman*, and *Abu Dawood* 40:4759) Muhammad predicted that his followers would become divided into 73 sects. He said that every one of these sects would go to hell, except one sect which followed the religion professed by himself and his companions. However today there are more than 150 different Islamic sects which far exceed Muhammad's prediction. Each of these sects claims that they are the one true sect that follows the religion of Islam. In this lesson we will look at the six major sects.

Sunni Muslims

Sunni Muslims are followers of the four main schools of Islam. They constitute 90% of all Muslims everywhere, and are considered to be the mainstream traditionalists. Because they are comfortable pursuing their faith within secular societies, they have been able to adapt to a variety of national cultures, while following their three sources of law: the Qur'an, Hadith and consensus of Muslims.

Sunnis are by far the largest sect in the Muslim world. They take the title of *Najiyah,* meaning "those who are being saved." They acknowledge the first four caliphs as the rightful successors of Muhammad rather than through a hereditary line. The Sunni believe, based on specific provisions of the Qur'an and the *Sunna* or *Sunni Hadith*, that Muslim people are to be governed by consensus (*ijma*) through an elected head of state, the caliph, according to democratic principles. The Sunni emphasize the power and sovereignty of Allah and his right to do whatever he wants with his creation, and strict pre-determinism is taught. They follow what they call the "six correct books," which make up the Hadith or traditions about the prophet Muhammad. Much of what is written in these lessons is about Sunni Muslims.

Shi'ite Muslims

The Shi'ites split with the Sunni over the issue of the successor to Muhammad. This split occurred after the assassination of the fourth caliph in 661 AD. Shi'ites believe that the successor to Muhammad should have been Ali, his son-in-law, and that subsequent successors should have been through his lineage through his wife Fatima. The Shi'ites strenuously maintain that they alone are right in their understanding of Islam, and, like the Sunnis, they call themselves *al-Mu'minun* or the true believers. They believe in the divine right of the successors of Ali. His rightful successor is now concealed, but they say he will appear at the end of the world as the *Mahdi* or the one rightly guided by Allah, thus able to guide others. They reject the six correct books of the Sunnis, and have five collections of their own.

The Shi'ites are broken into three main sects: the Twelve-Imam sect in Persia, Iraq, Afghanistan, Lebanon, Pakistan, and Syria; the Zaydis in Yemen and the Ismailis in India, Iran, Syria, and East Africa. Each group has differences of doctrine.

Shi'ite theology includes a doctrine known as the "Five Supports." These are Divine Unity (*tawhid*), prophecy (*nubuwwah*), resurrection of the soul and body at the judgment (*ma'ad*), the Imamate (*imamah)*, and justice (*'adl*). The first three are found in Sunni Islam, albeit with some differences of emphasis. The Imamate, however, is the most important distinction of the Shi'ites, based on the passage of authority through the family directly related to Muhammad. The last is justice, which is an inheritance from the Mu'tazilite rationalist sect, whose system is in many ways perpetuated in Shi'ite theology.

Shi'ites are numerous in Iran, where they have deposed the Shah and in his place installed the Ayatollahs and enforced Islamic law as the rule of the government. The Ayatollahs have gone beyond that by declaring that their command is as good as that of the prophet Muhammad.

Wahhabis

The founder of the Wahhabi sect was 'Abd al-Wahhab, born in Nefd in A.D. 1691. He maintained that the Muslims had departed from the precepts of Muhammad. He accepted only the Quran and the Traditions, rejecting the two other foundations, *Ijma* and *Qiyas*. He condemned the worship of dead holy men at tombs. He said:

> *They run there to pay the tribute of their fervent prayers. By this means they think that they can satisfy their spiritual and temporal needs. From what do they seek this benefit? From walls made of mud and stone, from corpses deposited in tombs. The true way of salvation is to prostrate one's self before Him who is ever-present and to venerate him - the one without associate or equal.* (Sell, Edward, *The Faith of Islam*, London, 1907)

The war cry of the Wahhabis was, "*Kill and strangle all infidels which give companions to Allah.*" On the day of battle, the Wahhabi founder gave each soldier a letter addressed to the Keeper of Paradise. It was enclosed in a bag which the warrior suspended from his neck. The soldiers believed that by dying in battle he would go straight to Paradise, without being examined by the angels. Many Iranian prisoners today have confided to their captors that they were convinced that by hanging a small Quran around their necks they would become invisible in battle and not be seen by their enemies.

The Wahhabis condemn astrology, trusting in omens, and believing in lucky or unlucky days, as well as praying at tombs. They disallow the use of the rosary but attach great merit to counting the 99 names of God on their fingers.

Sufis

The meaning of the name Sufi is disputed, but most agree that it comes from the Arabic word for wool referring to the white robes that the followers of this religion used to wear. Sufis themselves think of the word as meaning pure, as in pure white wool. Sufis are a Muslim sect that has set aside the literal meaning of the Qur'an and Hadith for a supposed spiritual interpretation. Their system is a Muslim adaptation of Indian mystic philosophy. They believe that only Allah exists and all visible things are really part of him. They believe that there is no real difference between good and evil and that Allah fixes the will of man. In fact, transmigration of the soul from one being into another is accepted. The principal occupation of the Sufi is meditation on the unity of God and the remembrance of God's name so as to obtain forgiveness and cleanliness. Sufis may accept Muhammad, Buddha, Confucius and Jesus all as good teachers and all helping point towards the unity of God.

Sufis are most numerous in Iran, once called Persia. The three chief Persian poets, Jami, Sa'di, and Hafiz were Sufis who dwelt on love to God. Many of the writings of the Persian Sufis contain indecent passages. The Sufis are divided into innumerable sects which find expression in the numerous order of *Faqirs*, or *Darweshes*. *Faqirs* are divided into two great classes, those who govern their conduct according to the principles of Islam and those who do not, although they all call themselves Muslims. Many Sufis seek a mystical experience. Sometimes they read the Quran from cover to cover ten times a day. Sometimes they twirl themselves until they fall into a stupor. These are known as the "whirling dervishes". All of these mystical experiences are supposed to help them come closer to God.

Baha'ism

The Baha'i sect began with a man who was born in 1817 in Tehran and whose real name was Mirza Hussayn Ali. In 1847 he declared that he was the glory of Allah or Baha'ullah. His acquaintance with a religious movement led by a man called the *Bab* (or gate) convinced him that he himself was the prophet that the *Bab* had predicted would appear.

In 1850, the Persian government executed the Bab for his teachings, and Mirza took over the leadership of the movement. In 1863, ten years after he was banished to Baghdad, Baha'ullah declared he was the expected prophet. From 1868 until his death in 1892, he lived in a prison colony in what is now Akka, Israel. He tried to unite the three monotheistic religions of Judaism, Christianity, and Islam through his writings, which comprise 100 volumes.

Bahais believe in good works, nondiscrimination, and a federated world government. Their headquarters are in Haifa, Israel, and they have over 17,000 local councils, called local spiritual assemblies, with 1,500,000 adherents. Ten percent of them live in India.

Ahmadiyya

The Ahmadiyya sect began at the end of the 1800s. Mirza Ghulam Ahmed, an Indian, proclaimed himself to be the "Reformer of the Age." He claimed to have fulfilled the prophecy of the return of Jesus. He and his followers claimed that his advent was foretold by Muhammad and also by many other religious scriptures of the world. In 1889, Mirza Ghulam Ahmad laid down the foundation of his community, which was later given the name of Ahmadiyya Muslim Jamaat. Since its inception, the Ahmadiyya Muslim Jamaat's objective has been the revival of Islam. Soon after the death of Mirza the movement split into two sects. The Lahore Ahmadiyya Movement affirmed the traditional Islamic interpretation that there could be no new prophet after Muhammad and viewed itself as a reform movement within Islam. The Ahmadiyya Muslim Community however, claimed that Mirza Ghulam Ahmad had indeed been a prophet (albeit a non-law-bearing one) and that mainstream Muslims who rejected his message were guilty of disbelief.

Some of the first people to convert to the Ahmadiyya movement were highly educated people from secular and religious circles. These included many Indian civil servants and military members. The Ahmadiyya Muslim Community has established offices in 189 countries and claims to have a population exceeding tens of millions. The Lahore Ahmadiyya Movement has branches in 17 countries.

Overseas Ahmadiyya missionary activities started as early as the 1920s. For many modern nations of the world, the Ahmadiyya movement was their first contact with Islam. The Ahmadiyya movement in America was very influential among African-Americans until the 1950s, when the Nation of Islam gained support among black communities.

In some countries it is an offence for the Ahmadiyya Movement to preach their religion as Islam. In Pakistan, the parliament has declared all Ahmadiyya to be non-Muslims. Due to this strong clash of beliefs, many Ahmadiyya have been the target of attacks led by various religious groups. As a result of the cultural implications of the laws and constitutional amendments regarding Ahmadiyya in Pakistan, persecution and hate-related incidents are constantly reported from different parts of the country. In Bangladesh, fundamentalist Islamic groups have demanded that Ahmadiyya be declared as *kafirs* or unbelievers. Ahmadiyya have become a persecuted group, targeted via protests; and acts of violence. According to Amnesty International, followers have been subject to house arrest and several have been killed. In 2003, several large marches were directed to occupy Ahmadiyya mosques. These marches were supported by thousands of protesters, armed with sticks, bricks, and other weapons, they chanted slogans of hate-filled and violent rhetoric.

Ahmadiyya beliefs mostly mirror those of Islam in general, including belief in the prophethood of Muhammad, reverence for historical prophets and belief in a single creator God. They accept the Qur'an as their holy text, face the Ka'aba during prayer, and accept the authority of hadiths.

Several Ahmadiyya beliefs are unique. For instance they, believe that Mirza Ghulam Ahmad fulfilled in his person the prophecies concerning the coming Mahdi, Messiah and the return of Jesus. They believe that the Hadith are second to the Qur'an and that any Hadith that appear to contradict the Qu'ran are not acceptable. They also believe that Jesus, contrary to mainstream Islamic belief, was crucified and survived the four hours on the cross. He was later revived from a swoon in the tomb. Jesus then traveled to India and later died in Kashmir of old age while seeking the Lost Tribes of Israel. Jesus' remains are believed to be entombed in Kashmir under the name Yuz Asaf. Ahmadis believe that Jesus foretold the coming of Muhammad after him, which Christians have misinterpreted.

Ahmadiyya Muslims also believe that the followers of Mirza Ghulam Ahmad will defeat the Anti-Christ or *Djajal* in a period similar to the period of time it took for Christianity to rise (300 years) and that the *Dajjal's* power will slowly melt away like the melting of snow, heralding the final victory of Islam and the age of peace. They also teach that the history of mankind is split into seven great ages, parallel to the seven days of the week. History is seen as periods of light and darkness with Mirza Ghulam Ahmad appearing as the Promised Messiah at the end of the sixth epoch, heralding the seventh and final age of the world. According to Ghulam Ahmad, this age is destined for a global gathering or assembly in which the world is to unite under one universal religion which, according to him, was Islam.

Biblical View

Many Muslims accuse Christians of being divided. They claim that if Christianity were really a true religion then we would not have divisions. Many Sunni Muslims are unaware of the multitude of offshoots and breakaway groups in Islam.

As Christians, we must know how to explain the divisions in the Christian church and the difference between union and unity. Here is a quick illustration: One day a group of boys caught two cats. The boys tied the cat's tails together and hung them over a clothes line. The two cats had union, because they were tied together, but they did not have unity as they scratched and fought with each other.

The Bible always calls on Christians to have unity with one another. It does not require us to belong to the same organized church. Rather we are to have unity, because we each follow the Bible and seek to be led by the Holy Spirit as he leads us into understanding it.

Paul calls us to be like-minded, having the same mind as Christ: In Philippians 2:1-5 he writes:

> If you have any encouragement from being united with Christ, if any comfort from his love, if any fellowship with the Spirit, if any tenderness and compassion, then make my joy complete by being like-minded, having the same love, being one in spirit and purpose. Do nothing out of selfish ambition or vain conceit, but in humility consider others better than yourselves. Each of you should look not only to your own interests, but also to the interests of others. Your attitude should be the same as that of Christ Jesus. Who, being in very nature God, did not consider equality with God something to be grasped, but made himself nothing, taking the very nature of a servant, being made in human likeness. And being found in appearance as a man, he humbled himself and became obedient to death-- even death on a cross!

This is the kind of unity of mind that we are called to. Every Christian should be united in purpose, willing to die to self and serve Christ and others.

It appears that in the Philippian church there were two women who were at odds with each other. Paul appeals to them in chapter 4:1-2: *Therefore, my brothers, you whom I love and long for, my joy and crown, that is how you should stand firm in the Lord, dear friends! I plead with Euodia and I plead with Syntyche to agree with each other in the Lord.* The important emphasis here is to agree with one another in the Lord; not to compromise, but to seek the Lord, and strive to agree with one another as each seeks the Lord.

Over the years, as Christianity has spread from country to country, different groups of Christians have sprung up. Each of these groups is slightly different from the others, but true Christians are those who accept the Bible as the word of God and look to Christ for salvation. These groups may differ on some minor interpretations of the Bible, but they all agree on the major things and accept one another as fellow believers.

Paul urges us in Ephesians 4:1-6:

> As a prisoner for the Lord, then, I urge you to live a life worthy of the calling you have received. Be completely humble and gentle; be patient, bearing with one another in love. Make every effort to keep the unity of the Spirit through the bond of peace. There is one body and one Spirit-- just as you were called to one hope when you were called-- one Lord, one faith, one baptism; one God and Father of all, who is over all and through all and in all.

Questions for Reflection and Group Discussion

1. Is Christianity mystical like the Sufis believe? How would you answer a Sufi's claims of experiencing God through trances and physical trauma?
2. How would you deal with folk Islam that claims power over demons?

Chapter Fourteen
Muslim Objections

Muslims have many questions and objections when they interact with Christians. Learning how to anticipate their questions and answer their doubts is an important part of sharing the gospel with Muslims. In this lesson we will look at some of the common objections or questions that Muslims ask, and consider ways of answering them. Each question will be followed by one or more responses. This material has been adapted from the book *KEYS: Unlocking the Gospel for Muslims* by Colin Bearup, 2008 (available from http://stpt.ca). Used here with permission.

Q1. Is Jesus Christ the Son of God?

This is the most complicated question. Many Christians don't realise that to simply say 'Yes' is not sufficient or even good. Muslims consider this expression to be blasphemous. One mustn't lose sight of the goal: present them with the truth about Jesus and encourage them to search for the truth.

Here are several suggestions. There are many other possibilities.

Response 1:

The Lord Jesus has many titles, and each one is important. (Read 1:1) He is called the Son of Abraham and the Son of David. Often he calls himself the Son of Man (e.g. 8:19-20). Let's look together in this book (3:17 and 17:5). Here God is speaking. We can't argue with God. We must ask him to help us understand. Whether we understand it or not, the term 'Son' is used to show that once for all God has revealed himself through Jesus. (See 11:27). Do you know that we can know God personally?

Response 2:

My brother, you're not the first one to ask this question. (Read 26:63-64). Jesus is the Son of God, but he is also the Son of Man. If you want to understand, let's read together and think deeply about the text. But if you are only interested in discussing the meanings of words, I'm not interested in that.

Response 3:

Be careful. Don't listen to the rumours and lies that certain people pass on! (Read 1:18-23). Absolutely no Christian believes that God married Mary in order to produce Jesus. It is a false accusation. (Read 14:22-33). Why, in this passage, did they believe that Jesus is the Son of God? It's because of his works, not because of his birth. (3:17). God himself declares that Jesus is his Son, but that is not in a fleshly sense. To understand, read and ask God to show you the truth.

Response 4:

Let's read together (16:13-17). There were many opinions. Everyone was in agreement that Jesus was not an ordinary man. Simon Peter knew the truth because God had opened his heart. If God doesn't open your heart, you won't understand either. I commit myself to pray for you while you are reading the word of God.

Q2. The Trinity: Do you really believe that? Three gods? (And so on.)

The word Trinity isn't found in the Gospel of Matthew. The idea of the Trinity can be illustrated from the text, but it's not very useful for explaining or proving the Trinity. In general, it is better to say that to experience the Trinity, one needs salvation. It can't be explained to someone who doesn't have salvation.

Nevertheless, there are certain aspects of the question that can and must be raised.

Q2a Do we worship only one God, or do we worship three gods?
Response:

Let's read together (4:10). Every disciple of Jesus must worship God alone. Let's read here (6:9-13). Jesus teaches us to pray to God our Father and not to anyone else. Jesus came to give us the possibility of a new relationship with God, a relationship of a child with his father, not a slave with his master. What joy, what a privilege!

And look at this (22:34). Jesus teaches that God's first commandment is to love God, our Lord, with our whole being. There's no point in believing that there is only one God if we don't obey this commandment. My friend, you know that God is one, but can you do what he requires of you? We all fall short and need the mercy of God. Jesus came to teach us a new way.

Q2b. You worship three gods, don't you – Allah, Mary and Jesus?
Response:

May God Most High forgive you and purify your tongue and your thoughts! There's not a Christian in the world who would affirm such a thing! Who told you this? Let's read the word of God together (12:46-50). We see here that Jesus never even placed his mother above the disciples. And, look, he treats those who become his faithful disciples like members of his own family. The Lord Jesus treats his followers as family members. Isn't that something you would like if it were possible?

NB. Don't even try to explain the Trinity. It is much more useful to speak of Jesus as Saviour (1:21).

And consider this (20:28), Jesus did not set out to make people worship him. He came to save people from their sins and to reveal God to the humble (11:25-30). Wouldn't you like to ....

Q3. You Christians worship idols, don't you?
Response:

We follow the Lord Jesus who said this (read 4:10). We serve the invisible God. (Read 6:17-18). Come look in our church; there are no idols. Why should we pray to an idol or even a lucky charm which is incapable of doing anything good or bad, when God, the all powerful one, has become a compassionate Father for us? Let's read (10:29-31). God has shown his great love for us through Jesus Christ. We have no need for idols or even objects to give us luck or ward off evil. Actually, when I say 'we', I mean everyone. Read this book. You will find that Jesus came to offer the blessing of God to everyone.

Q4. Why do Christians say that Jesus died on the cross?

This is also another complicated question. Muslims are all sure that Jesus was neither crucified nor killed. There are three main reasons.

1. The Qur'an says so in a well-known verse (Surat al-Nisa, v156).
2. It is against the Muslim mind-set to think that God would allow his prophet to be so humiliated.
3. Muslims don't understand the value of his death as a sacrifice.

In addition, they think we are saying that Jesus is dead.

Response 1:

Like you, we believe that the Lord Jesus is alive and that He will come back to this world. With regards to His death, God sent an angel so that we couldn't be mistaken. (Read 28:5-7). Here we see that, according to the angel of God, Jesus was crucified and even buried, but that He came back to life.

We agree wholeheartedly that it is difficult to imagine that God would allow his prophet to suffer in this way. Even Jesus' disciples didn't understand it. (Read 16:21-23). Pay close attention to what Jesus himself said! And let's read these passages as well (17:22-23 and 20:17-19).

Response 2:

Jesus our Lord is alive and able to help us in all circumstances. The Jews thought they had won, but absolutely not. Let's read (26:2). Jesus knew everything that was going to happen to him. And here (26:24) it says that he must suffer, because God had planned it that way and had revealed it in the scriptures. Here (26:26-28): Jesus understands that, according to God's plan, he must submit himself to death and shed his blood so that our sins could be forgiven. He chose to accept the will of God. (Read 26:53-54).

Response 3:

Some people say that God put someone else in the place of Jesus, that a replacement of some kind suffered and died in his place. If your friend suggests such a thing, you can reply like this:

Let's read together, and you show me at which point the replacement arrives.

Read from 27:1 (or even earlier, if you want to) through to the end of chapter 28. From time to time ask your friend if he understands and if he is sure that it is still Jesus that is being talked about. If he starts to say that this isn't any longer Jesus, don't say anything, but keep going to be sure. At the death of Jesus certain events indicate that a very serious event took place, and then, of course, in chapter 28, there is the testimony of the angel, etc.

To conclude: God didn't provide a replacement who suffered in the place of Jesus. It is Jesus that God sent to suffer in our place. He didn't deserve the punishment, rather it is each one of us that is guilty before God (20:28).

Q5. Injil al-Masih (The Gospel of Christ) has replaced Tawrat Musa (The Books of Moses). In the same way that the Qur'an has replaced Injil al-Masih.

Response:

Let's read this passage (5:17-18). Here we see that the Lord Jesus neither replaces nor annuls nor rejects the ancient scriptures. Reading the Gospel, you will see that Jesus often quotes the ancient books, declaring that the scriptures must be fulfilled. That's why, in faith and humility, we Christians read the books of Moses as well as all the prophets of olden times. The books of Moses serve as the foundation, the books of the prophets are the walls and the Gospel is like the roof, finishing off the house. Enter the house and meet with the person who lives there – Jesus Christ.

Q6. The Bible has been changed/falsified. The true scriptures no longer exist.

Response:

That is an extremely serious charge. Where did you get that idea from? Do you realise that you are accusing believers of a huge evil? You may even be accusing God of incompetence and weakness. Isn't God capable of protecting his own word? Let's read together what the Lord Jesus tells us. (Read 5:17-18.) It declares that not one little part of God's word will disappear so long as the world exists, and that his own words will last forever (24:35). Please be careful, my brother. If you have the word of God and you don't put it into practice, you are on a dangerous path. (Read 7:24-27).

Q7. The Prophet Jesus predicted that Mohammed would come, didn't he?
Response:

I have never seen this. Read this book and show me any passages that talk about the coming of Mohammed.

Q8. Mohammed came after Jesus. Why don't you believe in Mohammed?

In responding to this question, don't criticise Mohammed. We want to turn their thoughts to the Lord Jesus, not talk about Mohammed.

Response:

Now let's see. Are you saying that each prophet had his own period of history? (They will say yes.) But here (28:20), it is written that the time of Jesus isn't yet finished. He is with us and will be until the very end. His period of history hasn't finished yet. And until now, no other prophet has offered to us what Jesus gives (9:1-8). It doesn't make sense for us to follow anyone else.

Q9 We believe in all the prophets, but you, you only believe in Jesus.
Response:

Not at all. We believe in the prophets of God (read 11:13). Even in this small book, one portion of the Gospel (Injil), the names of 15 prophets are referred to. In the complete Bible there are even more. All these prophets have something to tell us; that's what this parable means (read 13:52). And these prophets from long ago predicted many things that happened when Jesus came, and they encourage us to trust him. Read this book and see for yourself.

Q10. You Christians, don't you know that when Jesus comes again he will preach Islam?
Response:

Really? It seems smarter to us to listen to what the Lord Jesus himself says about his return than to listen to what someone else has to say. Let's read what he said (24:29). Think how dark it will be the day he arrives. (Now read 24:30-31). See, he will come back to gather together his own. Let's also read here (25:31-33). He will return to judge the world and not to preach one religion or another. The question is are we ready for the Judgment? (See also 16:27).

Q11. Moses for the Jews, Jesus (Isa) for the Christians, right?

Response:

Not at all. Jesus himself wasn't sent to the Christians or to the West. God sent him to the Jews. (Read 15:24). In other words God sent him to people who already had a religion given by God. Then, at the right time, he sent his apostles to all the peoples in the world. (Read 28:18-20). First he sent them to those who believed in God but then on to those who didn't believe in God. He declared that his message, the good news, would be proclaimed everywhere before the end of the world. (Read 24:14). Today, this task is almost finished. No matter which nationality or ethnic group you are from, the message is for you.

Q12. Do Christians pray?

Every day Muslims are seen praying in public. Sunday is the only time Christians are seen praying. Many Muslims believe that Christians only pray one time a week.

Response:

Let's read the words of the Lord Jesus. (Read 6:5-8). He teaches us to pray in a secret place where no one sees us. We pray often, whether you see it or not. We pray with the assurance that God is listening to us. We don't need to keep making repetitions. He loves us. Jesus came in order to give us a new relationship with God. Our relationship is no longer like that of a slave coming before his master, but like beloved children coming to their father.

I don't want to give you the impression that this is some kind of exclusive privilege – it is available to you too. You say you believe in Jesus, well then, read his word and let him teach you.

Q13. Do Christians fast?

Response:

Let's read the word of the Lord Jesus. (6:16-18). He teaches us to fast in secret so that those around us won't even know. God sees us, and that's enough. It's the same thing as with prayer. Our religious practices are different from yours because Jesus came to give us a new relationship with God. (From this point on, use the Q12 material.)

Q14. Does the New Testament (Injil) teach an eye for an eye and stoning for adultery?

Many Muslims are interested in questions of law. One story that some Muslims are aware of says that the Jews wanted to hide the biblical texts that prescribe severe punishments.

Response:

People in this world are very interested in how to go about punishing other people. But Jesus teaches us to make it our aim to be righteous and to live with pure hearts. It is ourselves that we need to judge. (Examples: 5:38, 5:21-22, 5:27-28) These aren't new laws. Jesus explains the true nature of sin, the reason that the Great Judgment awaits us all. We are all guilty before God, but he sent us a Saviour. (Read 1:21 and 20:28). Laws might punish sinners if they get caught, but what we all need is mercy that transforms us and makes us better.

Q15. Questions about marriage: Why do Christian men only take one wife? What do you think about divorce? Can a man marry his cousin? (And so on.)

This type of question is of interest to Muslims because, in their way of thinking, life is divided into what is permitted and what is forbidden.

Read with me (19:1-11). Every time that someone asked Jesus a question about marriage, he quoted what God had done and what he said at the beginning. It is true that God has allowed certain things at certain times, but Jesus throws out a challenge. Do you want what is permissible or what is best in the eyes of God? You have to ask God: 'What is your will for me?' instead of saying 'This is what I want, is it permitted?' This passage (Read 22:37) teaches us that we have to put God before our own plans and projects. Is that how you are leading your life? Do you have need for forgiveness? It is Jesus that helps us.

Q16. For you, it's all right; you are Christian. But my family will not allow me to follow Jesus.

Response:

It has always been like that. Whoever wants to follow the truth with his whole heart will encounter opposition, even within his own family. Let's read together (10:26-39). You have to think about what is eternal, not just about earthly things. The Lord will strengthen you. Believe his word.

Q17. Why do Christians drink alcohol?

Good Muslims do not drink alcohol because it is forbidden. Whether you personally drink alcohol is not important here. They know that some Christians drink alcohol.

Response:

Alcohol causes a lot of problems and pain in this world. In places where it is banned, criminal gangs grow powerful by trafficking it. Alcohol on its own does nothing. The problem is in people, both the evil that alcohol lets loose and the weakness people have to meet temptation. The Lord Jesus did not come to make laws that we impose on people. He called each follower to be responsible for his own actions. Read this (18:7-9). Whatever causes us to sin we must reject utterly. The people who go out and get drunk are not people following Christ.

The Lord Jesus did not come to remind us of what is sinful, but to enable us to live differently. Look at what the prophet John the Baptist (Yahya) says here: (3:11). John called people to turn away from wrong doing, but he announced that the Lord Jesus would give people the Holy Spirit, that is the power of God in their hearts to live new lives. He brings forgiveness for the past and power to live as we should.

Q18. Why do Christians eat pork?

Muslims do not eat pork because they are taught it is unclean. The rejection of pork has a strong emotional dimension. It is not just a matter of religious requirement.

Response:

People who want to please God have always been concerned with what is clean and what is unclean. In our hearts we know that we need to be clean to approach Almighty God. The Lord Jesus showed us a truth that surprised many people at the time and still does today: (15:10-11).

What do you think he meant? (They will probably get this wrong!) That is what many thought he meant, but he explained here (15:17-18). The sinfulness of our hearts is much more unclean than any food or substance. As it says elsewhere in the scriptures, all food is clean if received by believers with thanksgiving and prayer. Our real need is to purify our hearts. God sent the Lord Jesus as the one through whom people become clean and this is demonstrated by the miracles that he did. For example: (8:2-3, 9:20-21). People who had conditions that made them unclean were made clean through faith in Christ. These miracles are signs for us, not just events that happened.

Q19. Why do Christians support Israel?

Most Muslims are not accustomed to making the sharp distinction between religion and politics that westerners make. For them, religion and politics are pretty much the same thing. For Muslims, the state of Israel is a quasi-criminal state imposed by foreigners in Muslim territory, a perfectly logical position from their point of view. Christians hold a variety of views on Israel, but here we are not supporting one view or another but rather looking at how we move from the question to gospel presentation.

Response:

God is great. Nothing happens in this world without his knowledge or permission. And everything that people do will be judged. Jesus spoke of the judgement of Israel(19:28). It is easy to see the sins of other people and feel righteous because they seem so bad. But we must remember that all of us face judgement. Consider this (12:36-37). It is not just the big sinners who are in trouble, it is everyone. But Jesus did not just come to warn us of God's judgement on all sinners, he came to save us (1:21). OK, you believe in Jesus as a prophet, but have you received all he came to bring?

Q20. Why are the Christians waging war on Muslims?

This is not the sort of question you try and answer standing nose to nose on the street. The question is provoked by actions not words and so our actions need to speak before our words do. So the first thing to do is to say you are happy to talk, but you need to find somewhere suitable. Either buy or make your friend a cup of tea. Be friends.

Response:

My friend, please be patient because I want to give you a good answer.

Please do not be taken in by the idea that the West is Christian. Even if Western leaders use religious words to justify their actions, they are not following the Lord Jesus. Let's look at what Jesus himself said: (26:51-54).

The Lord Jesus did not permit his followers to use weapons, not even to defend him. (Leave the 'fulfilment of the scriptures' hanging unless he asks). No true Christian takes up lethal weapons to fight for Christ, although they might to serve their country.

You and I are not enemies, are we? And even if we were, the Lord Jesus said something really amazing (5:43-48). People are always finding reasons to be angry with each other and to hate each other. The only way to break the cycle is to love your enemies. There is nothing special about loving your own people. You do not need faith to do that! Now, imagine how the world would be if everyone put the teaching of Jesus into practice? Wouldn't you agree that this is a better way?

Of course, not everyone will accept this teaching and Jesus told us that wars would continue up to the end of the world (24:6-8).

There will be hard times for everyone. Let's read on (24:9-14). Do you see what this means? The end of the world is delayed until the good news of Jesus is preached everywhere. This is not speaking about the crazy wars people are fighting. It is speaking about you and me sitting here looking at the words of Jesus together. Are you ready for his return? Check it out. Read the Gospel for yourself.

The material in this chapter was published previously in the book KEYS, Unlocking the Gospel for Muslims by Colin Bearup, 2008.
(Available in ebook format from http://stpt.ca) Used here with permission. This book is a practical teach-yourself guide to opening up the Gospel for Muslims and is recommended as a practical next step for those wanting to share their faith with their Muslim friends.

Understanding Islam
(Through Daily Life)

Chapter Fifteen
Modern Jahiliya

Islam teaches that there is only one way in Islam: the way of Allah as revealed to Muhammad. Islam believes that man has ills that cannot be solved except by the keys which Allah has provided through Islam. This is done by submitting to Allah's will and doing the things that Allah commanded, both religious duties and living a good life according to the directions set out in Islam.

When Muslims consider society, they think in terms of two basic divisions: there is Islam and there is something they call *jahiliya* or ignorance. In the Muslim mind, the world before the prophet Muhammad was governed by *jahiliya*. Chaos reigned and everyone lived for themselves and their own pleasure. This is because man was not guided. In Islam, animals are better off than man, because they are bound by their nature and cannot break out of it. Man on the other hand has a choice to either obey Allah or live in *jahiliya*. Through Islam Muslims believe Allah can purify mankind, man's heart, his emotions, his thoughts, Muslim homes, Muslim lives, and most importantly Muslim communities. Islam is all about setting up communities of Islam on earth; for it is only in the Islamic community that Islam can really transform lives.

The concept of jahiliya is very important because all of Islam is a reaction to what came before it. For example, Muslims believe that before Islam there were four kinds of marriage. Aisha, Muhammad's child bride describes them as:

• The ordinary kind where a man was engaged to a woman, he paid a dowry and then he married her.

• The a practice where a man would order his wife to lie with another man until she was pregnant. He would not touch her until it was obvious she was pregnant. Then he would lie with her. This was called *istabdha'* or "trading." It was considered a noble act, and often used when a man could not father his own children.

• A third kind of marriage, according to Aisha, was when a group of men had intercourse with a woman. When she gave birth she would summon the whole group and point out the man who was supposed to be the father. The child would then take on the name of this man. In this case the man could not deny that this was his child and had to support the child.

• A fourth kind of marriage was connected with prostitutes who would allow any man into their house.

Muslims believe that in the period of jahiliya before Muhammad, a woman had no rights, no inheritance and if her husband died or divorced her, she could not marry another. The woman was herself inherited as property. If her husband died, her husband's father or her own eldest son had rights over her and could keep her, demanding she ransom herself. Whoever inherited her could marry her or marry her to someone else.

In the time of jahiliya there was also a practice of burying female infants alive. Some females were killed this way because they were deformed, blue at birth, or dark skinned, were leprous, or lame. These were all considered bad omens. Sometimes babies, even males were killed if the baby was deformed or if the family could not afford to raise him or her.

> *Whenever the news of a female child is announced to any one of them, his face darkens and he chokes with inward gloom. He hides himself from his people because of the bad news he has heard, asking himself whether he should retain her with disgrace or bury her in the dust. Beware! Evil is the judgment they make about Allah.* Sura 16:58

The other option was to let the girl live until she was old enough to look after camels. She would then be sold like an animal, forced into marriage (and probably prostitution), or dressed in a cloak of wool and be sent into the desert to take care of camels. This work usually meant being away from home for weeks or even months on end, with no education and no chance at marriage because she was considered simple, and usually unavailable. Even today the work of being a shepherd is considered the lowest work on the Bedouin social scale.

Many Muslim teachers believe that we are entering into another time of Jahiliya. In our modern world (or modern Jahiliya) women must work in factories and are often abandoned by their fathers and raised by single mothers. Slavery was common until 100 years ago, and today businesses take advantage of workers and exploit them. These modern Muslim teachers tell us that Islam came to change all of this. Islam, and especially Islamic community is the answer to modern Jahiliya.

While the western world is promoting equality between women and men, Islamic clerics are protesting. This is not Allah's will. According to Islam, women are to be wives and mothers. They are created and designed for this. Islam protects women and honors them in these roles. In Islam, women are to remain at home and look after the family and men are to go out and work. Islam believes that it is bringing freedom to women today - freedom to be the women that God created them to be - and at the same time protecting them from exploitation by the modern world. One example to which numerous Islamic teachers refer is that in the west women lose their last names at marriage. This is not so in Islam. They believe that in the west women lose their rights, especially during a divorce. The woman usually loses and the man wins.

The focus of Islam is on the family unit, which is well defined and protected. Men have obligations to their wives. They must protect their wives and provide for their wives and children. In the midst of moral breakdown all over the world, the Muslim family survives and is held up by Muslims as one of the great successes of Islam.

Foundation blocks for Muslim marriage
- First, Muslims are forbidden to marry non-Muslims.
  "Wed not idolatresses till they believe for a believing bondwoman is better than an idolatress though she please you. And give not your daughters in marriage to idolaters till they believe, for a believing slave is better than an idolater though he please you." Sura 2:221

In Islam there are only two kinds of people: those who submit to Allah, and those who are going to hell-fire. How can there be union between these two? How can there be union between those who live in Jahiliya or ignorance and those who have come into the light of Islam? It is simply not allowed.

- The second foundation stone of Muslim marriages is that a dowry must be paid. They believe this gives women value. Men cannot just convince women to join them; they must act honorably and produce a dowry, some to be paid to her parents, and some to the woman herself. The woman then keeps the dowry all her life. She cannot lose it unless she herself chooses to get rid of it.

• The third foundation established by Muhammad was that women could be captured in battle, but even captured women and other women of low status were to have a dowry paid to them, thus giving them status even in their low estate.

• Fourth, the Islamic religion organizes the family and the entire community. It has clear commands about not marrying relatives. Nine kinds of marriages are forbidden. This makes it clear what is forbidden or permitted. These are always based on Allah's commands in the Qur'an.

• Fifth, a Muslim bride and groom must see each other before the wedding. They must be allowed to see each other's face and hands to make sure that the other person is healthy. They must reveal any sickness before entering into marriage with someone else.

• Sixth, in Islam, marriage should be based on mutual consent. The woman should be able to say yes or no. No woman should be forced into marriage without her consent.

• Seventh, Islam is a religion of the family, and the couple must relate to their families. Their own home is protected, and they can develop it as they wish within the bounds of Islam. The home is one of the fortresses of Islam. The strength of Islam is in the home. Islam does not rest on the man or on an individual, but on the home the family creates.

• Last, the Qur'an talks of building a community on earth. Islam is not about individuals; it is about communities. The family is the fundamental cell or building block of the community, and the entire community should be Islamic so that society can function in an Islamic way.

The Dowry

As noted earlier, Islam focuses on the state of things as they were in jahiliya and improves on them. It thus provides a set of laws concerning the payment of a dowry and emphasizes how this protects the bride. Muslims believe that in jahiliya the woman had to pay for the man, but Islam made this better by reversing it so now the men have to pay for the women. Many Muslims believe that once the dowry is paid the couple can enter into a physical relationship. The paying of a dowry helps regulate that a poor man cannot marry a rich woman. If he is not capable of paying the dowry price for her, he is not capable of supporting her at the level she or her family expects.

Married Life

Islam has much to say about marriage. In Sura 4:34 men are in charge of the women, because Allah made the man to excel more than the woman, and because men spend from their money to support the women. Good women are seen as being obedient, guarding the sanctity of the home.

In Islam men and woman are considered equal, and they believe that God honors the man and the woman the same in their rights, possessions, inheritance, rewards, independence and freedom. But the man is the guardian of the family. He is the arbiter in the family. Since he is the primary provider, he is the primary overseer. It is interesting to note that Muhammad did not teach this until his first wife died. This was because his wife provided him with money and a means of living. However, once she died, he inherited her riches and was independently wealthy.

Islamic Laws Regarding Intimacy

Islam has much to say about intimacy. The relationship between a man and his wife is linked directly to God - to his anger and his pleasure and to the giving of punishment and rewards. So Islam lays down rules for intimacy between men and women. As an example, Islam forbids sexual intercourse during a woman's menstrual period in Sura 2:222.

Several hundred years after Muhammad, Islamic teaching started to circulate that sex could be a focal point of a man's life. The sexual act was seen as providing a connection to God. So much emphasis was put on sexual pleasure that schools for singing began to also educate women in performing acts of pleasure for men. The women from these schools were purchased by wealthy men throughout Arabia and were very popular for several centuries. (Caswell, Fuad Matthew, *The Slave Girls of Baghdad: the Qiyan and the Early Abbasid Er*a, MacMillan, 2011)

208

Modern Jahiliya

Islam believes that modern society strips people of God's adornment of righteousness and respect, and then calls this new society "civilization" and "renewal" and labels pure people as "old fashioned." Today clothing stores, cosmetics businesses and the fashion industry are the masters which control people, whether it is a new style of clothing (whether suitable or not) or new beauty helps (whether helpful or not). Other master in today's society are the people behind films, magazines, pornography, and newspapers.

Many Muslims believe that the Jews are the people behind modern jahiliya. They believe that Jewish people own the clothing, entertainment and news businesses and thus influence all circles of power. They believe that the pursuit of sex in modern jahiliya is a product of Jewish Zionism which encourages this so widely that the Jews won't be accused as being the only people who have been stripped of all values and morals except materialism. Muslims believe that Jews want all people to bow to the coming king of Zion. Thus they believe that Jews are behind movements of Darwinism, Freudism, Marxism, and even Socialism in an effort to destroy the world and allow Zionism to conquer.

As the Muslim considers modern jahiliya, he sees thousands of people die each year of syphilis and AIDS. The family unit is in crisis and a normal family is almost unknown today. Single parent families are on the rise. Prostitution is expanding. Unwed mothers are common. Free love, swingers and nudism are on the rise. Pornography is pervasive. Drugs and alcohol are ubiquitous. Literature and films have degenerated into pornography. Homosexuality is rampant. Homeless people wander the streets. To the Muslim, this is modern jahiliya. Islam has come to set all this straight. It is Allah's wish to conform society as a whole. If everyone were to submit to Islam, all of these evils would disappear.

For instance, consider the wearing of veils. Sura 33:59 says: *"Oh prophet, tell your wives and your daughters and the women of believers to let down upon them their over-garments. This is more proper, so that they may be known, and not be given trouble."* The wearing of veils would discourage men who might have depraved desires in seeing and lusting after women. The veil covers women because men have a problem, not because women have a problem.

For the Muslim, the home is sacred. Islam speaks much of the sanctity of the home and keeping the things that happen in the home in the home. There are many rules and regulations in Islam. It even instructs when those inside the home can uncover their private parts for sex.

Islam aims at cleansing society as a whole and controlling sexual desires. Even glances and staring are to be controlled. Sura 24:30 says, "*Tell the believing men to lower their gaze and be modest. That is purer for them. Lo! Allah is aware of what they do.)*" Islam is seen as the best way for purifying society.

It is obvious from the Qur'an that Muslim regulations aim at purifying society. Islam did not wait until it became a community at Medina for this to start. Muhammad gave instructions in Mecca before the move to Medina, such as Sura 17:32, "*And do not commit adultery. Lo! It is an abomination and an evil way.*" In Medina however, Islam moved from being a group of individual followers of Islam to a community that had rules and structure. In Mecca the followers of Muhammad had no authority and could not punish offenders, but in Medina they began exercising punishment for infractions. Islam does not see itself as "law" as many suppose, but it endeavors to rescue people from jahiliya by helping them govern themselves and protect them from each other. Muslims today believe that there is no true control in society except for the teachings of Islam. It is Islam that teaches people to honor one another and honor authority. This is the greatness of Islam. Islam does punish, but it does so in the name of God, not in the name of a person or group. It is not people's authority, it is God's authority. In Islam God desires to rid community of obstacles to good.

Islam recognizes the sexual urge as legitimate and so has laws to help man satisfy these urges in legal ways, by various forms of marriage. Islam encourages early marriages so that man's desires are catered to in a legal setting.

In the Muslim mind modern jahiliya discourages marriage and makes crime more likely. When Islam governs, these factors shouldn't exist; there should be no poverty, and the criminal should have no excuse for his crime. In Islam criminals are punished. Muslims believe that there is no other system like Islam in all the world. Outsiders see Islam as all blood and punishment, but Muslims believe that Islam curbs crime in Islamic countries. Muslims believe that western countries fear this, because they are all guilty of wanting to revel in lust and greed.

Muslim theologians teach that Islam doesn't punish randomly, but always punishes with regard to the situation. This gives it a unique position among all the systems of man. Islam decrees that the adulterer should be stoned, but only if there are four witnesses. Crime will not be wiped out, but the percentage should drop greatly. Then there are stages of punishment:

> *"As for those women who are guilty of lewdness, call four witnesses against them and then confine them to their houses until death takes them or until Allah appoint for them a way through new legislation. And if two are guilty punish them both. And if they repent and improve, then let them be. Lo! Allah is Relenting and Merciful."* Sura 4:15

Non-Muslim men cannot witness against a Muslim woman, because they are not under Islamic law, are not considered trustworthy in the matter of dignity, and are not trusted in honesty and piety.

Flogging is for people who are not married, while stoning is for those who are married and fornicate. But this is a subject for long, detailed Islamic debate.

Islam recognizes that man has little power over his sex drive, and so it teaches that it is not good to repress it or kill it; so Islam does not try to stop the natural instincts God put there. Islam however fights against animal instincts that will ruin man by introducing a system of external control.

Islam teaches that sin is always individual and repentance is individual. There is no such thing as inherited sin, as in Christianity, and there is nothing of propitiation as taught in Christianity. Muslims do not believe that Jesus died for the sins of men. In Islam Adam's sin was only Adam's sin. Adam was saved by immediate repentance - simple and easy. God is the forgiving, merciful God will not punish another for the sins of a guilty person. In Islam God only punishes the guilty.

In Islam there is an emphasis on how much God desires to honor and purify people. Muslims believe that in Islam God exalts women and wants to preserve their nobility and honor and that no woman can really appreciate this unless she has love for Allah and his religion. They believe that one of the ways Islam honors women is that, unlike Christianity which opposes divorce, Islam provides a complete sura that deals with all aspects of divorce. This illustrates that Islam is superior and that it came from God not people. Just the presence of the Sura on divorce proves this to Muslims. The Sura begins with the importance of the family in the Islamic system. Those who study the legislation in the Qur'an realize how important the family unit is in Islam

211

and the respect it has for women. The sura on divorce emphasizes how God combines piety and respect for women: *"Be careful to your duty towards Allah… and of the wombs that bare you."*

Polygamy

Sura 4:3 in the Qur'an says

> *"And if you fear that you cannot do justice to orphans, marry such women as seem good to you, two, or three, or four; but if you fear that you will not do justice, then marry only one or that which your right hand possess. This is more proper that you may not do injustice."*

Most Muslims understand that this means up to four wives, although not all Muslims agree that the Qur'an limits Muslim men to four wives.

Muslim theologians tell us that divorce and polygamy are practiced in Islam because Islam meets mankind where he is and lifts him up to great heights, without denying his nature. Man's nature is not seen as 'fallen' but rather as God created, and therefore his nature is catered to in Islam rather than denied.

Muslims also argue that often women outnumber men. Many men die in battle or on long trips or from hard work, so the only honorable thing to do is to marry more than one woman. Otherwise many women will be unmarried, and thus unfulfilled in their natures, or they will be forced into prostitution.

Muslim theologians also argue that a man's fertility goes on until he is in his 70's, while the woman stops in her 50's. So, if the man wants more children, he must either take another wife or divorce his present wife. Polygamy is better than divorce.

Another reason given by Muslim theologians is that men should have access to more than one woman, so they will not be tempted to visit prostitutes when their wife is not available or not willing. This protects society and makes it a better place.

As for women taken in war, Islam sees polygamy as a way of giving them dignity. Women are not meant to be slaves and abused. If their captors take them as wives, they have rights and dignity.

Thus, Muslims believe that when God desired to lift man out of jahiliya he gave him the system of Islam complete with polygamy. Sura 4:26 says *"Allah would explain to you and guide you by the examples of those who were before you, and would turn to you in mercy. For Allah is all knowing and wise."*

In this way, Islam endeavors to shape society. Islam is not simply a religion for individuals; it is a way of life for all people. The power of Islam is demonstrated in its ability to structure society. This began in Medina, not Mecca, and today Muslims yearn to change society all over the world and want to assist Islam in overcoming the systems of the world that lead to jahiliya and replace these systems with Islamic government.

Biblical View

The Old Testament gave laws and regulations to the children of Israel so that they could manage the nation of Israel. Once they were carried off into captivity, however, many of these laws no longer applied, as the temple was destroyed and all forms of Jewish government disappeared. Even in New Testament times, the land of Israel was under the control of the Roman Empire.

In the New Testament, John the Baptist announced the arrival of the kingdom of God. Jesus then began preaching about this new kingdom. It was not a physical kingdom but rather a heavenly kingdom. As a result, the New Testament is filled with teaching encouraging the followers of Jesus to consider this world as only a place they are passing through. Christians are to be pilgrims and sojourners in this world. We are not to look for an earthly kingdom, but rather a heavenly one. As a result, the Bible does not seem to speak clearly about how Christians should form governments and what kinds of laws Christians should put in place to guide society. The purpose of Christianity is to change individuals, and then those individuals will change society. Christianity is not about bringing a religious system that will control society from the outside, but rather bringing change from the inside, individual by individual. In the eyes of Islam, Christianity looks weak. Islam provides rules and regulations for setting up society. Christianity does not.

As a result, Muslims have always longed for true Muslim government. However all down through history politicians, not clerics ruled the Muslim world. Sultans, kings and emperors rose. They used Islam for their own means to gain power. This changed however, when Ayatollah Khomeini took control of Iran. The ruler before Khomeini, the Shah of Iran, sided with the west, and opened his country for western development but he was not prepared for non-Islamic culture. As soon as his country was open, business people began to market their goods. Alcoholic drinks and drugs became widely available. Pornography was made available. There were few laws to control or eliminate these things, as they were unknown before. Very quickly people succumbed to the evils of outside society. At this point the religious Ayatollahs rose up with Khomeini as their leader. They overthrew the Shah of Iran and declared the first truly Islamic government in recent history. Muslim clerics now ran the court system. All the judges, all the members of the parliament, and everyone in any position of power was to be a Muslim cleric. Knowledge of the Qura'n was required. Muslims all over the world were excited. Finally a Muslim country existed. They expected that soon it would be paradise on earth. Within a few short years they were disappointed to discover that Islam had not brought in paradise.

Shortly after this, the people of Afghanistan were invaded by Russia. The mullahs declared a holy war, and warriors poured in from across the Muslim world. Together the Afghans and the Muslim fighters fought back, and as they pushed out the Russians the Muslim clerics took control of Afghanistan. In this case they were known as the Taliban. Things did not improve, however, they got worse. All over the world, Muslims voiced their concern. Here was the opportunity for Islam to really shine. Islam had the opportunity to transform these countries into paradise. Instead, Muslims around the world accused Iran and Afghanistan of abusing their power and not really following Islam. How else could they explain Islam's failure to turn these countries into paradise?

Silently, Muslims in Iran began to question, and then to seek other answers. In the last few years thousands of Muslims in Iran have turned to Christ. Many others have simply become nominal Muslims not wanting to cause trouble for themselves.

Questions for Reflection and Group Discussion

1. Read Galatians 5:19-24. Look at the list of sins in verses 19-21. From what you know of Islam, what sins do you think that Muslims strive to overcome and what sins easily overcome them? What sins have Muslims disguised and made acceptable?

2. Compare the Muslim idea of setting up a religious community or system on earth to control sin, and what the Bible says in John 18:36: *Jesus said, "My kingdom is not of this world. If it were, my servants would fight to prevent my arrest by the Jews. But now my kingdom is from another place."*

3. How would you explain to a Muslim that there are no Christian countries in the world when you know that Muslims consider all countries as either Christian, Buddhist, Muslim or atheist?

4. How would you explain the kingdom of God to Muslim? What verses would you use?

Chapter Sixteen
The Muslim Family

Daily Life in a Muslim Family

Most Muslims pray at least once a day. Often this happens in the evening. Muslim children are taught how to pray, so that they can go through the exact motions and utter the exact words that Islam requires. Some families gather together to pray, but usually prayer is left to individuals until the family gathers in the afternoon or evening to eat. This is the most common time for Muslim families to pray. Often women will pray in one room while men line up and pray in another. Children are often taught to recite verses from the Qur'an as a normal part of daily living, and often when visitors come the children are encouraged to stand before the guests and recite from the Qur'an.

Most good Muslim men try and visit the mosque to pray on Fridays. In Islam there are small local mosques and then there are more prominent mosques. Most mosques are simply places to pray. Muslims do not become members of the mosque, although there is usually a group of recognized elders who control what happens in the mosque.

The month of Ramadan is loved by many Muslims. Although they must fast during the day, families gather together in the evenings to eat. Thus, the entire month is focused on gatherings of families and friends. Added to this, there is a sense of unity with Muslims all over the world, as Muslims fast together and meet each evening for prayer. This sense of unity is very powerful and very meaningful to many Muslims.

Around the 27th night in the month of Ramadan is what is known as the Night of Power. Islam teaches that on this night the Qur'an was brought down from the highest to the lowest heaven. (Sura 2:185).

We have indeed revealed this message in the night of power: And what will explain to you what the night of power is? The night of power is better than a thousand months. In that month come down the angels and the spirit by Allah's permission on every errand: Peace!... This until the rise of morn. (Sura 97:1-5)

According to this sura, Muslims understand that the angel Gabriel revealed the first part of the Qur'an to Muhammad on this night. Many Muslims believe that this Sura teaches that if they pray to God on this night and ask with a pure heart, God will grant whatever they ask.

Another common Muslim practice is saying the name of God as often as possible. This is the direct opposite of what the Jews believed. Jewish people would refrain from uttering God's name as it was too holy. Christians are also told never to use his name in a vain or vulgar way. Muslims, however, are encouraged to use God's name all the time. They believe that the more they use his name the more blessing they will receive. Therefore, the name of Allah is used in everything.

If you ask, "How are you?" They answer, "Praise be to Allah" which indicates, "I am fine." Muslims seldom say, "I wish…" They usually say "If Allah wills." Muslims seldom say thank you, they often say, "May Allah bless you." In this way, Allah's name is used over and over in their everyday speech.

Organization of the Muslim Family

From the outside, most Muslim families look like conservative Christian families. They usually comprise of a husband and wife and several children. The husband goes to work, and the women stay at home and raise the children. Everything seems to appear as good and normal.

Several differences exist, however, between a normal Muslim household and a Christian household. First, in a Muslim household the husband is the ruler. He has total control of the house, and everything in the house revolves around him and his wants. A good wife will be waiting for him when he returns home from work. She will greet him warmly, have comfortable clothing ready for him to slip into, and then she will serve him and the family a warm meal. She sees her role in life as being available to please her husband. The home, the family, and especially the marriage bed are all there for his pleasure and to bestow honor on the husband. The woman's security is in knowing that she pleases her husband and he is happy with her. It is to this end that she works hard every day, cleaning, cooking and raising the children. The state of their home and the appearance and conduct of the children all bestow great honor on the husband. He is the focus of the home. In many ways, he is the Sultan of his house, just as God is the great Sultan, and everything that happens in the universe is for God's pleasure.

Once a Muslim man decides to take a second wife, he is faced with a dilemma. Should he take his new wife into his old home, or should he establish two homes? Often his choice is strongly influenced by what other Muslim men are doing in his community. In more modern Muslim countries, Muslim men often establish a second home. In this case they may own or rent two apartments and establish a family in both places. Thus his children may grow up with little contact with their step-siblings. This arrangement provides less stress between the two women and the young children, but often older teenagers feel slighted or upset by the father who is only present half of the time, and sometimes there is rivalry between the groups of children.

In some rural Muslim settings, such as the mountains of Yemen, family life is structured much differently than in other countries. In Yemeni villages extended families all live in one house. The father, grandfather and married sons might all live in the same house. In this case the men occupy a three or four storey building or tower, and the women, children and animals occupy the lower, single storey buildings around the tower.

In the tower, the men all sleep in a common room on the top floor. This room is also the sitting room during the day. The first floor has the same use as the single storey buildings, housing women, children and livestock. The bedrooms on the middle floor are only used when a husband sends a message to the women's section of the house (known as the harem) that he would like to visit a certain one of his wives in one of the bedrooms. She then leaves her work and goes to her husband.

In this case, men and women live very separate lives. In some villages men and women have developed different dialects because they never talk to each other, except for the occasional visit in the bedrooms. Young men move from the harem into the men's quarters when they reach puberty or before. At this point, some Muslim boys are circumcised to demonstrate that they are now becoming men. In Yemen the boys are circumcised and given a large knife that they wear all the time, and move into the men's section of the house where they begin to receive instruction on how to act honorably and how to fight to defend the family or tribal unit.

Divorce

In Jahiliya, men could easily divorce their wives. The prophet Muhammad was questioned about this in Sura 33 when a woman complained that the prophet had taken no action against her husband who had divorced her in the pagan way. Muhammad announced that God's penalty for the man was: no intercourse for a limited period of time, free a slave, or fast two consecutive months, or feed 6 poor people for a period of time. After this was completed then normal married life could resume.

Divorce is allowed in Islam. Sura 2:222 tells us that if the husband swears that he and his wife did not have intercourse for four months he may divorce her. Then the Qur'an adds, if they change their mind, Allah is forgiving. If they decide upon divorce, then Allah accepts. In Islamic armies men were not to be away from their wives for more than four months, because it was a threat to their marriages.

The basis of the family is that both the husband and the wife have submitted to Allah. They both agree to follow the rules Allah lays down. Their marriage is based on mutual submission.

Marriage is called *ihsan'* or *making chaste, fortifying,* or *maintenance.* It is not pleasing to God for a man to remain without *ihsan* even for a short time.

Islam addresses Muslim men. They are to be patient with their wives, even when they feel resentment. Sura 4:19 says *"But consort with them in kindness, for if you hate them it may happen that you hate a thing wherein Allah has placed much good."* Divorce is not an immediate option according to Sura 4:35: *"And if you fear a breach between the two, appoint an arbiter from his people and an arbiter from her people. If they desire amendment Allah will make them of one mind."* However, according to Sura 4:128 *"If a woman fears ill-treatment from her husband or desertion, it is no sin for them both if they make terms of peace between themselves. Peace is better. But greed has been made present in the minds of men."*

219

After being divorced a woman must wait three months (or menstrual periods) before she can remarry. This is to determine if she is pregnant. Islam also teaches that if a woman's husband dies, she must be in mourning for four months. (Again to determine if she is pregnant or not.) Then she can remarry.

Jealousy

A young missionary once noticed that whenever he purchased something at a store, the storekeeper would stop him and insist that he put the items in a bag before leaving the store. The young missionary did not want to use a plastic bag if it wasn't necessary, because he didn't want to create extra garbage. He preferred just to carry his goods home, but the storekeeper insisted. While this might not matter to most of us, what was actually happening was that the storekeeper was helping the missionary with two Muslim traditions.

First, the storekeeper knows that if the customer has an item in his hands and he meets someone on the way, courtesy demands that he offers the item to that person. They may be courteous and refuse profusely, but perhaps they might accept and take his purchase. If the things are in a bag, it is hidden from view, and his chances of getting his goods home without giving them away are much better.

Second and more sinister is the idea of *hasad*. Many Muslims believe that there are evil jinn or spirits who desire to wreck anything good or beautiful. These are spirits of jealousy or *hasad*. Muslims are always invoking the name of God and speaking blessing whenever they see anything nice, such as a new car or a new child or a child's new toy. It is thought that if you see something and recognize it as nice or beautiful and do not invoke the name of God you have left the door open for an evil spirit to damage or harm that person or object.

Doubly dangerous is when a person with *hasad* in their heart envies someone or is jealous of something and they cooperate with an evil spirit to wish harm on that person or the object of their jealousy. The results can be devastating. People can become sick or cars can be destroyed in accidents. This level of interaction with unseen forces is common in many Muslim communities. Curses are frequently placed on persons, so people wear Muslim clothing or *hijab* to protect themselves, and they put new purchases in bags when they leave the store just to reduce the risk.

The Bible clearly tells us in Galatians 5:20 that jealousy is part of the sinful nature of all mankind. In fact, the first murder recorded in human history was when Cain became jealous of Abel his brother and killed him.

One time a group of Christians tried to help a Muslim widow woman in a small village. They did not realize how *hasad* would affect the widow lady. When they saw the widow lady's great need, they arranged with the son of the Mullah in the mosque to get permission for the lady to live in an abandoned school building in the village. The missionaries then helped with repairs, fixing windows, toilets, electricity, getting her a small fridge and setting up some simple heaters for her in the winter. However, a grudge of envy (because she was getting housing for free) affected some of the men in the village and they took action and asked the authorities to give her an eviction notice.

Hasad is the particular curse where if a person sees someone else get a break or blessing that they did not receive, they will wreck the blessing for the other person just because of envy. The curse of 'hasad' has ruined many efforts of well-meaning Christians. It has sometimes even stopped governments from providing some services and has complicated many attempts to provide assistance to the poorest people.

It is always amazing that a people who are so rich in the tradition of hospitality and having blessed others with it so many times could be so enslaved to the curse of *hasad*. Grace and mercy come from God, but many Muslims who are always speaking of God "the Merciful One" need to be transformed so that they can live a life that demonstrates God's mercy and grace.

Biblical View

Since many Muslims openly practice their religion in their homes and in their community, Christians also need to learn to be open in their faith. Sometimes Muslims will stop what they are doing when the call to prayer goes out, and they will pray in the place of business or even at the side of the road. Since Christians don't make a big display of praying, many Muslims wrongly believe that Christians never pray.

While Christians should not seek to find public ways to 'show off' their faith, they should be ready to pray in their homes and in the homes of their Muslim friends. Christian children should be encouraged to memorize the

Bible and recite it before visitors and guests. This may be the only way some Muslims will ever hear the words of the Bible.

The best way for Christianity to be displayed, however is in the relationships between Christians. John 13:35 says: "By *this all men will know that you are my disciples, if you love one another.*" This love between Christians is demonstrated in two ways: first, through the church, which loves and cares for each other, and second, through the existence of Christian families. The glue that holds Christian families together is the expression of love and concern for one another. The Christian family serves each other, not only the husband and father.

Most Muslims have no idea how Christian families operate. They may enjoy visiting the home of Christians just to observe and understand how the Christian family is different, and how they love and respect one another and love and respect God.

Christian Marriage

The Christian view of marriage is very simple. First, the Bible teaches in Genesis 2:24, *"Therefore a man shall leave his father and mother, and shall cleave to his wife; and they shall be one flesh."* The husband and wife become a team together, and a new, separate entity from the families they came from.

The book of Ephesians instructs husbands to love their wives (5:25), wives to submit to their husbands as to the Lord (5:22), and all Christians to submit to one another (5:19-21). All Christian relationships center on mutual submission to one another, and corporate submission of all to God.

> *For this cause shall a man leave his father and mother and shall be joined unto his wife and they two shall be one flesh. This is a great mystery but I speak concerning Christ and the Church. Nevertheless, let everyone of you in particular so love his wife even as himself, and the wife, see that she reverence her husband.* (Ephesians 5:31)

The Christian home and marriage reflect the relationship between Christ and the church - mutual love, respect and submission, each giving him or her self for the other.

This is why God hates divorce. Divorce speaks of unyielding rebellion and conflict. It opposes everything God is. He loves and gives of himself. Even when it hurts him, he still gives sacrificially. This is the path that God wants us to take.

In Malachi 2:16 it clearly says *"I hate divorce."* The New Testament teaches:

> *To the married I give this command (not I, but the Lord): A wife must not separate from her husband. But if she does, she must remain unmarried or else be reconciled to her husband. And a husband must not divorce his wife. To the rest I say this (I, not the Lord): If any brother has a wife who is not a believer and she is willing to live with him, he must not divorce her. And if a woman has a husband who is not a believer and he is willing to live with her, she must not divorce him. For the unbelieving husband has been sanctified through his wife, and the unbelieving wife has been sanctified through her believing husband. Otherwise your children would be unclean, but as it is, they are holy. But if the unbeliever leaves, let him do so. A believing man or woman is not bound in such circumstances; God has called us to live in peace. How do you know, wife, whether you will save your husband? Or, how do you know, husband, whether you will save your wife?* (I Corinthians 7:10)

A man or woman is allowed to marry again in the case of death.

> *The woman who has a husband is bound by the law to her husband as long as he lives; but if the husband is dead she is loosed from the law of her husband. So then, if her husband lives and she is married to another man she is called an adulteress, but if her husband is dead she is free from that law so that she is not an adulteress; though she be married to another man.* (Romans 7:2)

On the other hand the Muslim world is filled with divorce and remarriage. While some marriages seem stable, other men divorce and remarry at will, sometimes to as many as a dozen wives during their lifetime. In the midst of this, Christian marriages should be solid and long lasting, demonstrating what true love and commitment are like.

On one occasion, a group of Sadducees came to Jesus to question him. They asked him about a case where a woman's husband died and she married again. This happened seven times. Their question was, if there is a resurrection from the dead, whose wife will she be? Jesus gave a very surprising answer to their question. Jesus said: *You err, not knowing the scriptures, nor the power of God. For in the resurrection they neither marry nor are given in marriage, but are like the angels of God in heaven.* (Matthew 22:29-30)

This is an important part of Christian teaching about marriage. Marriage between people on earth is temporary, not eternal. Contrary to the Muslim view, there is no marriage or sex in heaven.

Marriage on earth is good. Paul emphasizes this in I Corinthians 7. Even singleness is good. Each should seek to be led by God. However, Paul suggests that if there are those who struggle to control themselves, they should marry, for it is better to marry than to burn with passion.

In all things, however, it is important for the married couple to remember what the Bible teaches in Hebrews 13:4: *Marriage is honorable in all, and the marriage bed undefilable.* There is no shame in the marriage bed. Husbands and wives are free to explore and enjoy each other, as long as their sexual activity is limited to just the two of them. The Bible clearly adds *"but fornicators and adulterers God will judge."*

It is very important that men and women who go to serve in Muslim areas have dealt with their sexual passions. There is much in Islam that caters to sexual passion. Sexual matters are often spoken about openly, and because of multiple marriages and the presence of homosexuality (usually covered over) sexual temptations can be a real struggle for the Christian missionary.

Questions for Reflection and Group Discussion

1. Read I Corinthians 7. Why does Paul suggest that young people consider remaining single?
2. Read I Timothy 5. Why do you think Paul suggests that people consider being single in I Corinthians, and here in I Timothy he suggests that some marry?
3. If a woman is married, how can she serve both her husband and Christ? Will this bring conflict? How can she deal with this, especially if she is married to an unbeliever?
4. Why do you think Proverbs 31:10 and onward speaks so highly of a virtuous wife? Summarize what strengths you think the writer is highlighting that apply to wives today.

Chapter Seventeen
The Spiritual World of Muslims

Most Muslims are aware of the spirit world, but few have worked out how it operates. While Muslims are aware of Satan, angels and spirits, they are generally not too concerned with them. Rural Muslims have more of a sensitivity to this subject, although they are generally not too clear on how spirits, angels, man, and God relate to one another. For most Muslims, God is ultimately in control but and there are two responses to spirits: first, spirits must not be antagonized; second, when they do attack, the answer is Islam.

Fear of Spirits (Jinn)

All through the Muslim world there are many superstitions about jinn. These vary from country to country, depending on what sort of practices existed before Islam arrived. However, even in the heart of Arabia, Muslims are aware of jinn. For the Muslim, the jinn are simply another race of beings. They live, propagate and die like any other race. They live in the invisible world around us and Muslims try not to antagonize them.

Do you remember what was taught in lesson thirteen?

• Muslims believe that God created the jinn 2,000 years before Adam. (Sura 15:27)

• Muslims understand that there are believers and infidels among jinn as there are among men. (Sura 72:1-2; Al-Muwatta 54:33)

• The Qur'an teaches that jinn were created from smokeless fire so they are spirit beings, while humans were created from clay, so they are physical beings. (Sura 15:26-32)

- Muslims believe that jinn are peaceable, that they eat and drink and propagate their species.
- The Qur'an teaches that the chief abode of jinn are the mountains of Qaf which encompass the whole earth. (Sura 18)
- The Qur'an does not forbid communication with the jinn. They are simply another race of people. However, it is understood that some of them are evil and some are good. (Sura 72:1-2)
- Muslims are taught that Satan is the father of the jinn, and that he is generally evil. (Sura 18:50)
- All through Sura 55 of the Qur'an the jinn and mankind are addressed as equals.
- Sura 72 teaches that the jinn have heard the Qur'an and are amazed by it, and that many have followed Islam. Sura 72 also teaches that many jinn became arrogant because men turn to them for protection or help.

Protection against Evil or Trouble-making Jinn

Early Muslims believed in the jinn and were concerned about them and those who were affected by the jinn. Abu Daood relates:

> *Aisha once said: The apostle of Allah said to me: Have the mugharribun been seen among you? I asked: What do the mugharribun mean? He replied: They are those in whom there is a strain of the jinn.* (Abu Dawood 2421)

Muhammad ibn Abu Yahya said that:

> *... his father told once that he and his companion went to Abu Sa'id the Khudri to pay a sick visit to him. He said: Then we came out from him and met a companion of ours who wanted to go to him. We went ahead and sat in the mosque. He then came back and told us that he heard Abu Sa'id al-Khudri say: The Apostle of Allah said: Some snakes are jinn; so when anyone sees one of them in his house, he should give it a warning three times. If it returns after that, he should kill it, for it is a jinn.* (Abu Daood 2508)

Abdullah bin Umar tells the story:

> *I never heard 'Umar saying about something that he thought it would be so-and-so, but he was quite right. Once, while 'Umar was sitting, a handsome*

man passed by him, 'Umar said, "If I am not wrong, this person is still in the religion of the pre-Islamic period of ignorance or he was their foreteller. Call the man to me." When the man was called to him, he told him of his thought. The man said, "I have never seen such a day on which a Muslim is faced with such an accusation." 'Umar said, "I am determined that you should tell me the truth." He said, "I was a foreteller in the pre-Islamic period of ignorance." Then 'Umar said, "Tell me the most astonishing thing your female Jinn has told you of." He said, "One day while I was in the market, she came to me scared and said, 'Haven't you seen the Jinns and their despair and they were overthrown after their defeat and prevented from listening to the news of the heaven so that they stopped going to the sky and kept following camel-riders?' " 'Umar said, "He is right," and added, "One day while I was near their idols, there came a man with a calf and slaughtered it as a sacrifice for the idol. An unseen creature shouted at him, and I have never heard harsher than his voice. He was crying, 'O you bold evil-doer! A matter of success! An eloquent man is saying: None has the right to be worshipped except Allah.' On that the people fled, but I said, 'I shall not go away till I know what is behind this.' Then the cry came again: 'O you bold evil-doer! A matter of success! An eloquent man is saying: None has the right to be worshipped except Allah.' I then went away and a few days later it was said, 'A prophet has appeared.'

These passages clearly illustrate that belief in the jinn is a part of orthodox Islam, and not something from folk-Islam. All over the Muslim world, people's action demonstrate how important jinn are to their daily lives.

Jinn and Water

Today many Muslims believe that the jinn live in the ground, and if water is thrown on the ground the jinn will jump out and attack the person. Therefore they must say "*In the name of Allah*" before the water hits the ground in order to be safe. Many times when a person is demon oppressed those around will say that they have "thrown out water."

Ali ibn Abu Talib relates: Allah's messenger said:

"The screen between the eyes of jinn and the private parts of the sons of

227

Adam as one of them enters the privy is that he should say: In the name of Allah." (Al-Tabaraani, Al-Kabeer, 22/214)

It is for this reason that Muslims say "In the name of Allah" to keep away evil spirits. Qatadah related from 'Abdullah ibn Sarjas who said:

"The Messenger of Allah forbade urination into a hole." Qatadah asked, "What is disliked about urinating into a hole?" He answered, "It is the residence of the jinn." (Fiqh us-Sannah 1.18b)

Demon Possession

Islam teaches very little about demon possession, although everyone has heard of it. The Arabic language is full of words that deal with jinn. For example there is a word for the experience when a jinn sits on a person's chest and will not let him breathe, and there is a word for when a jinn trips someone and holds them on the ground. There are many words and stories that deal with what happens when jinn interfere with the lives of humans. Remember that jinn are not seen as evil but simply another race of invisible beings that live all around.

Jabir ibn Abdullah said that the Apostle of Allah was asked about a charm for one who is possessed (nashrah). He replied: It pertains to the work of the devil. (Abu Dawood 1766)

Usually when a jinn affects someone, the Muslim mullah will be summoned from the mosque. This mullah will recite the Qur'an over the person until he is released by the jinn. This sometimes takes more than half an hour.

The Evil Eye and Jealousy

As introduced in the last lesson, jealousy is a major problem in the Muslim world. Muslims believe that when someone is jealous of someone or something they open the door for the evil eye to damage the beautiful object or person. The prophet Muhammad encouraged his followers not to become involved with charms and spells that animistic people use. He did acknowledge the evil eye, however, and said that charms could be used to thwart the evil eye and protect against snake bites and scorpion stings. The following quotes demonstrate that belief in the evil eye is clearly a part of orthodox Islam.

Sahl ibn Hunayf relates the story: I passed by a river and entered it and took a bath in it. When I came out, I had a fever. The Apostle of Allah

was informed about it. He said: Ask him to seek refuge in Allah. I asked:
O my Lord, will a spell be useful? He replied: No spell is to be used except
for the evil eye or a snake bite or a scorpion sting. (Abu Dawood 1780)

Ibn Abbas relates the following: The prophet used to seek refuge with Allah
for Al-Hasan and Al-Husain and say: "Your forefather Abraham used
to seek refuge with Allah for Ishmael and Isaac by reciting the following:
'O Allah! I seek refuge with your perfect words from every devil and from
poisonous pests and from every evil, harmful, and envious eye." (Sahih
Bukhari 4:590)

Um Salama reported that the prophet saw in her house a girl whose face
had a black spot. He said. "She is under the effect of an evil eye; so treat
her with a charm or incantation. (Bukhari 7:635)

Abu Huraira reported that the Prophet said, "The effect of an evil eye is
a fact." (Bukhari 7:636)

Al Mawatta also related the following story: A man came to Muhammad
with the two sons of Jafar. He said to their nursemaid, 'Why do I see them
so thin?' Their nursemaid said, 'Messenger of Allah, the evil eye goes quickly
to them. Nothing stops us from asking someone to make talismans (charms
using pieces of the Qur'an) except that we do not know if you would agree.
Then Muhammad replied 'Make talismans for them. (Muwatta 53)

Because of these stories about Muhammad, the use of talismans or charms
to ward off the evil eye is very common throughout the Muslim world, and
it has spread to other practices. Often a Qur'an is kept on the dashboard of a
taxi to keep it from having accidents. Sometimes an incantation is said over a
child's shoe, which is then attached to the bottom of an automobile to keep
the car from running into children. Love potions can be obtained from special
workers of magic in order to make someone fall in love. It is common for young
men and young women to use this before marriage to attract someone to them,
so that they will be asked for in marriage, or it can be used by women after
marriage to try and attract their husbands to themselves. Often older women
will "read" tea leaves or coffee grounds. This is often done as a simple thing,
with lots of laughter, but it does promote the whole concept of magic and the
power that Islam has when it comes to the worlds of men and jinn.

Biblical View

"Father we pray against the power of the enemy. We pray that as the listener continues with this lesson, that you would bind the enemy and thwart his plans, and release the Holy Spirit into the listener's life. We also pray that you would reveal to the listeners your true feelings about the Muslim religion and your compassion for the millions of Muslims who are locked into this system of belief. We pray in the name of Jesus, Amen."

The Bible teaches us that there are good angels and evil demons. In the beginning God created angels. Hebrews 1:7 tells us that angels are spirit beings that serve God. It appears from the scriptures that angels were given a choice about following God. Jude 6 and 2 Peter 2:4 tell us that some angels left their 'first estate' and now remain under condemnation. From Revelation 12:4 it appears that one third of the angels rebelled, but this is not very clear. Matthew 25:41 indicates that Satan or the devil is the leader of the rebellious angels.

From Isaiah 14:12-16 we learn that Satan was cast out of heaven because he tried to exalt himself above God:

> *How you have fallen from heaven, (O Lucifer) morning star, son of the dawn! You have been cast down to the earth, you who once laid low the nations! You said in your heart, "I will ascend to heaven; I will raise my throne above the stars of God; I will sit enthroned on the mount of assembly, on the utmost heights of the sacred mountain. I will ascend above the tops of the clouds; I will make myself like the Most High." But you are brought down to the grave, to the depths of the pit.* (NIV)

It seems that God did not provide a plan of salvation for the fallen angels. Having seen the glory of God, having known God face to face and having served him, their rebellion brought final and lasting judgment on them. So God created again. This time he created a physical world and placed on it humans who had a body, soul and spirit. (I Thessalonians 5:23) This time mankind also had a choice, but he must choose without knowing God and seeing his glory and majesty. And so, from the very beginning God planned a method of redemption. Ephesians 1:4 tells us that he *"chose us, in Him, before the foundation of the world, that we should be holy and without blame before him in love."* (KJV) In John 20:29 Jesus said to his disciples, *"Because you have seen me, you have believed; blessed are those who have not seen and yet have believed."* (NIV)

God also provided us a way of salvation. This salvation is only available through the death and resurrection of Jesus. When Jesus' blood was shed and his life given as a ransom for many, the power of death and the power of the forces of evil were broken.

However, God has not finished his work of completely destroying the forces of evil. He is still gathering to himself a great nation of people who will rule the universe with him. Every one of these people will have chosen to follow God even though they do not see him or know him. Because of this, God will exalt them to a place higher than the angels, and it is they who, with Christ, will rule the universe forever and ever.

So, can curses and charms hurt the believer? Should we be afraid of the power of the enemy? Can we be affected by the forces of evil? Not every Christian believes exactly the same thing. We all agree that Jesus has triumphed over death, and that he defeated the forces of evil at the cross. However, the forces of evil still wield considerable power. They not only affect non-believers, but sometimes believers are influenced by them. None of us are free from the influences of sin or the influences of the enemy, as long as we live in this sin-ridden world. So we must all learn to walk in the light. I John 1:7 tells us:

> *But if we walk in the light, as he is in the light, we have fellowship with one another, and the blood of Jesus, his Son, purifies us from all sin.* The Bible also warns us: *If we claim to have fellowship with him yet walk in the darkness, we lie and do not live by the truth.* (1:6 NIV)

The letter of I John was written to Christians. It clearly teaches them in the next verse:

> *If we claim to be without sin, we deceive ourselves and the truth is not in us. If we confess our sins, he is faithful and just and will forgive us our sins and purify us from all unrighteousness.* (I John 1:8, NIV)

Christians who want to be free from the power and influence of the enemy must learn to walk in the light, confessing their sins and allowing God to purify them daily. Then we will not only have power over the enemy within our own lives, but we will have power over the enemy in the lives of others. In Luke 10:17-20, Jesus sent out the seventy-two disciples two by two.

> *When they returned they reported, "Lord, even the demons submit to us in your name." Jesus replied, "I saw Satan fall like lightning from heaven.*

So I have given you authority to trample on snakes and scorpions and to overcome all the power of the enemy; nothing will harm you. However, do not rejoice that the spirits submit to you, but rejoice that your names are written in heaven."

Jesus is very clear that we are not to rejoice in or focus on the power that is available to us through his name. This would cause us to become puffed up with pride. Rather we are to rejoice in what God has done for us in providing us with salvation. In and of ourselves we can do nothing. We ourselves cannot confront the enemy. Even as believers we do not have the personal power to confront the enemy. It is only through the person of Jesus, and his shed blood on the cross that the enemy responds to our prayers, for through Jesus we have power over demons, snakes and scorpions. Notice that these are the similar to the reason why Islam uses charms. The story in Luke continues in verse 21:

At that time Jesus, full of joy through the Holy Spirit, said, "I praise you, Father, Lord of heaven and earth, because you have hidden these things from the wise and learned, and revealed them to little children. Yes, Father, for this was your good pleasure. All things have been committed to me by my Father. No one knows who the Son is except the Father, and no one knows who the Father is except the Son and those to whom the Son chooses to reveal him." Then he turned to his disciples and said privately, "Blessed are the eyes that see what you see. For I tell you that many prophets and kings wanted to see what you see but did not see it, and to hear what you hear but did not hear it." Luke 10:21-24 (NIV)

Today, as followers of Jesus we are blessed and privileged. We not only know and understand the plan of salvation, we also share in the power of the plan. Twice in the Bible (Matthew 18:18 and Matthew 16:19) the followers of Jesus are told that they have the power to bind and loosen. This is our role in spiritual warfare. Through prayer we may ask the Lord to bind the enemy, and through prayer we can loose the Holy Spirit into a life or a situation.

As ministers to Muslims, you must be prepared to face the powers of the enemy. Through prayer, God will grant you opportunities to pray for Muslims you meet, binding the enemy and loosing the Spirit of God and the word of God into their lives. Prayer is the real work of the missionary. It is only through prayer that lives are transformed and churches planted.

Questions for Discussion and Reflection

1. Why do you think the reciting of the Qur'an will cause a jinn to release the person he is affecting? How is this different from praying in the name of Jesus? Think in terms of the permanent effect these have.

2. Why was Jesus full of joy in Luke 10:21 when the disciples returned and reported that even the demons were subject to them?

3. Discuss together what you believe Matthew 16:19 and 18:18 mean. How does this practically affect your ministry?

4. Have you experienced an attack of the enemy in your life as a Christian? How did you respond? What verses in the Bible have strengthened you, and helped you withstand the attacks of the enemy?

Chapter Eighteen
Paradise

In this lesson we are going to compare the Islamic view of paradise or life after death with the Christian view of heaven. Be prepared, the Islamic view is very different from what the Bible teaches us about heaven.

The Muslim Paradise, a Sexual Heaven

According to the Qur'an, life after death presents the beginning of progression and advancement far beyond anything conceivable in this world. Sura 17:21 says *"And certainly the hereafter is much superior in respect of degrees, and much superior in respect of excellence."* In the hadiths there is another account which relates the following story:

> *Anas related this story: Um (the mother of) Haritha came to Allah's apostle after Haritha had been martyred on the Day (of the battle) of Badr by an arrow thrown by an unknown person. She said, "O Allah's apostle! You know the position of Haritha in my heart and how dear he was to me, so if he is in paradise, I will not weep for him, or otherwise, you will see what I will do." The prophet said, "Are you mad? Is there only one Paradise? There are many paradises, and he is in the highest paradise of Firdaus."*
> (Bukhari 8:572)

What makes Firdaus a special paradise is that it is a physical paradise. All of the general descriptions of Paradise are literal and material. Some passages of the Qur'an sound strange and perhaps revolting to Christian ears because of their sensual aspects. Muhammad's paradise can be summed up as a garden in which there are beautiful women, couches covered with rich cloths, flowing cups and luscious fruits, in which God does not appear at all. The Muslim idea of heaven bears no similarity to the Christian teaching of a saved believer, purified and changed into the likeness of Christ and worshiping a holy God.

Muslims believe that there are seven divisions to heaven, the highest being paradise. Man moves from one level to another until he finally attains paradise. God's throne is above them all, for God does not mix with men.

The following quotations have been taken from the Muslim source, *"The Geography of Pleasures-Sex in Paradise"* by Ibrahim Mahmoud. Listen to what Muslims teach:

The Chief of Pleasures

The most important of all the pleasures in paradise are the sexual pleasures. The other pleasures in paradise are given to serve this chief pleasure. This is God's reward for the believer who has had faith, patience, and has served God in word and deed. This man will have the chief place in paradise. We must be careful when studying this subject. Sexual relationships are not the only thing in paradise, they are only a stage for man to pass through. There is wisdom in the Qur'an for creating the role of sex in paradise, and a strategy to it.

Since the believer has given his allegiance and obedience to Allah, and because sexual pleasures are so stimulating, then it is not strange that he should be rewarded with these in the end. Bodily pleasures are what exercises a person when he is on earth, and these are completed in paradise where he will be completely liberated from all fetters. Sex in paradise will be within God's will, regulated, and without sexual slander. There will be a change in the understanding of sexual pleasures. There will be continuing youth complete with a fullness of sensations. Many Muslim commentators have focused on the beauty of the women in Paradise. This is to show the believer on earth, that what he desires will be accomplished in paradise.

To form an accurate picture of pleasures in paradise, we must study the famous Muslim commentators. For instance in Ya Sin 36:55 it says: "Verily the companions of the Garden shall that day have joy in all they do." So this then is the chief occupation of the inhabitants of the Garden, they shall have joy and sexual bliss. The Qur'an repeatedly refers to the sexual power that the male believers will enjoy in paradise. This will be sexual power that will be

235

renewed continually. This word refers to fertility and taking what one desires. In addition there is the Qur'anic use of the word "fruit." It has a symbolic meaning. It symbolizes what stimulates the desires. (Sura 55:68) uses the world 'fruit' and puts us in a world teeming with stimulants.

If we follow this with the verse in Ya Sin 36:55, we see rich symbolism and meaning. We see a whole world in itself, all there for the pleasure of the male believer. At the head of this is pleasure of the body. Al-Tabari explains that the Arabic words used in this section actually mean to "break the hymen" or to have sex with virgins. The chief pleasure is sexual. A man's sexual powers will not be diminished in this perfect environment. All the pollution of a man's powers on earth will be purified in paradise.

The picture of fruit being picked, and then replaced by other fruit, refers to renewal of man's sexual powers. A great number of virgins await the Muslim man in paradise, and the Qur'an refers to a man's special place there and doesn't erase his special position as a "man."

There will be a great festival of women in paradise. One cannot imagine how many women known as perpetual virgins will be in paradise. Each one will have great beauty. Writers of hadith add to the short, symbolic descriptions in the Qur'an to place a picture in the minds of Muslims so that paradise will always be in their imaginations. In many ways this is the paradise that man was created in before he was expelled from it.

The person who contemplates the depths of the virgins of paradise, will know that he cannot understand these things except by the mind, the mind that goes beyond merely sensory perceptions. In light of this truth, the commentators focused on the manifestation of the depth of the beauty of the virgins of paradise, and their charms. The commentators expound greatly on the particulars of the virgins. They are the pivot around which other pleasures of paradise revolve. Al-Tabari writes extensively on this, and calls the virgins the 'pure white ones.'

The Muslim man in paradise will marry 4,000 virgins, 8,000 widows, and 100 hurs. The question may come to your mind: how can one man maintain contact daily with all these? The Hadith says that man will have power of 100 men and will be able to have sex with 100 virgins. A strong hadith says that man will have a tent hollowed out of a giant pearl 60 miles *long. Virgins will be returned to virginity after sex. How will this happen? The man's sex organ will never go limp, the woman's vagina will never be sore, and his sexual passion will never abate. Also, there will be no "sperm".*

The hurs are a special creation of Allah, obedient to their husband and faithful to him. If any wife on earth tries to harm her husband, his hur will rebuke her "May Allah kill you."

All focus in paradise is on the man--the companions and women follow him. He is the focus in paradise and is characterized by strength and authority. While the main emphasis in Paradise is on the pleasures of the man; the companions are restricted to anything that he desires.

As we can see, the Muslim paradise is all about earthly pleasure. The Qur'an and the Hadiths have much to say about this place.

It is interesting to notice that there are three kinds of women in paradise. First there are the virgins, then the widows and lastly the hur who are created by God and gifted to those whom he deems deserves them. These women are owned by the men and serve their every desire.

There is a verse in the Quran that mentions boys in paradise. Muslim scholars have long argued over the meaning of this verse. Sura 52:24 says: *"Round about them will serve, devoted to them, youths, handsome as pearls, and well guarded."* Who are these boys, and is the Muslim man`s relation sexual?

The Qur'an says these youth serve the believer. This is in addition to the others who will serve him. What is the nature of their service? There is not a complete and specific answer. But there have been great efforts at exposition, which infer that there is a sexual relationship there between the youths and the believer. The most specific and boldest of commentators on this subject is Sayyid Abdul Hamid Kishk, who has stirred up much controversy and opposition, as he is a Muslim jurist from the esteemed Al-Azhar University. He has emphasized the sexual nature of this relationship: *"The one who has been chaste during earthly life, who has suppressed his sexual desires, does he not deserve a release in Paradise? Just as the Hur are the fulfillment of the "adultery" he did not do on earth, in fear of Allah, so are the "youth" in paradise.* (Kishk, Abdul Hamid, *Thoughts of a Muslim and the Subject of Sex* Edited by the Muslim Heritage Library, Muslim Research Institute, Cairo) (Arabic).

These words agree with those of Ibn Qayim Al-Juzia who wrote that *"those who did not indulge in forbidden desires on earth will be rewarded these things in paradise in a much more complete fashion. In paradise, there is not a cancellation of desires, but anticipation of fulfillment and a "kindling" of the passions and desires."* (Ibn Qayim Al-Juzia, *Zad al-Ma'ad* (Provision of the hereafter) (Arabic).

All over the Muslim world, men look forward to dying and arriving in paradise. Some people willingly give their lives to advance the cause of Islam believing that this will provide for them a better place, or more women in heaven.

But what of Muslim women? Because paradise is described in largely male terms, the exact nature of an equivalent reward for women remains unclear. Married women who pass the purity test will be reunited with their husbands and children and will live a life of ease. A woman who married more than once would have to choose which husband she would prefer to join her in the after-life. She, however, remains reserved for her husbands, if one chooses to keep her.

Men who married more than once will remain free to keep all their wives while also having the privilege of being attended to by the women God awards them. Although Muhammad was heard promising that *"round about them will serve boys of perpetual freshness: if thou seest them, thou wouldst think them scattered pearls"* Muslim scholars are emphatic that the pretty virgin boys in paradise are not there for the women.

Biblical View

For the Bible believing Christian, heaven is very different from what a Muslim is taught. First of all, the Bible teaches us that God is Spirit. In John 4:24 Jesus tells us that God is a spirit and we must worship him in spirit and in truth. Secondly, in Hebrews 1:14 we are told that the angels are ministering spirits. And even we humans have a spiritual component. I Thessalonians 5:23 tells us: *May God himself, the God of peace, sanctify you through and through. May your whole spirit, soul and body be kept blameless at the coming of our Lord Jesus Christ.* (NIV)

While we as humans live in a physical world, God and the angels live in a spiritual world. We live in bodies that lock us into the physical world. Our bodies can only hear a limited range of sounds and see a limited number of colors. We cannot see the spirit world. But the spiritual world affects the physical world. There are many examples in the Bible of angels or demons interacting with mankind.

When we die, our physical body dies and decays but our spirit lives on. The moment we die we are released from the physical body and become spirits in a spirit world. The Bible tells us that at death one of two things happens: If we have been redeemed by the blood of Christ and our names are written in the Book of life and if the Holy Spirit of God is in us as a seal of our redemption, then at the moment of death we will be absent from the body and present with God. If we are not saved, at the moment of death we will pass into eternal judgment. The Bible never speaks of God judging the dead to see if they are fit for heaven or not. That is decided right now. The Holy Spirit is our seal, preserving us and ensuring that we will go to heaven.

So what about God's judgment? The Bible does refer to an event in the future when God will judge the nations that are alive on the earth when he returns. This is in Matthew 25:31-34. The Bible also refers to the Judgment Seat of Christ that will be for believers. We will look at this in a few moments.

So those people who die now will have an experience in heaven as a spirit among other spirits in a spirit world. But the day is coming when the resurrection happens. At this point in time, those who are in heaven will receive their resurrection bodies.

> *Now we know that if the earthly tent we live in is destroyed, we have a building from God, an eternal house in heaven, not built by human hands. Meanwhile we groan, longing to be clothed with our heavenly dwelling, because when we are clothed, we will not be found naked. For while we are in this tent, we groan and are burdened, because we do not wish to be unclothed but to be clothed with our heavenly dwelling, so that what is mortal may be swallowed up by life. Now it is God who has made us for this very purpose and has given us the Spirit as a deposit, guaranteeing what is to come. Therefore we are always confident and know that as long as we are at home in the body we are away from the Lord. We live by faith, not by sight. We are confident, I say, and would prefer to be away from the body and at home with the Lord. So we make it our goal to please him, whether we are at home in the body or away from it.* II Corinthians 5:1-9 (NIV)

The Bible makes it plain that while on earth we have earthly bodies. But there is a coming resurrection. On that day we will receive our resurrection bodies. I Thessalonians 4:14-17 tells us:

> We believe that Jesus died and rose again and so we believe that God will bring with Jesus those who have fallen asleep in him. According to the Lord's own word, we tell you that we who are still alive, who are left till the coming of the Lord, will certainly not precede those who have fallen asleep. For the Lord himself will come down from heaven, with a loud command, with the voice of the archangel and with the trumpet call of God, and the dead in Christ will rise first. After that, we who are still alive and are left will be caught up together with them in the clouds to meet the Lord in the air. And so we will be with the Lord forever. I Thessalonians 4:14-17 (NIV)

So we will go to meet the Lord in the air, whether we as Christians have lived near to God or far from him, whether we have worked for him, or never opened our mouths for him. At that moment the dead in Christ shall rise, and on that day he will change us to be like his son Jesus.

The resurrection of our bodies from the dead is not our own work, it is Christ's. At Calvary, Jesus paid the price for our salvation. This included our spirits and our bodies. We will go to heaven based on our acceptance of his salvation while we were alive on earth. No judgment is needed to tell if we are saved or not. God knows that right now.

The moment we accept Christ, several things happen.

- Our sin is removed (Psalm 103:12)
- Salvation is declared for our spirit (I Thessalonians 2:13)
- Our name is written in the Lamb's Book of Life (Phil 4:3, Rev 20:15)
- God gives us the Holy Spirit (II Corinthians 1:21-22)
- We are sealed with the Holy Spirit. (Ephesians 1:13, 4:30)
- Salvation is declared for our bodies (I Corinthians 15:42)
- We are adopted into God's family (Romans 8:17)
- Heaven is guaranteed

So can we live as we please? No, because all believers will face the Judgment Seat of Christ.

Out of the 260 chapters in the New Testament, the coming of the Lord is mentioned 318 times. And the Bible teaches us that when the Lord returns, he will set up his judgment seat…, not for sinners, but for believers!

Now there is a method in God's judgment and a reason for everything God does. I Peter 4:17 tells us that *judgment begins in the house of God.* If we are judged first, how can the unbelievers complain when they are judged?

So believers will be judged of God:

- Why did you do this?
- Why did you not do that?
- Did you know that every idle word that men will speak will be taken into consideration on the Day of Judgment? (Matthew 12:36)
- What did you do with the ten pounds I gave you? (Luke 19:13)
- What did you do with the five golden talents? (Matthew 25)
- What did you do with your time?
- What did you do with your responsibilities?

God will judge us and will reward every Christian according to his works.

After the Judgment Seat of Christ we will proceed to the Marriage Supper of the Lamb. This is described in Revelation 19. At this point, we will be united with Christ and formed into a group of believers who will rule the universe with Christ.

Revelation 21:1-27 and 22:1-6 describe the new earth and the great city, the New Jerusalem that God is making for his people. This is the place that Jesus talked about in John 14:2. He is preparing this for us right now. The new earth and the new Jerusalem will be a place perfectly fitted for us. Each believer will have a resurrection body. This body is just like the body that Jesus had. Jesus is described as the first Adam of a new race of beings, and each of us will be just like him. We will be a new race of beings with bodies perfectly suited for a physical as well as a spiritual world. And we will enjoy the new earth, and from there be joint rulers of the universe with Christ.

For the Christian, heaven is a wonderful place where we live with God in perfect harmony. We will love and serve God throughout eternity. Sexual activity will pass away. Matthew 22:30 clearly tells us: *For in the resurrection they neither marry, nor are given in marriage, but are as the angels of God in heaven.* (KJV) So while the Muslim man looks forward to a paradise of sensual pleasures, Christians look forward to being transformed into the image of God's son and living and working in harmony with God forever.

Questions for Reflection and Group Discussion

1. Read the following verses and discuss what they teach us about the Judgment Seat of Christ: Romans 14, I Corinthians 3, I Corinthians 4, II Corinthians 5.

2. Read the following passages and discuss what rewards God has for faithful Christians: 1 Peter 5:2-4, I Thessalonians 2:18-20, Philippians 4:1, 2 Timothy 4:8, I Corinthians 8:25-27, James 1:12 and Revelation 2:10.

3. How important is faithfulness? Read the following and discuss. Matthew 24:13, Luke 12:35-40, Luke 16:9-12, Luke 19:17, Hebrews 13:4, Revelation 2:26.

Chapter Nineteen
A Nomadic Religion

Millions of Muslim people are nomads and have been outside of the influence of most missionary efforts. In this chapter we will discuss the life of nomads and some of the challenges of reaching them with the gospel.

Researchers have noted that there are three different types of nomads. The first type are the *hunter-gatherers*. These people move because of changes in their food supply. They move from place to place because their food supply runs low. Once they move on, the food supply replenishes itself. Often hunter-gatherers have little contact with the outside world. Few hunter-gatherers are Muslims; most are animistic.

The second type of nomads are the *trade workers*. These people move from place to place offering their particular work or trade. Because of their work they require contact with people. Some of these trade workers have a set route that they follow, and they often take advantage of events, weather, harvest seasons and so forth. Sometimes these trade workers are craftsmen, entertainers, or merchants. Traveling craftsmen are quite common in Muslim countries. Often these craftsmen offer a range of services and products. The man might be a worker of metal, sharpening knives and mending pots. Young people might sell goods. The women might offer traditional medical advice, (often mixed with superstitions, such as burning the skin to drive out demons), making charms, casting spells, telling fortunes or offering sexual services.

The third type of nomads are the *pastoralists* who have flocks of sheep or herds of cattle or camels. These people move from pasture to pasture. They are interested in managing the natural resources of animals and pasture without necessarily having much contact with other people. Many pastoralist nomads are Muslims.

No matter what type of nomad we are thinking of, they almost always move purposefully, going from resource to resource. Some nomads move continually, living in tents, wagons or boats all year round. These are known as continual nomads. If they are pastoralists they often have a winter and a summer camping spot, usually moving from highlands to lowlands.

Some nomads move only occasionally. These are known as semi-nomadic. Many of the Bedouin of Arabia are now semi-nomadic. In the cold winters they live in small villages throughout the desert. In the summer part of the family will move into the desert or farmland. There are many reasons for nomads to be semi-nomadic. In many cases, the desert does not support the entire family, so women, young children, and elderly may live in the desert looking after the animals while the men and older children live in the town so the children can attend school. Sometimes the entire family lives in the town, and they only move into the country during planting and harvest time.

Finally, there are sedentary nomads, who may now work in industry, mining or tourism, but they still have the ethnic identity and values of the nomads. Many of these would prefer to live in tents but economics dictate that they live in the town or city.

Nomadic Worldview

Nomads have a particular worldview that differs from people who live in towns or villages. Usually nomads prefer the nomadic way of life and consider themselves independent people, separate and superior. The nomads of northern Arabia have been known to say, "We graze our sheep over the ruins of many civilizations, Greek, Roman, Byzantine, Turkish, and more. Some day we will graze our sheep over the ruins of today's cities. Our way of life is sustainable. We will survive. All of these cities will not."

Most nomads have a complex social structure with unique values, social identity and tribal lines. They are interested in relationships between people, not what people own. They can often trace their ancestors far back into history and they know how they are related to other nomads. While many cannot read or write, they value their complex social structures and their nomadic identity.

Many nomads view houses as prisons. Once you have a house, you cannot move. You are locked into a specific area and lose touch with the wider world. Nomads know the hills, forests, and deserts. They enjoy knowing things that settled people do not know.

Most nomads are "invisible people" in that they are not noticed by the majority of the civilized people. Their tents blend into the rural countryside. They work away from most people and once they move on, they are forgotten.

But the nomad seldom forgets. Nomads notice things. They are masters at using marginal renewable resources. Land that others would consider useless has value to them, but only for a short period of time. Nomads notice plants and animals. They notice weather patterns and remember where the rain fell, so they can return weeks or months later for the grass. They remember people, faces, names, and events. They are masters at living with very little, moving through life leaving little evidence that they were there, and yet they can enjoy life when the opportunity presents itself. They enjoy meeting other nomads, sharing together, and exchanging information. In many ways theirs is an easy life, with many quiet hours interspersed with a few hours of interaction with others.

Most nomads value their lifestyle, and one of their goals is to maintain their distinctive identity and values, along with a measure of self-sufficiency. For this reason they are slow to adopt outside ideas and they question the 'advice' offered by those who are not nomads, and who do not face the challenges of using marginal renewable resources.

As we said earlier, the majority of Muslim nomads are pastoralists, herding their animals in the deserts of Arabia, Asia and Africa. How many pastoralists are there?

In the Middle East	1.1 million
In East & Southern Africa	9.3 million
In North Africa	1.2 million
In West Africa	6.8 million
In South Asia	2.3 million
In Central Asia	2 million

This comes to a total of around 23 million nomads, most without a gospel witness.

Misconceptions about Nomads

Most settled people assume that nomads are doomed to die out because of the advance of civilization. Since most settled people think in terms of ownership of land and resources, they assume that a nomadic lifestyle is non-viable, and that nomads are "second class." Most developing nations want to appear to be modern and progressive and since nomads don't fit this picture these governments try to restrict or curtail nomadic practices. Thus nomads can become hostile to outside intervention, especially when governments or development projects encourage or force them to settle down. Most modern development projects, even those offered by Christians are designed for towns and villages and do not really consider or apply to nomadic people.

Missionary Challenges

Almost all missionary efforts are focused on reaching cities and villages. Since this is where the majority of people are, missionaries usually start in the cities. Often the nomads go unnoticed, even to the local city people.

Those who have tried to minister to nomads have found it very difficult. Visas are very hard to obtain and most missionary families struggle in a nomadic setting. Children's schooling is often a problem when a missionary family attempts to reach nomads.

The emerging church in Muslim lands is usually in urban settings. Churches are in buildings, with chairs, musical instruments, and set programs. This makes our churches out of reach for the nomad. A nomad once told a missionary, "When you can put your church on the back of a camel I will listen."

Islam and Nomads

Islam began as a religion for semi-nomadic people. The Quraysh family were merchants who traveled by camel caravan in Arabia. Since they were traveling many months of the year they could be considered semi-nomadic. Many of the people living around Mecca and Medina were also semi-nomadic or fully nomadic. So from the very beginning, Islam was strongly influenced by nomads.

Much of Islam's simplicity has to do with the demands of nomadic lifestyle. Formal prayers were about words and actions not about the place where a person prayed. Friday meetings at the mosque were never obligatory. Qur'anic study was not so much about reading as it was about memorization, poetry, and chanting.

It was only as Islam expanded that architecture, formal education and bureaucracy became important. Even so, these are not at the heart of Islam, and so the nomads of the desert found an identity with Islam that they did not find in the formal churches with their icons and bearded priests. The challenge that missionaries face today is understanding Christianity in a nomadic sense.

Biblical View of Nomadic Theology

Most Christians today live in houses and attend church services that are held in buildings. Since few Christians are nomads, few have noticed how much the Bible talks about nomads. Few Christians have noticed how God calls us today to be more 'nomadic' in our attitudes towards God's plan for mankind and the normal Christian life. But as we look at the Bible, we will notice that God speaks to nomads and has a special place in his heart for nomads.

The book of Genesis contains the story of Abraham, who was called from being a settled person to being a nomad. Few Christians realize that this is still God's call on Christians today. We are to abandon the call of the world to wealth, success and prestige, and follow the Lord wherever he leads us. Much of Genesis has to do with the life and events of a nomadic family who maintain a separate identity from the people around them. God's missionary purpose for the world began with a promise to a nomad that God would lead Abraham and his descendants in their journey. This was the start of a period of over two hundred years that God led the nomadic patriarchs and their families.

The book of Genesis in particular and other Old Testament references are full of truths that nomads appreciate. The only lasting evidence of Abraham's passing were the piles of stones he set up as remembrances. Abraham and his descendants did not own houses or property, but they considered all the land as theirs, even if it was claimed by settled people. Abraham and his family kept themselves separate from the settled people and did not intermarry with them or enter into business with them.

In Genesis we find that God created the earth, and yet he allows the earth freedom, even though he still has transcendence or power over it. God is supremely nomadic and has no need of creation and is not limited by it. He is free to move through the universe as he wishes. Yet he is revealed as the creator-shepherd, who has chosen to have fellowship with a people traveling with him through time.

In Genesis 45:15-16 Israel blesses Joseph and says:

> *"May the God before whom my fathers Abraham and Isaac walked, the God who has been my shepherd all my life to this day, the angel who has delivered me from all harm--may he bless these boys. May they be called by my name and the names of my fathers Abraham and Isaac, and may they increase greatly upon the earth."* (NIV)

In these verses God is referred to as the shepherd. This concept is continued throughout the Bible, with God choice of the shepherd David.

In 2 Samuel 5:2 the people of Israel proclaim David king with these words: *"In the past, while Saul was king over us, you were the one who led Israel on their military campaigns. And the LORD said to you, 'You will shepherd my people Israel, and you will become their ruler.'"* David understands this concept intimately and writes in Psalm 23, *"The Lord is my Shepherd."* Many Christians who study this psalm think in terms of the shepherd and the sheep, rather than the nomadic characteristics of the shepherd himself.

God revealed his nomadic purposes for mankind when he called the nation of Israel to walk through the desert, leading them by a pillar of cloud in the day and a pillar of fire by night. At this time the Bible begins to unfold God's plan for the nation of Israel. It would be a revelation of the relationship between God and mankind, demonstrating a people walking by faith with God. This is a powerful picture of a nomadic God living in a tent.

God's dwelling place was with nomadic people. He moved with them. They did not come to him, he came to them and dwelt with them. His presence, confirmed by a covenant, made them his people, and he acted as the shepherd, leading them and providing food and water for them.

The Bible seems to indicate that God never desired to have a temple built for him. He seemed to have preferred the tent. Moses and the people of Israel never built anything for themselves, and the tent of meeting was built from free will offerings.

But David built a temple after he completed building his own house. Second Samuel 7:2-7 tells us David said to Nathan the prophet:

> "Here I am, living in a palace of cedar, while the ark of God remains in a tent." Nathan replied to the king, "Whatever you have in mind, go ahead and do it, for the LORD is with you." That night the word of the LORD came to Nathan, saying: "Go and tell my servant David, 'This is what the LORD says: Are you the one to build me a house to dwell in? I have not dwelt in a house from the day I brought the Israelites up out of Egypt to this day. I have been moving from place to place with a tent as my dwelling. Wherever I have moved with all the Israelites, did I ever say to any of their rulers whom I commanded to shepherd my people Israel, "Why have you not built me a house of cedar?"

God was not looking for anything other than a tent. The tent demonstrated what God wanted to demonstrate, that God moved with his people - but David and Solomon built God a temple. Moreover, Solomon used forced labor to do it. From that point on, the temple of God and its treasures were a target for invaders. The original tabernacle had been safe for all of its 480 years of history and it lasted longer than any of the later temples. Solomon's temple lasted only 375 years, often stripped bare by invading kings. When Herod built his temple it was condemned by Jesus as being a den for thieves.

Why did God prefer that his people be nomads? Because it isolated the Israelites from others so that they would be alone with God. In Exodus 33:15 - 16 we read:

> Then Moses said to him, "If your Presence does not go with us, do not send us up from here. How will anyone know that you are pleased with me and with your people unless you go with us? What else will distinguish me and your people from all the other people on the face of the earth?

Later in Leviticus 20:26 it says: "You are to be holy to me because I, the LORD, am holy, and I have set you apart from the nations to be my own."

Even when Israel was more settled in the promised land, many of the prophets were sojourners, moving around the country without a permanent home. Elijah and Elisha are excellent examples of itinerant prophets.

The New Testament presents us with Jesus, the promised Messiah. All through history the followers of God looked forward to the coming Messiah. But when Jesus came, he was a nomadic Messiah, not a settled Messiah. The announcement of his arrival was not made in the temple, rather God chose to announce his birth to the nomads living in the hills around Bethlehem. Jesus' parents were poor. Joseph was a craftsman who worked with his hands. He did not have enough money to provide a lamb for the sacrifice, so they offered two doves, the offering of a very poor person.

When Jesus came, he lived the life of a nomad. His followers were known as the "*People of the Way.*" Jesus himself did not own houses or land. Indeed, the Bible tells us in Matthew 8:20: "*Jesus replied, foxes have holes and birds of the air have nests, but the Son of Man has no place to lay his head.*" (NIV)

Jesus' lifestyle was one of moving from place to place. He often preached on a hillside or on the seashore. He withdrew into the wilderness to pray. Jesus called his disciples to come and follow him. It wasn't just come to him and study at his feet, but rather it was to follow him as he moved around the country. He trained them to be nomads, moving as the Lord directed them. Their traveling was an expression of obedience to the Father. Jesus would say things like "*I must go to Jerusalem.*" It was God who was directing his movements. The disciples were called upon to give up their sedentary life and to follow Jesus wherever he took them, just as Abraham was called many years before this.

The New Testament letters are full of allusions to the disciples walking with Jesus. Ephesians 5:8 tells us: "*For ye were sometimes darkness, but now are ye light in the Lord: walk as children of light*" (KJV). Colossian 2:6 says: "*As ye have therefore received Christ Jesus the Lord, so walk ye in him.*" And Galatians 5:16 instructs us: "*This I say then, Walk in the Spirit, and ye shall not fulfill the lust of the flesh.*"

The church is also called upon to be nomadic. We are told that each believer now becomes a mobile sanctuary. Listen to these verses with nomads in mind.

> I Corinthians 3:16 - 17: *Don't you know that you yourselves are God's temple and that God's Spirit lives in you? If anyone destroys God's temple, God will destroy him; for God's temple is sacred, and you are that temple.* (NIV)

> I Corinthians 6:19 - 20: *Do you not know that your body is a temple*

of the Holy Spirit, who is in you, whom you have received from God? You are not your own; you were bought at a price. Therefore honor God with your body. (NIV)

2 Corinthians 6:16: *What agreement is there between the temple of God and idols? For we are the temple of the living God. As God has said: "I will live with them and walk among them, and I will be their God, and they will be my people."* (NIV)

I Peter 1:1: *Peter, an apostle of Jesus Christ, to the strangers scattered throughout Pontus, Galatia, Cappadocia, Asia, and Bithynia.* (NIV)

I Peter 2:11: *Dearly beloved, I beseech you as strangers and pilgrims, abstain from fleshly lusts, which war against the soul.* (NIV)

The nomadic expressions of scripture have important lessons to teach us in our Christian lives. First, we should have a commitment to relationships rather than to property or places. Our primary relationship is to a nomadic God who is always on the move, and calls us with the words: "Come follow me." This requires an act of faith, daily dying to self, and seeking God's guidance. It comes with the call to leave the things of the world behind and travel unhindered and unburdened. The life of sacrifice is actually a life of abandoning the things that will hinder us on our journey.

Second, we are called to maintain a distinct social identity from the surrounding society. God calls us to be separate from the world. Our lives should be the lives of the nomad, and it should not surprise us if they are filled with typical nomadic experiences such as alienation, hunger, cold, poverty, and even shame. Romans 8:35 – 39 have a special meaning for nomads who are outcasts from society:

Who shall separate us from the love of Christ? Shall tribulation, or distress, or persecution, or famine, or nakedness, or peril, or sword? As it is written, For thy sake we are killed all the day long; we are accounted as sheep for the slaughter. Nay, in all these things we are more than conquerors through him that loved us. For I am persuaded, that neither death, nor life, nor angels, nor principalities, nor powers, nor things present, nor things to come, nor height, nor depth, nor any other creature, shall be able to separate us from the love of God, which is in Christ Jesus our Lord. (KJV)

God is not found at the end of our journey, rather we experience God as he journeys with us through each of these experiences. The world will hate us, because they don't understand us, just as they didn't understand our Master and what he called his followers to do.

Years ago an illiterate nomadic woman found a Sunday School lesson book for children. As she couldn't read she carefully studied the pictures and became a follower of Jesus. What had she learned from the pictures? She told others that Jesus was poor like she was. He came to crossroads and wondered which way to go, he was moved on by the authorities of his day, he had no knife so he broke his bread, and he had only a candle for light. She concluded that Jesus was a nomad like herself.

Why do we find reaching Muslim nomads such a big challenge? Usually it is because we as Christians do not see ourselves as nomads. We ask Muslim nomads to become settled so they can join our religion and attend our churches. Today God is calling for his servants to rediscover their nomadic spiritual heritage and take up the nomadic lifestyle. It is time we took the gospel to the nomads and share with them about a nomadic God who sent the Messiah into the world. The Messiah calls us to "come and follow him." And best of all, through the death and resurrection of Jesus, it is possible to enter into a relationship with God, wherein we can walk with him on this journey through life.

Questions for Reflection and Group Discussion
1. Read the following verses and discuss God's call on us. How could we share this with a nomadic person? Genesis 12:3, 17:4,5; 18:18; 22:18; Galatians 3:8, Hebrews 11:8
2. Read the following verses and discuss the walk of faith that God calls us to. Genesis 12:3; Matthew 12:15-21; Acts 15:14-17. Romans 1:5, 16, 2:9,10, Galatians 3:8

Chapter Twenty
Understand and Sharing with Muslims

We have now reached the very last lesson in this series on Islam. Let's go back and review the gods that were worshiped in pre-Islamic Arabia. Do you remember them?

Al-Uzza	The god of power
Al-Dushares	The god of rocks
Al-Kutbe	The god of writing
Al-Qaum	The god of war
Al-Manaat	The goddess of fate
Al-Lat	The goddess of sex

Think back over what you have learned about Islam since starting these lessons. Muhammad cleverly combined the worship of all of these old gods, along with some of the teachings of Jews and Christians to create a religion that sounded like and looked like all of them.

If you worshiped Al-Uzza, the god of power, you found all of his attributes in Allah, the one and only God who ruled like a great emperor, able to do whatever he wanted, whether it was for good or evil. Allah was in total control.

If you worshiped Al-Dushares, the god of the rocks, you could find in Islam the worship of a rock, but only one rock: the black stone in Mecca. Every day, five times a day, millions of Muslims around the world face the black stone and pray.

It you worshiped Al-Kutbe, the god of writing, you would be pleased to discover that Allah sent down books to earth. Each book was written in God's own hand. The last and greatest of these, the Qur'an, was revealed by the prophet Muhammad. This prophet never claimed to write the book, and he never claimed the words in the book were his. He only claimed to reveal what God had already written.

If you worshiped Al-Qaum the god of war, you would find in Islam the call to fight for Allah. Allah loves those who fight for him and who defend or spread the faith of Islam.

If you worshiped Al-Manaat, the goddess of fate, you would find in Islam the theology of fate. Everything was ordained before hand by Allah. Everything is written. You cannot go against God.

And if you worshiped Al-Lat, the goddess of sex and fertility, you would find in Islam many rules and regulations about sex, when it was to be performed, how it was to be performed, and with whom. And not only this, you were promised an everlasting future of sexual bliss. This surely would have attracted the followers of Al-Lat.

But there is more than this in Islam. Islam teaches that people should accept all the prophets including Adam, Abraham, Moses, David, Solomon and many more. It builds on the stories revealed in the Bible, and it can be attractive to nominal Jews as well.

And even for Christians, Islam has its attractions. Islam accepts Jesus as a great prophet and teacher. It acknowledges his teaching and miracles. It teaches that the Gospel is a book that Jesus brought… and it introduces only one other greater than Jesus, the prophet Muhammad. All down through history there have been Christians who have converted and joined Islam.

So whether it is the theology, the warm caring community, the promise of sexual fulfillment, or the honor and respect one receives, Islam has been attractive to many people. Muslims pride themselves in having a religion that many have joined, from many walks of life.

Muslims pride themselves in having a religion that dealt with jahiliya and established a kingdom on earth. Christianity did not bring such a system and so Islam appears to be superior to Christianity. All over the world Muslims look down on Christianity and hold themselves aloof from Christians.

Christians on the other hand seem to have little interest in this world. They feel they are part of a heavenly kingdom and look forward to ruling with Christ some day in the future. It is all so strange and foreign to Muslims.

Biblical View

Christians see things differently than Muslims do. Muslims think of the physical both now and in eternity. Christians on the other hand think in terms of relationship with God and uphold this as the ultimate Christian goal or experience. We talk about entering into a relationship with God, but what do we mean by the term: a relationship with God?

In this lesson we want to consider three aspects of our relationship with God. All three of these are different than what is found in Islam. Herein lies the real difference between Islam and Christianity. Islam is a religion. It is a system of works that hopes to please God. Christ on the other hand came so that we might enter into a relationship with God. As we look at four aspects of our relationship with God, please compare them with your life. Do you have a relationship with God in all three of these ways?

Covenant Relationship

I Corinthians 11:25 says: *After the same manner also he took the cup, when he had drank, saying, This cup is the new covenant in my blood: do this as often as you drink it, in remembrance of me.*

Our Bibles contain two sections, the Old Testament or old Covenant, and the New Testament, or New Covenant. For thousands of years, God has dealt with mankind through covenants. This is something that Islam completely misunderstands. The first covenant was through Moses, and the children of Israel followed this covenant for many years. It involved worship in the temple as well as the messages of the prophets.

The second covenant is described in Hebrews 8:6-13. It refers to a promise given centuries earlier through the prophet Jeremiah (31:31):

> *But the ministry Jesus has received is as superior to theirs as the covenant of which he is mediator is superior to the old one, and it is founded on better promises. For if there had been nothing wrong with that first covenant, no place would have been sought for another. But God found fault with*

the people and said: "The time is coming, declares the Lord, when I will make a new covenant with the house of Israel and with the house of Judah. It will not be like the covenant I made with their forefathers when I took them by the hand to lead them out of Egypt, because they did not remain faithful to my covenant, and I turned away from them, declares the Lord. This is the covenant I will make with the house of Israel after that time, declares the Lord. I will put my laws in their minds and write them on their hearts. I will be their God, and they will be my people. No longer will a man teach his neighbor, or a man his brother, saying, 'Know the Lord,' because they will all know me, from the least of them to the greatest. For I will forgive their wickedness and will remember their sins no more." By calling this covenant "new," he has made the first one obsolete; and what is obsolete and aging will soon disappear. (NIV)*

If you are a true Christian, then you have entered into this covenant relationship with Jesus. You are included in the promises that are part of the New Covenant. Jesus offers all the gift of eternal life, but it is attached to a covenant relationship. If we surrender to him and follow him with our whole hearts, we can enter into this covenant relationship.

How many covenants have you been involved in during your life? A covenant is simply an agreement between two or more parties. Each side agrees to do something. Perhaps you have had a rent agreement with a landlord; perhaps you have a loan from a bank or another person. Perhaps you have entered into a marriage agreement with a spouse. If you have a covenant with someone, you have a relationship that is based on the covenant between you. Jesus is also offering us a covenant relationship. Every person who desires to be a messenger and to take the gospel message to Muslims must have a covenant relationship with God. Every missionary should be able to take a seeker through the scriptures and show them how they can also enter into a covenant relationship with God.

Lordship Relationship

There is a second kind of relationship with God. First, our relationship with Jesus should begin as a covenant relationship. But it should not stop there for there is a second, deeper relationship that we should have with God. This is the kind of relationship where He is Lord and we are servants. This is what is meant by the term "Kingdom of God" that is talked about so much in the New Testament. Jesus is the King, We are the servants.

As soon as a sinner enters into a covenant relationship with Jesus, he also enters into the Kingdom of God where Jesus rules supreme above all. However, not every new believer fully accepts Jesus as Lord and ruler of every area of his or her life. The Christian life is a process where God reveals areas of our lives to us that we have not yet fully surrendered to him. We either surrender that area, or we enter into a spiritual struggle with God who is not pleased until we surrender all of our life to him.

Philippians 2 tells us that some day: ... *at the name of Jesus every knee should bow, of things in heaven, and things in the earth, and things under the earth; And that every tongue should confess that Jesus Christ is Lord, to the glory of God the Father.* *(KJV)* Today, not every area of our lives is surrendered to him because we don't know ourselves as God knows us. Every believer everywhere is in the process of becoming aware of areas of his or her life where he or she has not given God complete Lordship. We are learning to die to ourselves and surrender ourselves to God. As we enter into a covenant relationship with God we discover that he wants to be Lord of every area of our lives. He wants to lead us and guide us as a shepherd guides his sheep. John 10:27 says: *My sheep listen to my voice; I know them, and they follow me. I give them eternal life, and they shall never perish; no one can snatch them out of my hand. My Father, who has given them to me, is greater than all; no one can snatch them out of my Father's hand.* (NIV)

Unfortunately some believers grow satisfied with their level of commitment to the Lord and get sidetracked by the cares of life or the things of the world. Some are satisfied to only have a covenant relationship with God and try to ignore God as Lord and Master. They want to be part of the Kingdom of God, but do not want to be submitted to the King. If you want to minister the gospel to Muslim people, you need to review your own life and make sure that you are fully surrendered to God so he can powerfully use your life as a witness of what God can do.

Friendship Relationship

There is a third aspect to our relationship with God. We not only have a covenant relationship and are part of the Kingdom of God, but God invites us to a further, deeper relationship with him. In John 15:15 we read, "*I no longer call you servants, because a servant does not know his master's business. Instead, I have called you friends, for everything that I learned from my Father I have made known to you.*" (NIV)

This is the most amazing part of our relationship with God. It is something that Muslims struggle to understand. How can God, the great Sultan of the universe, be interested in me or you as a person? We are like ants in his sight. We are nothing to him. This is one of the great mysteries of the gospel. The God of the universe invites us into a personal relationship with him. He wants to walk with us, talk with us, and personally lead us through life. He demonstrated this in sending his son to this earth to walk and talk with the disciples. He made this kind of relationship possible through the death and resurrection of Jesus. The book of Hebrews 2:9-18 tells us:

> *But we see Jesus, who was made a little lower than the angels, now crowned with glory and honor because he suffered death, so that by the grace of God he might taste death for everyone. In bringing many sons to glory, it was fitting that God, for whom and through whom everything exists, should make the author of their salvation perfect through suffering. Both the one who makes men holy and those who are made holy are of the same family. So Jesus is not ashamed to call them brothers. He says, "I will declare your name to my brothers; in the presence of the congregation I will sing your praises." And again, "I will put my trust in him." And again he says, "Here am I, and the children God has given me." Since the children have flesh and blood, he too shared in their humanity so that by his death he might destroy him who holds the power of death-- that is, the devil-- and free those who all their lives were held in slavery by their fear of death. For surely it is not angels he helps, but Abraham's descendants. For this reason he had to be made like his brothers in every way, in order that he might become a merciful and faithful high priest in service to God, and that he might make atonement for the sins of the people. Because he himself suffered when he was tempted, he is able to help those who are being tempted.* (NIV)

Jesus, the very son of God came to this earth as a human and was tempted, hungry, cold, abandoned and abused. He did this because he was entering into a relationship where he would call us brothers.

As a missionary to Muslims, God calls you to a ministry where you have the privilege to partake in the sufferings of Christ. You will be misunderstood, discouraged, tempted and abused. But in this, you will find that Jesus will never leave you nor forsake you. He is your brother, as well as Lord and Master. Through everything you experience, your life will be a witness to the Muslims around you of the type of relationship that God is inviting them to enter into.

The Future

Muslims and Christians look forward to very different futures. For the Muslim, his future is very physical. Good food, comfort and physical bliss are all that Islam offers him. Christ offers so much more. He offers us a very different future.

The Bible tells us that when we die, we will be changed. I Corinthians 15:50 – 58 tells us:

> *I declare to you, brothers, that flesh and blood cannot inherit the kingdom of God, nor does the perishable inherit the imperishable. Listen, I tell you a mystery: We will not all sleep, but we will all be changed-- in a flash, in the twinkling of an eye, at the last trumpet. For the trumpet will sound, the dead will be raised imperishable, and we will be changed. For the perishable must clothe itself with the imperishable, and the mortal with immortality. When the perishable has been clothed with the imperishable, and the mortal with immortality, then the saying that is written will come true: "Death has been swallowed up in victory." "Where, O death, is your victory? Where, O death, is your sting?" The sting of death is sin, and the power of sin is the law. But thanks be to God! He gives us the victory through our Lord Jesus Christ. Therefore, my dear brothers, stand firm. Let nothing move you. Always give yourselves fully to the work of the Lord, because you know that your labor in the Lord is not in vain.* (NIV)

This is the great difference between Islam and Christianity. Islam offers physical fulfillment. Christ offers change. Here on earth we only begin the process of change. But one day, the Bible tells us that in a flash, in the twinkling of an eye we shall be changed! This is the power of the gospel. It is the power of God through Jesus Christ. Islam has nothing like this. There is no thought of change. Islam as a religion hopes to change the situation on earth to make it more bearable, but it does not offer the power to change hearts. Christ on the other hand came to offer us change. He begins by the transforming work of the Holy Spirit in our lives. Bit by bit he works on our lives, slowly bringing every part of our life into conformity to God. This is the daily experience where we learn to make him Lord and Master of every part of our lives.

But we look forward to a coming day when we shall be changed. The daily fight against the flesh will be over. Our very flesh will be transformed, and we will be set free from these bodies that hold us back, these bodies that bring us such turmoil and struggle. Every Christian looks forward to the day when he will be changed and set free.

Muslims on the other hand have no idea what we are talking about. They look forward to the day when they can indulge in all the things that are forbidden in this world.

And so when comparing earthly religions Islam might seem superior, but when comparing our eternal state, Christianity offers so much more.

May the Lord Bless you as you seek to prepare yourself for ministry to Muslims.

Prayer for the Muslim World

1. Gather information about various Muslim people groups and pray for them.
2. Find other people who are interested in ministry to Muslims and praying for them. You may want to pledge to pray daily for each other.
3. Discuss together what God has been saying to you personally as you have gone through these lessons. Do you feel God's calling or direction in your life to seek out and witness to Muslims? Is he directing you to go somewhere so you can witness? Share these things and then pray together for each other.

www.ingramcontent.com/pod-product-compliance
Lightning Source LLC
Chambersburg PA
CBHW051716020426

42333CB00014B/1006